Other h

Paul

Publi

Boundary

The Breath of God (Book 1 in Moana Rangitira series)

For Want of a Shilling (Book 2 in Moana Rangitira series)

Gunpowder Green

Into the Shade

Falls Ende short story eBooks
1. The Oath
2. Courser
3. The King

Falls Ende full length novels
Falls Ende – Primus (eBooks 1,2 & 3)
Falls Ende – Secundus
Falls Ende – Tertium
Falls Ende – Quartus
Falls Ende – Quintus

Leonard Hardy's
A Sinister Consequence
A Questionable Virtue

First published in 2023 by Mellester Press
Copyright © 2023 Paul W. Feenstra

A Questionable Virtue
ISBN 978-1-99-118244-9 Soft Cover
ISBN 978-1-99-118245-6 Hard Cover
ISBN 978-1-99-118246-3 Epub
ISBN 978-1-99-118247-0 Kindle

Published in New Zealand.
A catalogue record of this book is
available from the
National Library of New Zealand.
Kei te pātengi raraunga o Te Puna Mātauranga
o Aotearoa tewhakarārangi o tēnei pukapuka

With heartfelt thanks.

Allanah Kalafatelis
Jane Petersen
Cover Design by Mea

http://www.paulwfeenstra.com/

A Questionable Virtue ©2023 Paul W. Feenstra
Leonard Hardy © 2017 Paul W. Feenstra

Published by
Mellester Press

A QUESTIONABLE VIRTUE

By

PAUL W. FEENSTRA

Acknowledgements

My heartfelt thanks to Rowan Carroll, Director of the New Zealand Police Museum; The Greater Wellington City Council Harbour Master; the helpful staff at the Wellington Maritime Museum; the New Zealand Police; the New Zealand National Poisons Centre; IAG New Zealand Insurance, and to the countless people who answered my persistent questions and encouraged my creativity.

"A man of kindness, to his beast is kind,
But brutal actions show a brutal mind:
Remember, He, who made thee, made the brute,
Who gave thee speech and reason, formed him mute;
He can't complain, but God's omniscient eye
Beholds thy cruelty—He hears his cry!
He was designed thy servant, not thy drudge,
But know—that his Creator is thy judge."

Unknown author
Believed to have been penned circa 1820

A QUESTIONABLE VIRTUE

BY

PAUL W. FEENSTRA

Chapter One

Wellington, 1886

There was only one entrance into the *bullpen* of the *Evening Standard* newspaper offices. It was through an internal door, a plain varnished door that had darkened a little with age, and more so by the repetitive touching of ink-smudged fingers.

Over time, the door's latching mechanism had loosened and now had excessive play due to wear and tear. Not enough to affect the effectiveness of the latching apparatus, but certainly its clunky movement created significant noise when rotated. For the reporters of the *Evening Standard* newspaper, who spent much of their productive time in the bullpen, this noise allowed them about a single second of advance warning that someone was about to enter their domain. A second was plenty of time for an inquisitive reporter with keen hearing to adjust and almost instantly transform himself from absolute inactivity to industriousness.

But frequently that same warning sound would work in reverse causing a distraction. To these employees, the noise was a boon. When everyone was legitimately busy, as they all were this morning, they would raise their heads at the signal and turn to see who the unexpected visitor was. They could be forgiven, as being reporters, they were naturally curious folk. From the perspective of a visitor entering the room, he or she would often be greeted by the sight of a roomful of sorrowful and pathetic-looking men staring — frequently with mouths agape. For any normal person unfamiliar with nuances of the *fourth estate*, this wasn't a particularly delightful or welcoming sight.

And so, when the sound of the rotating doorknob broke the concentration of the assiduous newspapermen in the bullpen, everyone stopped what they were doing, including the *Evening Standard*'s aging senior reporter Mr Frederick Pembroke, and as one, in perfect synchronisation, their heads swivelled with curious regard to face the newcomer. With almost a full second of suspenseful anticipation they waited for the door to open and, on this occasion were rewarded by the sight of an austere, sharp featured woman who, without seeking permission or offering the courtesy of a cordial greeting, stepped confidently into their realm. Her dour proclivity was reinforced by her brazenness as she cast a disapproving eye around the room, ignoring its intrigued occupants.

She was in her mid-thirties and appropriately attired in a maroon *day*, or *morning* dress with shortened sleeves and kilted skirts over a moderate bustle. Although somewhat dated by current fashion trends, it appeared she'd made some effort to look presentable. Her choice of head-wear was an acceptable gable bonnet with a sharply peaked brim and she protectively clutched an expensive sealskin purse. Her sense of style did little to soften her appearance and plainly obvious to all, her expression contained no warmth nor invited anything more than a mere, and only very tepid salutation — it didn't extend to forgiveness for her unannounced and impolite intrusion. In this awkward situation the responsibility of confronting the intruder befell the newspaper's senior reporter, Mr Pembroke.

Behind her in the doorway, looking increasingly uncomfortable and apologetic, stood a secretary who'd failed to prevent the interloper from entering the most hallowed inner sanctum of the *Evening Standard*.

Mr Pembroke removed his reading spectacles and rose from his seat more quickly than he should, dislodging his chair pillow which tumbled to the floor, and giving the secretary a nod indicating he would deal with the unexpected encroachment. He forced a smile. "Ah, Mrs, uh — Mrs Bedsworth, good morning and what –"

She turned from appraising the bullpen's clutter and faced the elderly reporter with a look of disdainful scorn. "Bedingfield, Mr Pembroke, Mrs Bedingfield," she corrected him harshly.

With the identity of the hostile intruder now established and confirmed, all six of the *Evening Standard*'s reporters turned away and were again, diligently and with some enthusiasm, going about their business. No one was keen to engage with the woman as all had previously heard about her sharp tongue from past visits, and one or two, unfortunately, had experienced it.

The *Evening Standard*'s most junior reporter, Leonard Hardy, who sat at the very front of the bullpen where he could be keenly observed and productively managed, had his head down, mere inches from his desk where he grinned, thoroughly enjoying his superior's discomfort.

"Forgive me, Mrs Bedingfield, in my advanced years, my memory has lapses," apologised Mr Pembroke, with a token bow of his head.

"Then, let's hope age spares your acumen," she added coldly.

Leonard could feel, rather than hear Milton Camden, the reporter seated directly behind him, react to the acerbic barb.

"And how may we be of assistance to you this morning?" asked Mr Pembroke. His voice a little louder than necessary, highlighting his disquiet.

"He's absconded, Mr Pembroke. Mr Bedingfield has disappeared."

Mr Pembroke raised an eyebrow, but not out of concern. "Again?" he asked. His expression unreadable but bordering on angelic.

Leonard was not alone, all the dedicated newspaper men whose faces were buried in their work were amused, fighting to control their reactions and remain taciturn. A challenging task at best.

"But, er, you only recently found him…" he continued.

"Well, yes, of course, but Mr Bedingfield has, he has…" she leaned forward slightly lowering her voice, "continued his intemperance and returned to his wanton ways."

"Ah, yes. How unfortunate," commiserated Mr Pembroke. "Then I suggest you visit the constabulary and report his, uh…"

Leonard silently mouthed, *escape.*

"…disappearance, Mrs Bedingfield," offered Mr Pembroke as he shuffled a step closer to the door, a subtle hint she'd imposed enough on his valuable time. After all, he was a busy man with responsibilities and a deadline to consider.

"I have indeed solicited their help; as yet, they have been remiss and unable to locate him, which is why I thought this tabloid could assist me and the constabulary by publishing a front page composition detailing his disappearance."

Mr Pembroke thrust out his chest slightly at the offensive depiction of his beloved newspaper.

Not so long ago, the *Evening Standard* was struggling; failing in its task to deliver the high standard of journalistic excellence required of a leading city newspaper. But through Mr Pembroke's dedication and tireless efforts, the paper was now flourishing and moderately prosperous.

"Mrs Bedingfield, the *Evening Standard* is not a tabloid, but a respected and well-received metropolitan newspaper." He paused a moment, challenging her unflinching gaze with one of his own. He cleared his throat. "Your husband is most likely to be found with the other drunk– er, gentlemen on Courtenay Place where such ungodly men often congregate."

"He's been gone for three weeks, Mr Pembroke, what am I to do?"

Mr Pembroke conceded she did have valid reason for concern and slid a finger between his shirt collar and neck. It felt uncomfortably tight. Three weeks was a lot longer than the other three times the poor fellow had managed to stay away. He coughed to clear his throat. "Yes, I do accede your point." He looked around the bullpen at the back of his reporters heads who were hoping not to be noticed and now diligently engrossed in their work. His gaze settled and stopped at the back of a head. "We're so understaffed…" he mumbled.

"Mr Pembroke, I do not read lips, please speak up and enunciate," she scolded.

"We are very understaffed at present," he repeated, this time much louder. "We have a reporter who has taken ill. He's recuperating but has been absent all of a month."

Those in the bullpen used to the moods of the senior reporter could detect the angst in his voice. Not wishing to be singled out, their heads settled even lower hoping to blend in to the scarred woodwork of their writing desks and become invisible.

"I fail to see why this becomes my problem, this… newspaper serves the community, I am part of the community, am I not?"

"Oh yes, indeed you are, Mrs Bedingfield," acknowledged Mr Pembroke with a miniscule amount of sarcasm creeping into his voice.

She folded her arms, with the sealskin purse dangling from beneath her hand like an impenetrable shield. With lips compressed, she waited, like a serpent poised to strike again with another biting, poisonous rebuke.

Resigned to the superfluous task of assigning a reporter, Mr Pembroke came to a decision and exhaled slowly. "Mr Hardy, please retrieve your notebook and a sharp pencil and kindly escort Mrs Bedingfield to the conference room where you are to gather all relevant information about the unfortunate disappearance of her husband."

Leonard's eyes opened wide, he froze. He must have misheard. Milton Camden, the reporter seated behind, stifled a laugh with a poorly disguised cough.

"Mr Hardy!"

As the most junior reporter, Leonard's duties did not involve writing actual stories. His normal day-to-day activities included writing obituaries, advertising copy, and compiling shipping notices, the life-blood of a successful city newspaper. For Mr Pembroke to call on him to attend to Mrs Bedingfield was quite out of the ordinary and somewhat perplexing. *What have I done? Am I being punished?* he silently questioned.

Galvanised by the command, he scooped up his notebook, a pencil, including spares and headed towards his superior and Mrs Bedingfield, who still stood impatiently waiting near the open door. The embarrassed secretary had long gone.

"Mrs Bedingfield, this is Mr Hardy, he will record all pertinent details for you." Mr Pembroke smiled raising an arm like a divine holy man, indicating they should exit the bullpen through the doorway and receive redemption.

"Then let's hope he is competent," she added, thrusting her nose in the air.

"Please follow me, Mrs Bedingfield," Leonard said, ignoring her comment as he eased past her and Mr Pembroke. He could smell moth-balls; obviously Mrs Bedingfield didn't wear this dress often, he surmised.

The conference room was unremarkable. A plain mahogany table and half a dozen chairs filled the seldom used space, and few dusty paintings that graced the walls did little to brighten the dull atmosphere. The room's best feature was a row of windows along one wall that provided an impressive view over downtown Wellington and the busy harbour beyond.

"Please be seated, Mrs Bedingfield," Leonard politely invited, and as etiquette dictated, stood behind a suitable chair to offer her assistance in the event her bustle proved unmanageable.

She frowned disapprovingly, hesitating briefly as she tried to decide if his invitation was appropriate. Deciding no offence was intended, she gathered her skirts and slowly sat, perching herself on the chair's edge while still tightly clutching her purse. Leonard found a seat opposite her, then arranged his notebook and pencils and offered her a warm smile. She didn't reciprocate, instead looking at him coldly.

He cleared his throat. "May I have your husband's full name, please?"

"Harold Arthur Bedingfield."

"Do you call him Harold, or is he known as 'Harry'?" Leonard asked as he scratched away in his notebook.

"His name is Harold, why would I address him in any other way?" she snapped at him.

Leonard raised his eyes and resisted the temptation to respond. "Age?"

"Thirty-four, in July."

"And your residential address?"

"Number one-hundred-and-one Ellice Street, Mount Victoria." Her voice was flat and lacked emotion.

"Can you please describe his general appearance, height, hair colour and weight?"

"He isn't a particularly handsome man, but was a good provider until he began his immoral pursuits." She looked away and stared out the window as if her revelation was shameful.

Leonard again looked up and waited for her to continue.

"Mr Bedingfield is without hair, nor gifted with fine teeth," she continued matter-of-factly. "He stands at an acceptable five feet and nine inches tall, of average weight. Although lately he seems thinner and gaunt," she added as an afterthought.

"Occupation?"

"He calls himself a saddler, but he's lazy and refuses to work anymore."

Leonard kept his eyes on his notes. *This woman was virulent.* He'd not be doing Mr Bedingfield any favours if the article in the paper was useful in locating him. He took a deep breath and continued. "And when was the last time you saw him?"

She sighed. "Twenty-two days ago, on the afternoon of March tenth."

"And where was he when you saw him last?"

She looked away and didn't reply.

"Ahh, Mrs Bedingfield?..." Leonard waited.

She remained silent as she stared at a painting of a solitary horse on the far wall. It may have been a racehorse, Leonard didn't know, and cared less. As far as he was concerned it was just a horse, but it held her fascination.

He began to doodle on his notepad as he waited for her to respond. After a few moments he repeated the question. "Mrs Bedingfield, where was it you saw your husband last?"

"On Courtenay Place," she replied suddenly, tearing her gaze from the painting.

"And where exactly?"

"Near Cambridge Terrace by the tram shelter," she said, barely above a whisper.

Leonard recorded the information then raised his head to look at her. "For what reason was he in Courtenay Place? And can you tell me the names of his closest friends or associates?"

Her head spun and she glared at him. "He ran away; he abandoned me, preferring to be with those objectionable hobos who loiter without means or temperance, Mr Hardy," her voice icy.

Before Leonard could respond, she continued. "When he saw me, he, he … ran … I haven't seen him since." She stood suddenly, self-consciously arranged her dress and stepped toward the door. "I place little faith in your ability to find Mr Bedingfield, Mr Hardy, however it appears that I have no choice in the matter as you are all this newspaper has seen fit to provide." She gave him another stern, deprecating look, opened her mouth to say more, thought better of it and snapped it closed it again. Her expression returned to the familiar guise of austerity. "Good day, Mr Hardy."

Before Leonard could react she reached for the door.

"Do you love him?" He winced inwardly. Again, he'd opened his mouth without thinking. An unfortunate habit that frequently had unpleasant consequences.

She paused as he rose from his chair, then turned her head and made eye contact with him. Her gaze was chilling.

"I, uh, apologise Mrs Bedingfield, that was rude and inappropriate of me."

It mattered not, she was gone, the door closed before he'd finished.

Leonard returned to his seat with a groan. *If I was married to that woman, I'd run away too*, he thought.

Chapter Two

As they usually did first thing in the morning after arriving at work, the hard-working reporters of the *Evening Standard* were seated at their writing desks, engaged in their usual ribald banter before Mr Pembroke arrived. Today they were discussing the rather agreeable form of a young woman who was employed at the cobbler's, two doors down from the newspaper's offices, when the door knob began to rotate, triggering its dependable warning. All conversation immediately ceased and everyone appeared to be diligently hard at work when Mr Pembroke entered the bullpen.

He paused briefly, glanced quickly around the room and sniffed loudly. "I detect the vociferous odour of inactivity, a disgusting vile habit propagated by the slothful and maladroit. Inform me; surely, such a pitiful affliction has no foundation to fester within the sanctity of these sacred four walls?"

The reporters all knew his question was rhetorical and therefore didn't require an answer. Most of them were grinning. Mr Pembroke's overly dramatic monologue was a sign of his mood and disagreeable disposition this fine morn.

Rather than habitually fussing with his chair pillow before seating himself, Mr Pembroke remained standing and cleared his throat. "Gentlemen, if I may have the pleasure of your undivided attention!"

With their interest piqued, all present twisted in their seats to face their supervisor, for this was not a common occurrence and most unusual. They waited curiously for him to continue.

"Mr Hardy," began Mr Pembroke when he saw everyone facing

him. "I'm sure you can vindicate yourself and explain your tardiness this morning? Or perhaps your fertile mind was focusing on other matters, like the young miss at the cobbler's?"

Leonard blushed, *How did he know?* "No. Uh, yes, I do have an excuse, sir."

The aging reporter folded his arms. "Spare us no details, out with it," goaded Mr Pembroke to everyone else's amusement.

"I apologise, Mr Pembroke, I *was* unavoidably delayed this morning."

"A late night carousing?" Mr Pembroke lifted a solitary eyebrow as he waited for a response.

Leonard looked quickly around the room and saw all eyes were on him. "No, sir," he shook his head in enthusiastic support of his denial. "I was waylaid by a customer, sir."

A reporter snickered behind his hand.

Mr Pembroke inclined his head, a subtle hint for him to continue.

"Mr Christopoulos," stated Leonard simply.

Normally, he was never late for work. This morning, Mr Christopoulos, a frequent advertiser with the newspaper, stopped him to chit-chat. It was idle talk, but the man, eager to discuss all topics of social importance was reluctant to allow Leonard to continue on his way. Rather than appear rude and rush off, Leonard stayed to talk with him. After all, he was a regular paying advertising customer of the *Evening Standard* and it was important to maintain a healthy relationship. A tenet of the paper's publisher, of which Mr Beaumont keenly reminded his employees.

Satisfied with his response and unwilling to press the issue, Mr Pembroke nodded and looked around the room and untypically avoided making any further eye contact with his most junior employee. "I will keep this brief." He cleared his throat. "I am pleased to inform you all that we have a new staff member commencing work tomorrow. This should ease the burden somewhat. Mr Beaumont has agreed to increase our reporting staff and I'm sure you will all do your utmost to make Mr Neil Flanagan feel welcome."

A murmur rippled around the room. A few men looked in sympathy at Leonard. It was universally expected he would receive a promotion so it came as a disappointment to nearly everyone that he'd been overlooked.

"What will his duties be?" asked a voice.

"He will focus on issues of economic and financial significance, otherwise he will assist where he can and sit at the vacant desk beside Mr Hardy until I re-organise the current seating arrangements."

"And he has experience, sir?" someone asked.

"Considerably, he has been in the employ of leading newspapers in England."

"I ain't never heard o'him," commented another, while someone else muttered something unintelligible that didn't sound complimentary. If Mr Pembroke was expecting gratitude for hiring another reporter, then he must have felt discouraged, for none was forthcoming, and the mood in the bullpen turned decidedly glum. Ignoring the sarcasm he scanned the room, still avoiding eye contact with Leonard. "Unless you have further questions, please return to your work. That will be all."

All conversation trickled to a stop and heads obediently returned to their familiar positions. Leonard stared at his desk feeling the stab of discontent. He'd hoped to be considered for advancement and promoted to become a regular reporter for the newspaper. *Perhaps management has its reasons*, he thought morosely.

A polite cough emanated from the very rear of the room; it was a casual reminder to begin work. It was only 8.30 a.m., and already Leonard was looking forward to meeting his friends for a beverage at the Southern Cross Hotel after work. It couldn't come quick enough, he decided.

"What did you say to that detestable woman?" Bridgette Leyton asked between howls of delight.

Leonard looked sheepish. "I asked if she loved him."

Constable Tim Yates was doubled over in hysterics, while Mary Worthington, who sat beside Leonard, turned away and also began to laugh.

Mary and Bridgette were distantly related. Mary, an English immigrant, came to New Zealand after her husband became ill and died. She had few friends in her newly adopted country and only one relative on her mother's side, an elderly, frail aunt who resided in a community twenty miles north of Wellington. Mary currently lived in Bridgette's guest room as a boarder, an arrangement that pleased them both. Bridgette and her late husband Alex had decided that Mary was a suitable romantic match for Leonard, and introduced them. To everyone's delight, Mary and Leonard eventually became betrothed.

"I couldn't help myself," Leonard explained to his friends. "It's obvious the poor man has repeatedly attempted to leave her, and like a wayward puppy, she keeps retrieving him and brings him back home. It's plainly evident he wants nothing to do with her, and quite frankly, neither would I. She is a bitter, pitiless woman."

"And how did she respond?" asked Mary, managing to control her mirth.

"She stared at me as if I were the devil himself; that woman has not an ounce of love or warmth in her frigid and vacant soul."

"I'm sure she does love him but just has a peculiar way of showing it," Mary added. She released Leonard's hand and reached for the small glass of sherry on the table.

"Well, you've done your part, Leo, now it's up to the newspaper. Let's see if anyone comes forward with information," said Bridgette.

Leonard turned to Tim. "Where could he go to hide where no one could find him, Tim?"

Tim shrugged, "I suppose there are plenty of places, but to remain undetected for three weeks is odd, I grant you that. He could even be in hospital, or tragically, he may be dead."

"Isn't it routine procedure for police to investigate hospitals when searching for missing persons?" Leonard asked.

"Do you believe the constabulary would devote resources to locate a vagrant drunkard? They have more important things to attend to, dear boy," replied Tim.

"Well, it isn't my problem," stated Leonard after a moment of silence.

"And you won't put your sleuthing skills to the test and locate him?" Tim asked.

Leonard shrugged. "Isn't my job."

"I don't blame him for leaving her, she seems to be a very unpleasant woman," added Bridgette.

"And why would anyone wed a woman like that?" questioned Tim.

Leonard shifted to a more comfortable position on his chair. "Certainly there isn't reciprocal love between them. I wish the poor fellow all the best. He's better off without her."

The four friends were enjoying a drink at their favourite local establishment, the Southern Cross Hotel. The only one missing was

Meredith Smithson, who Constable Tim Yates had been calling on with some regularity over the last few months, but unfortunately she was scheduled to work this evening. Bridgette and Mary were nurses and worked with Meredith at Wellington Hospital.

"That's settled then," said Bridgette, keen to change the topic of their conversation. She looked at Leonard. "And speaking of love and marriage, have you set a wedding date yet?" She gave Mary a subtle wink.

Mary smiled and turned to her fiancé, who surreptitiously avoided her gaze.

"Uh, no, not yet, Mary and I are still discussing it." Leonard quickly added as his cheeks flushed, "Nothing has been finalised."

Mary's eyes narrowed slightly.

"Leo, you can't keep a lady waiting like this, you need to make a decision promptly, it's been months," Bridgette advised, trying to look stern.

"We just need to arrange some details and coordinate which family members can attend the wedding," Mary offered, coming to Leonard's defence.

Seeing Leonard's discomfort, Tim grinned.

"Worry not Bridgette, you'll get an invite," laughed Leonard.

She pushed aside an errant strand of her fiery red hair and sat back in her chair. "I hope so, as I'm so looking forward to your big day."

Leonard was a widower. His wife Mae had tragically died in suspicious circumstances when she fell beneath a swiftly moving Hansom cab. Coincidently, Bridgette's husband had died in a similar fashion when pushed in front of a cab on Adelaide Road only the year before. Leonard had struggled to fully commit to a new relationship as he still felt strong bonds for his dearly departed wife. *My big day, marriage,* Leonard sighed. His mouth tightened and he turned away. He didn't see the expression on Mary's face as she looked down at her hands resting in her lap.

A brisk, cold southerly wind blew over the hills surrounding Wellington, cruelly reminding the city's inhabitants that the beautiful days of summer were a distant memory. Overhead, as darkness reluctantly succumbed to the hesitant dawn of a new day, slate grey skies declared that rain was imminent, and the morning's typical discourse would undoubtedly turn to Wellingtonians favourite topic of conversation, the weather.

Leonard rose at his normal time of 6:00 a.m., dressed quickly and prepared himself for the day ahead. After a cup of freshly brewed coffee, he departed for work at his regular time, walking from his property, closing his gate, and pausing briefly as he turned up the collar of his coat to thwart the biting chill. With hands buried deep in his pockets, his satchel slung over a shoulder, he made his way down the steeply inclined Marjoribanks Street towards the newspaper offices, about a fifteen-minute walk.

At the bottom of the hill Hansom cabs, a variety of wagons and horses, clogged the swarming intersection of Courtenay Place and Cambridge Terrace. The mayhem from nearby produce markets always created congestion here in the morning, and while Leonard waited for a tram to pass through the intersection he followed the erratic flight of a wayward paper bag caught in the wind.

Propelled by the persistent southerly, the bag tumbled down the street, dodging people and obstacles, occasionally soaring upwards and then descending as the swirling wind eased slightly. Suddenly its roving journey came to an abrupt end as the bag blew against a branch of a Pohutukawa tree. Another gust saw the bag unfettered, and it continued merrily on its way, but Leonard no longer watched its fitful path, instead his eyes were fixed on a man seated on the ground, leaning back against the tree the bag had flown against. He could vaguely see another figure lying on a bench-seat near the tram shelter a couple of yards away. He immediately recalled his interview with Mrs Bedingfield and how she'd last seen her husband at this very place. Curiosity got the better of him and as soon as the traffic eased, he quickly walked across the road towards the two men.

The man seated on the ground leaning against the Pohutukawa tree was, quite obviously, intoxicated. He babbled incoherently and, although it was too difficult to determine his age, he appeared far too old to be Mr Bedingfield. The other man was definitely younger; to Leonard's eye he may have been anywhere between thirty and fifty years old. He lay atop a wooden bench cocooned in a large and very worn, buttonless overcoat. A length of twine wrapped around his waist kept the chill out and the coat from opening, but it did little to hide a half-empty bottle of methylated spirits that peeked out from beneath the filthy folds. From the description Mrs Bedingfield had given him, it was plainly obvious the drunkard wasn't her wayward husband. In spite of his appalling filthy, and dishevelled condition, the man appeared to be somewhat attentive so Leonard bent down to talk with him.

"Excuse me, ah, I wonder if you could assist me?"

The hobo shifted his head slightly and grunted.

"I'm looking for a man, his name is Harold Bedingfield. Have you seen him recently?"

The man rubbed his rheumy eyes, but they failed to focus. Dried spittle collected at the corners of his mouth, and his stained and dirty beard hid discoloured teeth. "Got a coupla bob[1] for me?" asked the man hoarsely. His eyes remained unfocused.

"Er, I'm looking for Mr Bedingfield," he repeated. Even in the wind, Leonard detected the unpleasant odour of vomit and faeces. He prudently decided to take a step back.

The drunk tried to laugh but ended up coughing; the wet hack caused Leonard to grimace and turn away as the man hawked. "Two bob?" he finally managed to rasp after his coughing fit subsided.

Leonard knew if he gave the man two shillings he'd spend it on alcohol. But then again, the man was already drinking high-powered methylated spirits. If he must drink, then surely whiskey would be better. He fished in his pocket for a coin.

The drunk watched him but did not see.

"When was the last time you saw Harold Bedingfield?"

Recognising the sound of jangling coins as Leonard dug in his pocket, the man raised a trembling, grimy hand, ingrained black with unwashed dirt.

Careful to not touch him, Leonard braved stepping closer and dropped a single coin into his outstretched paw. "Well … have you seen him?"

The man barked again; the wet hack made Leonard feel queasy.

"Harold, you said?" wheezed the man. His sightless eyes stared into nothingness.

1   *Bob, slang term for shilling.*

Leonard felt a measure of hope. "Yes, has he been here recently, are you acquainted with Mr Bedingfield and know where I may find him?"

The drunk nodded and opened his mouth to speak, then just as quickly, shook his head and changed his mind. "I ain't seen him." With another cough, he fumbled for his bottle then rolled over to face away.

Leonard stood. "Why can't you tell me?"

The drunkard didn't move or respond; feeling a little miffed, Leonard watched him a few moments longer before shrugging his shoulders and continuing on to work.

Chapter Three

The last reporter exited the bullpen, leaving Leonard alone. Everyone else was out covering stories. Mr Pembroke was at a City Council meeting, and the newest employee, Neil Flanagan, who'd begun his tenure at the *Evening Standard* this morning, was thrust immediately into the deep-end having been assigned to report on the expensive Wellington harbour reclamation project. Other reporters were going about their normal duties, which left Leonard to complete his work in solitude.

He stared blankly at the wall, directly in front, where a variety of old notices were pinned to a large corkboard. Some were memorandums reminding employees of a company picnic, a Christmas function, while others were humorous, representing the bawdy, off-colour, dry wit of reporters. The results of an office raffle held two-and-a-half years ago were still attached to the notice board; the paper yellowed and curled at its edges.

He had no enthusiasm for work and so, distracted, his thoughts drifted to Mary and the pressure he felt to finally agree on a wedding date. He knew he should feel happy about marrying her. She was beautiful, intelligent, had a well-developed sense of humour and was loving and supportive. *What more can I want in a wife?* he thought. But a part of him couldn't let Mae go. She had died – no, she'd been deliberately targeted and then killed by a Hansom cab. It wasn't an accident as the coroner initially stated. Later it was discovered that her death was linked to the illicit activities of an Oriental crime gang. Leonard shuddered and immediately felt overcome by the familiar feeling of loss.

It wasn't a good day. Actually, if he were honest, it hadn't been a good week. Mr Pembroke's decision to hire a new reporter instead of promoting him didn't sit well. He felt let down, used and disheartened, especially when he'd worked hard, well beyond the expectations placed on him. Management had ignored his fine efforts, and instead, they'd hired a total stranger. And to top it off, he was out of pocket and swindled out of a shilling by a hobo.

With a heavy sigh, Leonard half-heartedly resumed his work, and after an uneventful day, departed for home at his regular time.

"Do you remember me? I was here yesterday and gave you a shilling," said Leonard to the hobo the following morning.

The drunk was just as filthy and didn't appear to have moved since he saw him the previous day. The only difference was that he had another bottle of methylated spirits. He held it to his lips, taking a swallow of the poison.

Leonard grimaced, and received a rancid belch in response.

"Where can I find Harold Bedingfield?" he repeated.

"Can a good gentleman like yerself spare a bob or two?" Like a serpent, a filthy hand snaked out from beneath the coat. An appeal for more money.

"No! Please, as a generous gratuity, I gave you a shilling yesterday and you didn't tell me anything."

The drunk shook his head in confusion, pausing for a moment, his unseeing eyes unfocused as he appeared deep in thought. He coughed once, a sickly wet bark, and lifted his head to face Leonard. "He'd most likely be with Sweet Hazel."

Leonard recoiled. *Another woman*? "Who is Hazel and where

does she live?"

The drunk hacked again, then weakly shook his head. "I, uh, don't know any more." Realising no more money was forthcoming, he folded his arms, tucked his head into his chest and closed his eyes.

"Please, I need more."

The drunk didn't respond.

Again, Leonard lingered a few moments longer. Trams arrived disgorging passengers, Hansom cabs came and went and a few commuters looked curiously at him as they hurried past. Except for his wheezing, the drunkard remained silent, and it was plainly obvious he wouldn't communicate further. Disappointed, he gave up waiting and continued on to work. He found the notion that Mr Bedingfield was having an illicit affair with someone called Hazel rather amusing. He certainly couldn't blame the man, but Mrs Bedingfield indicated that Harold was intemperate. A drunkard having a *liaison amoureuse* seems most unlikely, he mused with a grin.

He walked quickly to the *Evening Standard* only to find the bullpen empty, all the reporters were out. He sat at his desk and again stared listlessly at the wall. Once again his anxiety over marriage resurfaced and he felt guilty for his doubts. Mary deserved better, much better than he could give her.

The sound of the rotating door knob reminded him to return to his duties so when the *Evening Standard*'s newest employee, Neil Flanagan, stepped into the bullpen, Leonard had his head down and appeared to be diligently hard at work.

"Good Morning Mr Hardy."

"Huh? Oh, indeed. Good Morning Mr Flanagan," greeted Leonard with little enthusiasm.

Neil Flanagan perched himself casually on the edge of his desk and looked down at Leonard. "Having a difficult day?"

Leonard looked up and frowned. "How about a terrible week."

The reporter offered a sympathetic smile. "How bad could it be? I've seen that look before and if I may impose on your privacy, then I surmise there is normally a woman involved."

Leonard met the reporter's gaze and remained silent.

"Ah yes, the tribulations and complexities of the fairer sex," suggested Neil.

Leonard felt awkward, he didn't share his private life with colleagues, let alone a stranger, however he could see that Mr Flanagan was only trying to be cordial. "Another of life's perplexing mysteries," he replied with a smile. In unspoken agreement, both men remained quiet for a moment.

"Uh, it will be luncheon soon, could I take the liberty and perhaps buy you a cup of tea and a sandwich?" offered the *Evening Standard*'s new reporter.

Leonard looked at Mr Flanagan. He was quite dapper for a newspaperman. Unusual really. Most reporters were not known for their style or sense of flair when it came to their appearance. Normally they looked hackneyed and dishevelled. Neil Flanagan's clothes were fashionable and appeared expensive, and for a large muscular man, he wore them well with a nuance of sophistication. *Perhaps there isn't any harm in having a cup of tea with a work associate,* he thought. "That is very kind of you, Mr Flanagan, that would be nice."

"Please, you may address me as Neil, more informal, eh?" he replied with a toothy grin.

Leonard smiled. "And my friends call me Leo."

"Splendid, then at twelve, we'll have a refreshment and a chat and get to know one another, Leo."

The door latching mechanism sounded its dependable warning and automatically Leonard's head dropped; to to any casual visitor he appeared to be studiously working. However, Neil Flanagan was unaware of the prerequisite of the audible door warning and was still half seated on top of his desk when Mr Pembroke entered the bullpen.

"Is it luncheon already?" the senior reporter innocently enquired as he placed his satchel on the desk and began arranging his chair pillow. "For I could easily mistake your indolence for a man unused to the rigours and entirely reasonable demands placed on him by this generous newspaper." Satisfied the pillow was suitably positioned, Mr Pembroke straightened and turned to face the front of the room – towards Neil who was only now trying to quickly manoeuvre around his desk so he could be properly seated. This time Mr Pembroke expected an answer.

Leonard kept his head down and grimaced. He felt pity for Neil.

"Forgive me, I do apologise Mr–"

"Here at the *Evening Standard*, we do not offer weak excuses for our torpidity, Mr Flanagan," interrupted Mr Pembroke. "We accept our shortcomings and always strive for betterment—and to never repeat them, isn't that so Mr Hardy?"

"I fully concur, Mr Pembroke," Leonard answered, doing his best not to laugh.

"Mr Flanagan, see to it that your time is purposely managed."

"Thank you for your wisdom and immensely profitable insights, sir, it shan't happen again."

Leonard raised an eyebrow, Neil returned Mr Pembroke's rebuke with equal fluency.

Mr Pembroke sat at his desk before delivering his final riposte. "Carry on, Mr Flanagan," he replied sternly, "time is money."

"Is he always like that?" questioned Neil as he stirred his tea and watched Leonard with some amusement.

Leonard was delicately spreading a liberal amount of whipped cream on top of the strawberry jam that he'd already smeared onto a scone. It wasn't an easy task, and by his own admission, he was attempting to defy the laws of physics. He explained to Neil that the challenge was to place as much cream as possible onto the scone, where its mass would be self-supporting and not be affected by motion. The motion, he clarified, was the distance the scone had to travel from the saucer to his mouth and retain the mass exactly where he'd placed it.

"Stiffer cream would help," Neil volunteered.

"Mr Pembroke takes great delight in his theatrical oratory, it's normally a sign of his disagreeable disposition." Leonard licked his fingers and stared hungrily at his creation. "But you see, you can't ever be far away from your desk, or not working when you hear the door knob rotate. When that knob turns you have a short amount of time to appear busy." Leonard lifted the saucer so it was near his mouth and with some care and practiced skill, gently lifted the scone.

Neil watched, his own mouth involuntarily opening.

A large portion of the scone disappeared into Leonard's mouth while his nose dislodged a substantial amount of cream. It hung precariously. Neil quickly offered Leonard a napkin and watched in amazement as Leonard devoured the first bite, placed the remainder of the scone back on to the saucer and wiped his mouth and nose.

"However, you will find Mr Pembroke fair and balanced, if not gruff," Leonard mumbled with his mouth full.

"Yes, somewhat typical." Neil watched Leonard for a moment as he licked his fingers before tackling the remaining portion of the scone. "And for entertainment, Leo, how do you occupy your time in Wellington?"

Leonard chewed with gusto. As he savoured the lingering tang and sweetness of the strawberry jam, he thought of his response. He swallowed, wiped the last vestiges of jam and cream from his mouth and then swept crumbs from his morning coat. "There are many activities, but mostly my friends and I have frequent get-togethers or a have a meal. Sometimes we go into town for a night out," he explained.

Neil nodded. "I have yet to make any acquaintances since I arrived here."

"Have you seen much of Wellington since your arrival?"

"No, not really, only Island Bay," Neil replied.

"Why don't you join us for a beverage at the Southern Cross Hotel on Saturday afternoon? I'm sure the group would enjoy meeting you." Leonard drained the last of his tea and stood. "We really should get back."

"Thank you for the invitation Leo, I think I will take you up on that offer, Saturday afternoon at the Southern Cross. You are indeed kind."

The wind was most unforgiving this morning. It's chill was penetrating and in spite of layered clothing to hinder its frigid advance, Leonard still had ruddy cheeks and a runny nose. To make matters even worse, it looked like rain again. He quickened his pace and then stood at the bottom of Marjoribanks Street with his hands buried deep in his pockets while he waited to safely cross the congested street. He raised his head and looked across the intersection as his thoughts turned to the hobo he'd spoken to the previous morning. It came as no surprise to see the figure huddled up in his coat on the same bench. He felt sympathy; the poor man must be freezing. As soon as there was a pause in the traffic, he cautiously navigated through the busy intersection to ask him a few more questions.

The eastern end of Courtenay Place, where the hobos congregated, was normally bustling with commuters as it was a major hub for trams and Hansom cabs, but no one generally spared any time for the intemperate men who loitered or made this place their home. Many pretended not to hear their languid appeals for gratuity and just walked past or looked away to spare themselves the burden of guilt. Although it was acknowledged these men chose to be here, and their lifestyle, free from the constraints of normal and acceptable social behaviour, openly consumed alcoholic beverages and solicited vociferously for coin or favour. To avoid the haranguing, most people, including Leonard, always walked on the other side of the street and were spared having to devote thought to the pitiless, undignified men who cared not for a place to call their own.

As Leonard approached, he saw the figure on the bench raise a bottle of whiskey to his lips and take a hefty pull. Leonard shuddered involuntarily - it was only about 7.30 a.m.. More astonishing was the fact the hobo wasn't the same man he'd spoken to for the last two mornings. He paused a foot or two away from the drunk, unsure of what to do.

"Is bloody c-c-cold today, sirrr, gotta c-c-coin r'two to help me get a hot meal?" stammered the hobo, slurring his words.

"Where is the other fellow, the one who was here yesterday?" Leonard asked as he glanced around hoping to catch sight of the man he sought.

The drunk was well prepared for disagreeable weather and wore a long coat, scarf, hat and gloves, all of which had seen better days, and evidently, not benefitted from a launder in quite some time. They were filthy. The drunk spent a moment or two focusing on Leonard, "You mean B-Balthazar?" He belched loudly without shame.

"Yes, the man who lay here for the last two mornings, where is he?" Leonard turned his face away as a medley of rank smells infused with cheap whiskey assaulted him.

"He's g-g-gone."

"Gone? Gone where?"

"He'd be d-d-d, he'd be dead, sir."

"What?" Leonard flinched. "No, surely not! I uh, I spoke to him yesterday and he looked health–" He realised the man certainly wasn't healthy when he saw him last. "Oh dear, that's terrible."

The sot casually shrugged as if death meant nothing and was just an expected outcome for the unfortunate, bereft of luck, kindness or a penny.

"Was it the methylated spirits?"

The drunk appeared to concentrate for a moment, a task he seemed to have some difficulty in achieving "N-no, sir, t'was the man who came to see him, told that to the c-c-constable, I did."

Leonard was taken back, his eyebrows furrowed together as he grasped what the hobo told him. He risked taking half a step closer and squatted as close to the drunkard as he dared. "Are you suggesting foul play? Was he killed? What man? Please, tell me what happened?"

The drunk raised his head uncertainly. "A soldier, he b-bent down, did something to him, then that w-w-was it."

"And he was dead, after the man bent down?"

The drunk nodded and lay his head down on the seat. "If you c-c-can spare a c-c-coin, sir."

"You said his name was Balthazar, and what is his family name?"

"You look flush, c-c-can spare a shilling or t-t-two for the penniless, sir?"

"Do you know his family name?"

The drunk looked confused as he tried to remember, then shook his head again.

"What about the soldier, who was he?"

"I'd seen him here a'fore, not familiar with his n-name, though." He unscrewed the lid of the whiskey bottle and took another pull.

"And the constabulary came?"

"As I said, sir, they c-c-came, took the body away and I g-got his spot," the drunk wheezed, then coughed.

"Could you be mistaken, I mean, then you're sure he was killed?"

"I saw what I saw, and told that to the c-c-constable," he stuttered.

Leonard needed to hasten or he'd be tardy for work and he didn't feel like being exhorted by Mr Pembroke. He stood, easing the cramp in his legs. "Are you familiar with Harold Bedingfield?"

Again the sot shook his head and stretched out an open hand.

Leonard dropped a sixpence into the filthy mitt, thanked him and with the cold forgotten, hurried away hoping to seek some facts from one of the reporters at work.

Chapter Four

"And who is this mysterious man you've invited to join us this afternoon, Leo?" asked Bridgette as she settled more comfortably into her chair at the Southern Cross Hotel.

"He is our newest employee, Mr Neil Flanagan," replied Leonard as he looked towards the door hoping to catch a glimpse of him.

"Is he the chap that took your job?" Tim asked.

Leonard shrugged, "I don't know, for whatever reason the newspaper deemed appropriate, they hired him instead of offering me advancement."

"I think you deserve a promotion, Leonard," Mary added. "After all you've worked very hard for that newspaper and performed admirably well, I might add. I think it's deplorable you weren't considered."

"It seems rather unfair. Can't you talk to your employer about it?" questioned Tim.

Leonard was becoming increasingly frustrated. "To what means? If they wanted to consider me for promotion, then I'm sure they would have discussed it with me."

"Then you should make your feelings known, speak to Mr Pembroke, he's a reasonable man," Mary offered.

"And what will that achieve?" Leonard retorted sharply. "Oh, yes, Mr Hardy, of course we will hire you as a reporter, forgive us for our misgivings. We will dismiss our new employee forthwith, and promote you instead!" Leonard replied with slightly more vigour and sarcasm than he intended. He reached for his glass.

Mary's cheeks flushed and she turned away.

Leonard looked towards the entrance door again.

"Excuse me," Mary suddenly said. She stood quickly and walked to the back of the room towards the women's water closet[2].

Bridgette glowered at Leonard then rose from her seat. "Leonard, that was callous and insensitive," she said disapprovingly. With her nose thrust in the air and with a rustle of skirts, she spun and followed Mary.

"You put the proverbial foot in it, old boy," admonished Tim with a shake of his head.

"What did I do?"

"That was a tad harsh."

Leonard looked contrite.

"Leo!"

Leonard looked up with a scowl, then recognized Neil Flanagan, who walked up to the table where they sat. With his previous churlish behaviour forgotten, he rose from his chair to greet his guest. "I'm pleased you decided to come, Neil. This is Constable Tim Yates. Tim this is Neil Flanagan who was recently hired by the *Evening Standard*."

"It's a pleasure to meet you, Mr Yates." Neil extended a hand and Tim shook it warmly.

"Please, call me Tim, and welcome to our Saturday afternoon *soirée*."

Neil looked puzzled, "Where's the music?"

"You just missed the performance," replied Tim with a grin as he looked at Leonard.

---

2   *Water closet or W.C, convenience, lavatory.*

"Ignore him, Neil, please have a seat," offered Leonard, feeling guilty for his earlier insensitive outburst at Mary.

An unexpected commotion at the other end of the room drew all their attention towards a group of brash young men who began quarrelling and shouting. Mary and Bridgette returned from the women's convenience in time to see four men begin pushing and shoving each other. Fuelled by alcohol and undoubtedly inebriated, two agitators were easily identified, and without ado, quickly marched from the premises. Hotel patrons, annoyed by their uncouth behaviour, yelled and cheered loudly in support of their expulsion.

Conversation returned to normal and Mary and Bridgette were introduced to Neil. Mary was still a little frosty towards Leonard and chose to ignore him, preferring to chat with Bridgette.

Neil purchased a round of drinks for them all and began to recount a humorous story around one of his experiences in London. He was a gifted storyteller and soon everyone was laughing and delighted in his company.

"I hope you are enjoying your new job at the *Evening Standard*?" Tim asked. "Leo says you are reporting on finance?"

Neil smiled. "I find writing about finance and the economy less than invigorating. I'd much prefer entertainment and recreation, is more to my liking and experience."

"Milton Camden has that portfolio and unlikely to hand it over any time soon," Leonard offered.

"That's what I was told when I applied for the position. But, one never knows, eh?"

The door to the Southern Cross Hotel flew open with a crash, and the two recently evicted larrikins returned, each brandishing a spade handle like a wooden club. They paused momentarily near the doorway, their heads swivelling from side to side as they searched for their quarry.

All conversation stopped and Tim, Leonard and Neil shot to their feet in alarm. The burly attendant who'd previously escorted the rabble-rousers from the bar, strode with determination and annoyance, weaving around tables and chairs, towards the two unwelcome intruders; his patience thin and intentions plainly obvious to all. One of the young men wielding the wooden club saw the large man lumbering towards them and waited with his weapon at the ready. Timing his move to perfection, he swung it forcibly, striking the attendant's upper arm, near his shoulder. With a howl of pain, the large man stumbled, quickly regained his footing and grabbed the young attacker, throwing him to the floor as the second young man prepared to bludgeon him with his own club.

Constable Tim Yates' expression hardened as his training took over. Without thought, he quickly stepped forward to block the attacker's path and intercede. However, he wasn't quite agile enough. The young man barrelled into him with some force, sending Tim sprawling over a chair. Bridgette and Mary were now directly in the path of the angry young lout and gasped as they saw their friend fall into a heap on the floor. Leonard was on the other side of the table and couldn't protect the women – he was helpless. Without hesitation, Neil sidestepped to stand directly in front of the club-wielding attacker. He bent slightly at the waist and waited until the last possible second before the lout collided into him. Neil's upper body swayed from side to side, offering a difficult target, and then with remarkable ability, his fist shot out. He struck the young man squarely on the nose, felling him instantly. A few patrons cheered in delight.

With his club forgotten, the brawler sat holding his injured nose as blood seeped through his fingers. Tim quickly regained his feet and secured the young man as Neil turned to the women to ensure they were unharmed. Leonard rushed over but could do little.

Both young men were restrained and now sat morosely on the floor. One held a bloody rag to his nose.

"What was all that about?" Leonard asked, once Tim had swiped dust and dirt from his clothes and returned to their table.

Tim shook his head, "It was nothing, one man believed another had insulted his mother. That's all it was." Tim looked over at Neil. "You handled yourself quite well … I see you've boxed before?"

All eyes were on Neil. He casually shrugged as if it were nothing. "I have spent a little time in the ring, mostly as a youth, but my immediate concern was for these fair ladies and their safety." He turned to Bridgette and Mary, offering a dashing smile and a bow with a dramatic flourish of his arm.

"Thank you, Mr Flanagan, is heart-warming to know chivalry still exists in these modern times," said Mary, returning his smile while still ignoring Leonard.

Leonard felt the rebuke.

Bridgette sat back in her chair observing the gallant hero carefully.

"Unfortunately, we were seated in the path of where the young man intended to go. I fear he may not have spared either of you as he barged through," replied Neil.

Tim made a second attempt to brush debris from his coat and trousers while Leonard observed Mary who began talking to Neil.

The two larrikins were given a stern talking to, and feeling somewhat remorseful, were marched away, and the afternoon continued without further incident.

Once Tim was again comfortably seated, Leonard scooted his chair closer to him. "Have you any information on the death of the man in Courtenay Place?"

Tim raised his glass to his lips and drained it, he wiped his mouth with his sleeve and met Leonard's inquisitive gaze. "One of your reporters was already sniffing around asking questions about it."

"I'm asking you—as a friend."

Tim exhaled. "I don't know much other than what was being spoken about at the depot. I agree, it is peculiar though."

Leonard glanced at Mary, who was in deep conversation with Neil. He turned back to Tim and leaned forward, lowering his voice. "And what *was* being spoken about at the depot?"

Tim eyed Leonard warily. Even though they were good friends, there was some information he just couldn't divulge. "The police are still investigating the matter … and need I remind you, Leo, I'm unable to share any of those details."

Leonard rolled his eyes. He'd heard this argument countless times, but he always found a way to make Tim talk. "I'm your friend."

Tim laughed. "However, what I *can* share with you …" he leaned closer and spoke quietly, "We are searching for a witness, a military man…"

"A witness? That isn't what I heard, seems this mystery military man may, in fact, be a murderer," Leonard interrupted rather loudly. Mary, Neil and Bridgette all looked towards him.

"And what do you know of this man, Leo?" Tim enquired, keeping his voice low.

Leonard noticed that Neil was now listening intently to their conversation. "Not much at all. I spoke to the same drunkard that the police spoke to, and he believes the man is a soldier. That's all I know."

Tim looked thoughtful.

Neil had his head cocked and listened with interest.

"Was the man actually murdered, or did he die of natural causes?" Leonard raised his eyebrows in question, "Or did that poison he drank kill him?" He knew Tim would provide him with information if he pushed him hard enough.

Tim sighed. "You don't give up, do you?" He laughed, then leaned forward and whispered. "Officially, we are still waiting on the results of the autopsy. However, I was told the victim had contusions around his throat, which suggests he was asphyxiated."

Leonard's eyes opened wide.

Tim continued. "In my opinion, I think he *was* murdered."

Leonard sat up. "Really? Why would anyone want to kill such a wretched man?"

Tim shrugged.

"Well, it certainly wasn't motivated by a robbery gone wrong. They're penniless." Leonard smirked.

"I agree," replied Tim with a smile. "Although, some are saying that we shouldn't take the testimony of a drunkard seriously."

"But the physical evidence supports his account, does it not?"

Again, Tim shrugged.

"And that's it, that's all you will divulge?" Leonard laughed.

The sky was overcast, and it was still a little chilly even though the wind had eased considerably when Leonard and his friends departed the Southern Cross. Warmly wrapped in coats, scarves and hats, they caught a tram back to Newtown, where Bridgette and Mary lived and where they planned to eat dinner together. They'd just alighted from the tram and were walking up the street towards Bridgette's home. Tim, Neil and Bridgette walked ahead, and Leonard urged Mary to drop back a bit so they could talk.

He waited a moment until the others were out of earshot and reached for her hand. "I apologise, Mary, it was rude and insensitive of me to say what I did earlier. I was wrong."

Although he clasped her hand, he did not feel a reassuring squeeze in return.

She turned to look at him, her eyes probed his, and they walked on in silence for a few more steps. "I sometimes worry that you don't want me as your wife, Leo." Her eyes welled with tears.

He wanted to reach out and hold her. "I do want to marry you, Mary, I love you dearly, and you will make a fine wife ..." He swallowed and turned away briefly as he sought to make sense of his emotions.

She pulled him to a stop. "Leo, it's quite all right to still love Mae, she was taken from this world unfairly, before her time, and I know you miss her terribly, but do not think of me as a replacement for her—I am not."

This discussion made him feel uncomfortable, and he wanted to change the subject. "I, uh, I have been distracted lately, and I apologise. Being overlooked for promotion caused me some distress, much more than I realised and, er, you are correct; I will talk to Mr Pembroke about it, just as you suggested earlier."

"Oh, Leonard, you just don't understand, do you?" she said in frustration.

He was puzzled, *what did she mean*? "We, uh, we should catch up to the others, they'll be worried where we are."

This time he did feel her squeeze his hand. She stepped closer, and their shoulders touched.

Chapter Five

Driven by powerful wind gusts, rain splattered against the windows of the bullpen and Leonard was pleased to be inside where it was warm and dry. Turning away from the windows he focused his attention back to the obituary he'd just written. The elderly gentleman had had a full and productive life, a loving family and a storied past. The deceased's family had provided some brief notes on him, and with some earnestness, he took the responsibility to write and honour the gentleman with an obituary the family would be proud of. He placed the completed notice in the 'For Approval' tray and turned to the next name on the list.

When the deceased had family, they would often provide a brief background on their dearly departed and request the newspaper write a few kind words on their behalf. Frequently, what the family member wrote and sent to the newspaper required modifying and revising to ensure grammar was acceptable and that the story did not stray from the simple parameters of *a notice of death* and become a rambling biography. Rewriting and creating the obituary notices were Leonard's responsibility and typically, Mr Pembroke fervently ensured they were concise and well-written.

Earlier, Leonard had visited the coroner's office and retrieved a current list of the deceased , double-checking to ensure the coroner's information matched the particulars sent to him by the deceased's family. His finger slid down the page to confirm the name of the next person. The list wasn't long and only contained a few entries — his finger stopped at the last name and he froze. The name Balthazar Ernest Gringle leapt out at him. This was the drunkard he'd spoken to at Courtenay Place over a week ago; it could only be the same man who had met with a suspicious death at the hand of the soldier. The name Balthazar was not common, and Wellington was not a large city... it could only be the same person.

With growing curiosity, he searched amongst the correspondence he'd received to see if anyone had sent him an obituary letter for Balthazar. It didn't take long, and there it was. The sender was Miss Agatha Gringle who lived in Te Aro.

The letter contained no useful information other than the normal, 'much-loved father and dearly missed'... *If he was so loved, then why did his family allow him to live on the streets and drink poisonous methylated spirits*? he wondered.

Taking advantage of being alone in the bullpen, he rose from his seat and stretched his back. The rain still sheeted down the windows, and the wind had not yet abated. He returned to the window and stared out. There was nothing to see but the liquid indistinct shapes of distant buildings and a smudge of dark grey to match his mood. *Perhaps I shall visit Miss Agatha Gringle,* he thought.

Earlier, Mr Pembroke had informed him that Mrs Bedingfield had unexpectedly visited them when he was at the coroner's office, and she demanded, in her typically brusque manner, an update on her missing husband. "I suggest that on your way home, you deviate from your normal route and visit her. Kindly remind and inform the madam of all this newspaper has done, and provide her with any developments or particulars you may have. I do not want that confounded woman here again, understood, Mr Hardy?" Mr Pembroke glared over the rim of his spectacles to reinforce his point.

"She may even take some pity on me for travelling in this abhorrent weather and offer me a cup of tea," replied Leonard.

Mr Pembroke waved his hand dismissively at him and uttered something incomprehensible.

With some reluctance, Leonard turned from the window and prepared to leave work. He organised his desk, grabbed his satchel, coat and hat, and observant of Mr Pembroke's request, determined to brave the elements and visit Mrs Bedingfield at her home. He shuddered at the thought of traipsing in the rain.

Leonard stepped from the tram and directly into a steady downpour, harsh winds and a deep puddle. Horizontal rain lashed across the street, and for a brief moment, he considered going directly home, but as his feet were already wet, he decided to continue. The address he sought was near the top of a steep street, and to seek some protection from the weather, he trudged up the more sheltered, south and even-numbered side. It was almost dark when he neared Mrs Bedingfield's house. He was about to cross the street when the front door of her home opened, and the light of an oil lamp spilled onto a spacious covered porch.

Leonard froze then quickly stepped onto the garden path of the nearest house to observe unseen. An overgrown hydrangea provided him with some concealment as a man stepped out onto the porch, followed closely by Mrs Bedingfield, who began helping him into his overcoat. In the dim light, he could see the man appeared to be wearing a military uniform of some kind. The flash of gold was an indication that the gentleman was possibly an officer of rank.

Once the coat was on, the man turned and faced her as she began buttoning it. When she reached the last button near his neck, he leaned down and kissed her on the forehead before securing his hat and walking into the rain. No one saw Leonard except an overweight tabby seeking refuge from the wet beneath the veranda of the house where he hid.

Should he follow the man or continue on to Mrs Bedingfield? Leonard was perplexed. Mrs Bedingfield was a married woman and certainly had no business canoodling with another man. And according to witnesses, a military man had allegedly killed the hobo at Courtenay Place. *Who was this man, was he the murderer*? Leonard waited for Mrs Bedingfield to return inside as the man hurried past then decided to follow him. Perhaps his destination will leave a clue to his identity, he thought grimly as he followed the soldier from a discrete distance. The man continued down Ellice Street, paused briefly at the Basin Reserve as if undecided which way to go, then turned right onto Kent Terrace, before crossing onto Cambridge Terrace and heading north with the rain at his back.

Leonard's right shoe was soaked and squelched when he put his weight down on his foot. Cold rivulets of water trickled down his neck and powerful wind gusts threatened to liberate his hat. He was cold, miserable and, with each sodden step, regretted making the decision to follow the stranger. He silently cursed him, Mrs Bedingfield, and finally, Mr Pembroke for sending him on this ridiculous outing. Twice the soldier looked back over his shoulder, but Leonard was convinced he'd remained undetected as he walked on the other side of the road and appeared only to be walking in the same direction and not following—or so he hoped.

As the soldier approached Courtenay Place, he suddenly stopped, stuck out an arm and hailed a passing Hansom cab. Leonard, displeased when the cab took off, turned around and headed back in the direction from where they'd just come. His decision to follow the soldier was a complete waste of time. He stopped and decided to visit Mrs Bedingfield another day. Thoroughly disappointed and wet, he squelched towards home.

Mr Pembroke exercised his discriminative prerogative as editor and with liberal strokes of his red-inked pen, slashed Leonard's story on the disappearance of Mr Bedingfield by one hundred words. One hundred words isn't much, but when the entire article is only three hundred words in length, the deletion is substantial. It wasn't that Leonard's pride was affected. He knew the revised version of the story was now nothing more than a brief community bulletin, far from the in-depth reporting, Mrs Bedingfield demanded of the newspaper.

The Wednesday edition of the *Evening Standard* containing the abbreviated bulletin was published that afternoon and unless he went to her home and spoke to her first, he knew she would come to the *Evening Standard* and complain. He'd rather deal with her at her house than suffer from her sharp tongue at work and risk embarrassment and further humiliation from Mr Pembroke. He'd visit her on Monday.

Neil Flanagan shook his head and stared unbelievingly at what Leonard was about to put in his mouth. "Leo, I don't believe you should be pursuing strangers, especially at night. You could easily be mistaken for a pick-pocket. Good Lord, what would you have done if he felt threatened and confronted you?"

Leonard's eyes were firmly focused on the heap of cream he'd placed on a scone and was trying to manoeuvre the ensemble towards his mouth. "He never saw me and didn't suspect he was being followed." The scone entered his mouth, and the motion dislodged a substantial portion of cream and strawberry jam which slithered from his chin and ended up on his shirt. "Damn!" he exclaimed after swallowing the first mouthful.

Neil handed him a napkin and tried not to laugh.

"You have to admit that it is a coincidence. A soldier is seen to have killed a man on Courtenay Place and–"

"Allegedly," Neil interjected.

"Alright, allegedly, and then witnessed by me, a soldier is kissing a married woman who is the wife of a man last seen in the vicinity of a victim, *allegedly* murdered by a soldier." Having finished wiping his chin and shirt, Leonard eyed up the remainder of the scone for a second attempt.

"I think you are feeling the effects of too much sugar."

The remaining portion of the scone disappeared without mishap.

"Leo, look, how many soldiers are there in Wellington? I can't begin to estimate … I think it's nothing more than a coincidence and totally unrelated."

"That doesn't explain why Mrs Bedingfield was kissing a man on her porch who wasn't her husband." Leonard dabbed at crumbs on the plate with his finger.

"So, the woman is having an affair of the heart, an *affaire de Coeur*. After all, her husband is an inebriate and she has good reason … is this not so? That doesn't mean she is frolicking in her *boudoir* with a murderer. And Leo, you have jam on your cheek."

"You haven't met her, and if you did, you'd think differently.

The woman is just outright disagreeable and I don't see her as being the amorous type." Leonard shuddered as he imagined her showing romantic affection to a man.

"And uh, are you any closer to finding this elusive man?" Neil asked with interest.

Leonard shook his head. "No."

"Keep at it, eh. Drink up, it's time to return to work."

Leonard finished his tea, wiped his face and stood.

"I hope you don't have to meet with any customers this afternoon."

"Why?" Leonard asked as he and Neil walked from the tea rooms.

"Your shirt."

Leonard looked down at the smeared stain of cream and strawberry jam.

Chapter Six

Leonard arose from bed feeling less than refreshed. He'd dreamt he was a hobo — homeless, destitute and a drunkard. He was relieved to wake in familiar surroundings, inside his home on Mount Victoria and not lying wrapped in a soiled blanket beneath a bench nursing a bottle of methylated spirits. However, his mind wouldn't rest, and Balthazar Ernest Gringle's name kept swirling around in his head, which made sleep difficult, if not impossible. He'd tossed and turned until daybreak and decided to visit Balthazar's daughter, Agatha Gringle, today. Perhaps she could shed some light on the relationship between her father and Harold Bedingfield.

The storm had passed leaving patches of blue sky and puffy white clouds, suggesting it would be a lovely day to stretch his legs and go for a walk. Although it was Saturday, and normally he would visit his friends for an afternoon drink at the Southern Cross Hotel. However Mary, Bridgette and Meredith had cancelled as they were all scheduled to work at the hospital, leaving the day free for him to do as he pleased.

The home of Agatha Gringle in Te Aro was easy to find, and Leonard gathered himself at the front gate of her home before he entered. He took a deep breath, unlatched the gate and stepped into a well-tended winter garden dominated by roses. Although not flowering, he could see the garden was nicely maintained and someone's passion. He knocked on the door, took a step back and waited. He heard the heavy footfall of a man before the door opened.

"Good morning, sir. My name is Leonard Hardy. I apologise for my untimely intrusion, but I seek Agatha Gringle. Is she available?"

The man's welcoming smile disappeared, and he looked at Leonard with suspicion that quickly changed to hostility. "We don't want your sort around here, shame on you. Be off!" He motioned with his hand and waved Leonard away.

Leonard's eyebrows furrowed together. "My sort? What sort would that be?" he asked. "I have come to your door, sir, where I seek to only ask Miss Gringle a question or two, nothing more. If I have offended you in some way..."

The door opened wider and a woman appeared. "Why do you wish to talk with Agatha?" she asked.

The man still stared malevolently at him, so Leonard turned his attention to the woman, who seemed less threatening. "I have some questions about her father, Balthazar Gringle."

The man's expression softened. "He passed a short time ago. So he can't help you, and neither can Agatha." He went to close the door.

"Wait, one moment, sir. Let me explain."

The man paused, and Leonard took it as an invitation to proceed. "I am searching for a man who went missing, and his wife, understandably, is desperate to ascertain his whereabouts. He was a known acquaintance of Mr Gringle, and I hoped that Miss Gringle may have information that will help."

"What did you say your name is again?" asked the man.

"Hardy, Leonard Hardy. I'm in the employ of the *Evening Standard* newspaper."

The man nodded. "I apologise, Mr Hardy. I thought you was one of them? We don't want, er, immoral, licentious characters darkening our doorway. We've had a few in the past, and I chased them off."

"Immoral — licentious?" Leonard's head turned in bafflement from the man to the woman.

"Mr Hardy, I assume you've never met Agatha, is that correct?" asked the woman.

Leonard nodded.

"Agatha, has uh, questionable virtues, Mr Hardy. She chooses to live an abhorrent lifestyle untethered to God and we continue to do what we can to lift her from pity and despair but to no avail."

It dawned on him. *Questionable virtues*! "I see –"

"She's a bloody tart, Mr Hardy," exclaimed the man with a sorrowful shake of his head.

"Peter!" admonished the woman.

"Well, call it what you like, it is what she is, and we don't approve."

"Were you acquainted with Mr Gringle?" Leonard asked, hoping to change the subject.

"We were; knew him well. It was very sad, he hit the bottle and became a swizzler after his wife passed, he couldn't cope with her death. We took care of Agatha and raised her like she was our own," he replied.

"Like a daughter," added the woman with a maternal smile.

"Do you know where I could find her, it is important that I ask her about her father's friends."

"Probably at that God-forsaken place, the Victoria Hotel, on Frederick Street," said the man angrily.

Frederick Street! Leonard nodded. "I'm grateful for the information and sorry for what you're going through. I can see you still care for her. Good day."

The woman wiped away a tear.

Leonard turned to walk away and stopped. He looked back. "It was you who wrote the obituary notice for Balthazar Gringle in Agatha's name, is this not so?"

"I did," said the man.

"I understand. Thank you," Leonard replied and walked past the unflowering roses towards the gate. Although he didn't know her, he felt saddened at what Agatha had become. He ambled towards home, lost in thought.

Frederick Street was notorious for its dubious avocations. He'd been there countless times to visit Uncle Jun, a Chinese merchant with a shop selling herbs and medicines. He knew better than to go into that area at night, amongst the squalid opium dens, seedy brothels, and loud gambling halls. However, Agatha Gringle's name played on his mind, and he couldn't forget her. On a whim, he decided to detour to Frederick Street and visit the Victoria Hotel when it was safer during day-time, where he hoped to find her.

Even during the day, Frederick Street was busy. He pushed past the hawkers, pedlars and opportunists, ignoring their brochure hand-outs and solicitations, and saw the familiar sign hanging obliquely from Uncle Jun's shop front. He paused briefly and considered going in. He realized he didn't want to be reminded of his past with Mae, especially when he was trying to focus on Mary and finalising the date for their marriage. He felt guilty as he quickly hurried past the shop.

Ahead, a run-down two-storied building masquerading as a hotel nestled between a tea shop and a pawnbroker. The hand-painted sign above the door advertised that the Victoria Hotel was homelike and economical. *It was nothing of the sort.* Leonard knew the establishment was a bawd-house where a man could procure love for money from wayward, unfortunate women. He stopped outside and looked self-consciously around, hoping he wasn't recognized.

Around him, people hustled past. They didn't care who he was or where he was going. Leonard's hand automatically went to his billfold to ensure it was safely in his pocket, then feeling quite uncomfortable, he stepped cautiously towards the garish pink door. Before he reached for the handle, it opened, and a rather burly man stepped out. He was an extraordinarily large and muscular man who, on first impression, appeared quite threatening and intimidating. Leonard had second thoughts.

"Afternoon, sir," said the man, his voice raspy and gruff. He gave Leonard a quick up-and-down appraisal. Seeing Leonard posed no threat to his charges inside and, by all appearances, was a gentleman of somewhat moderate means, he extended an arm, an invitation to enter.

"Uh, good afternoon," Leonard replied as he climbed a single step and entered the dank premises of the Victoria Hotel. It was dark and smelled of mould, sweat and cigar smoke. Already he regretted coming and was considering leaving when a woman stepped from behind a screen.

"Welcome to the Victoria Hotel," she said pleasantly. "Looking for some companionship, sir?" She was a substantial woman, and the extent of her voluminous clothes only made her seem larger. She stood before him with hands clasped over an extended belly.

"I'm looking for– um," he cleared his throat. "I'm looking for

Agatha Gringle."

"Who?" she asked.

"Agatha Gringle," Leonard replied, not feeling too sure of himself.

"There's no Agatha's here —Oh, wait, isn't that Trixie?"

The burly guard at the door behind him must have nodded.

"You mean Trixie." She gave Leonard a smile and a wink. "You saucy devil."

"I don't want her for, um … I just want to talk to her," Leonard added quickly.

"Of course, dear." Her smile vanished. "Pay now. One pound." She held out her hand and curled her fingers.

"Then she is here?"

"Where else would she be? Pay now or I will have to ask you to leave."

"One pound to just talk?" Leonard protested.

"I don't care what you do with her when you're in a room with the door closed," she wagged a pudgy jewelled finger at him in warning, "as long as you don't leave any visible marks or bruises. But, it will cost you—one pound," she reiterated.

Leonard felt the guard take a step closer. "Thank you, perhaps another day." He turned to leave. *One pound was ridiculous.*

"Alright then, ten shillings. You can have half an hour with her."

Ten shillings was still a lot of money, but... "Very well, ten shillings." He fished in his pocket for coins and counted out the money for her.

With the money safely sequestered, the madam indicated for him to follow. She led him past a staircase and into a parlour. "Wait here, Trixie will be out shortly."

Leonard was uneasy, he'd never been to a place like this before, although he'd passed by them on many an occasion. It was a world he was unfamiliar with, and felt out of his element. He was out of pocket by ten shillings, and already he regretted the decision to pay the madam. He looked around the gloomy airless room which held quality furniture that now looked worn and shoddy. Red velvet drapes hung in depressive past splendour and shielded the afternoon sun from adding cheer. He wanted to yank open the curtains, raise the windows and allow fresh air to blow away the foulness. A bouquet of wilting flowers stood forlornly on a small table, overflowing ashtrays and stained drinking glasses littered available surfaces. With his mind made up, he stood to leave when the door opened and a young woman entered the room. Closing the door she turned to face him.

He studied her carefully, her posture, the tilt of her head, the way she looked at him – her eyes. He stared and swallowed thickly, avoiding looking at what little clothing she wore. A hard life had taken its toll on her; that was obvious. His mouth opened. "Uh, um, Miss Gringle?" he finally managed to say.

The use of her real name came as a surprise. Her *faux* smile and assuredness vanished, and she paused with uncertainty. Leonard took a step closer to see her better. The room's dimness had obscured the lines around her eyes and mouth, but even in the poor light, he could now see her eyes were dull and lacked energy - she looked tired and disinterested. She began fidgeting with a ring, compulsively turning it around and around her finger. She didn't make eye contact, nor did she answer him. She looked like a frail bird, poised to take flight.

A muted cry, *a scream of pleasure, or pain?* – Leonard wasn't sure – drifted down from somewhere upstairs. It could have come from Agatha, but her mouth didn't move.

"Miss Gringle?" he repeated softly. "I, uh, I mean you no harm. I've come here to see you, uh, speak with you, as I have a few questions about your father, Balthazar. May we talk?"

She stood with doubt. Her chest rose and swelled beneath the looseness of her *peignoir*, and her fingers continued to toy with the ring.

"Please, it won't take long, and I promise I'm not here to cause you distress."

She looked at him intently for a heartbeat or so. "I'm known here as Trixie. Who are you?" Her voice was soft and mellow.

He leaned forward to hear her more clearly. "Forgive me for not scheduling an appointment with you, this establishment makes it… um… Er, my name is Leonard, Leonard Hardy, my friends call me Leo. Can we be seated?"

She turned to look at the door.

"I don't believe we will be disturbed; I paid for half an hour of your time." Leonard winced inwardly and immediately regretted his tactlessness.

She breathed out long and slow, pulled her flimsy robe tighter and sat on the edge of a chair. "How can I help you, Mr Hardy?"

Her voice lost its sensuous warmth and now contained an edge, a hardness, that wasn't endearing.

Chapter Seven

Leonard began with some mundane small talk — idle chatter, to ease her obvious discomfort — and it seemed to help as her harshness dissolved as she visibly relaxed. Occasionally she held her stomach as if afflicted by malaise, and at times she seemed confused by the simplest of questions. He was patient and didn't pressure her for answers.

"Miss Gringle," Leonard continued slowly. "Did your father ever speak of Mr Harold Bedingfield?"

She paused, averted her eyes, then shook her head and yawned.

"Did he ever mention someone called Harry?"

This time she nodded and gave a hint of a smile, "Often."

Leonard returned the smile. The name Harold was frequently shortened to Harry or Henry. He was finally getting somewhere. "What type of association did they have?"

She looked at him with vagueness, and then from somewhere deep within, she found clarity and focus. He saw the persona of Trixie slowly dissolve to be replaced by an attractive and endearing young woman called Agatha. She sat a little straighter and met his gaze. "Father told me that Harry was a confounded pest who wanted him to stop his immoral consumption of alcohol."

Leonard wanted to laugh. *One drunk telling another to stop.* "Was there a reason, or was Harry just being a good Samaritan?"

"He wanted Father's help."

"Help? Help in what?" he asked.

She shrugged. "He only mentioned a name, I know nothing

more." She looked away.

"Do you recall the name?" He watched her carefully as she tried to remember. She had paid the price for prolonged use of opium. With his eyes now accustomed to the low light, he could see her skin was pale, she had discoloured rings beneath her eyes and needed sleep. She struggled to maintain lucidity, and from what little he knew, deduced she exhibited all the characteristics of a habitual narcotics user.

"I believe it may be another woman, but I apologise, Mr Hardy, for I know not the reason why Father would be called on to help his friend. He addressed her as sweet Hazel. That's all I know."

Someone pounded on the door. "Times up!" came the muffled warning.

Leonard ignored the caution. *There was that name again, sweet Hazel. Who is Hazel*? he wondered. "Do you know Hazel?"

"No."

"Hey! Time's up!"

"One last query, Miss Gringle. What was your father's profession before he, uh, before…"

"Before the intemperance?" she volunteered.

Leonard nodded.

"He was an animal doctor. A veterinarian."

"A veterinarian? What — "

The door swung open and the burly guard stepped into the room. "C'mon, matey, you've had your fun, now clear off. Your time is up!" The gravelly sound of his voice added to the menace.

Leonard's head spun as he tried to make sense of what she told him. He shifted his attention to the guard. "Uh, yes, of course. I'm leaving now." He turned back towards her. "Thank you, you've been most helpful."

The guard stepped up, firmly grabbed Leonard's elbow and frogmarched him from the room, through the hall, reception area and finally deposited him outside.

He blinked in the afternoon sunshine as he was thrust dismissively onto the footpath.

"No need to be so brusque!" Leonard yelled to the back of the thug as he re-entered the hotel.

He straightened his clothes and stood in reflection, thinking about his brief encounter before walking home.

Moments later, someone grabbed his shoulder, and he spun. Believing it was a hustler, he shook the person off, but it was her, Agatha. "Miss Gringle! I must apologise, I thought–"

"Why are you doing this?" she asked, cutting him off.

Inside the brothel, she was meek and subdued, and in contrast, here on the street, she was confident and assertive. The change in her mannerisms caught him off guard. *Was it an act*?

Pedestrians stared as they walked past. It was not a common occurrence for a woman to be seen dressed in such a provocative manner on the street, especially during daylight. Outside and away from the confines of the Victoria Hotel's disreputable pursuits, she seemed more alert and lucid.

Ignoring the curious glances, he struggled for an honest reply. Reaching for her arm, he gently pulled her to the side. "I work for the *Evening Standard* and was asked to write about the disappearance of Mr Harold Bedingfield. When I visited the place where he was last seen, I spoke to your father. He was rather poorly, and then, later, I learned of his, uh … untimely passing."

For the first time, she didn't avert her eyes and met his with intensity. He saw it again, and it was more than a glimmer; it was a flame of life that blazed behind the troubled façade. Even through the harsh physical side effects of opium use, he saw past the tiredness of her drawn features. She was a most remarkable and striking young woman.

"But it wasn't an *untimely* passing, was it? He was slain." Her bottom lip trembled.

Leonard was taken back. She knew a great deal more than he first believed. He leaned in, and looked into her eyes. "What do you know of his death?"

She tore her eyes from him and looked around. "I cannot converse with you here, can you meet with me, tomorrow, midday, at Ivy's on Oriental Bay?"

With fists clenched, the Victoria Hotel's burly guard was striding towards them. He didn't look happy.

"Mr Hardy, you should leave," she urged.

"Tomorrow, Ivy's at midday," he said quickly and rushed off before the brute arrived. After a few paces he turned to look behind and saw him roughly escorting her back to the Victoria Hotel. *Poor, wretched girl*, he thought.

He walked home trying to untangle the information he had regarding the disappearance of Harold Bedingfield and his association with Balthazar Gringle. Both men intemperate and one man dead, possibly murdered. Then there was the military man. He stopped suddenly, almost colliding with a man walking behind who had to nimbly step around him. He and Mary were to meet tomorrow for Sunday luncheon, and without proper consideration, he'd foolishly agreed to meet Miss Gringle at the same time. He scratched his head. He couldn't cancel his meeting with Miss Gringle…

He reached into his coat and, pulling out a notebook and pencil, quickly wrote a brief note to Mary explaining how he would be unavoidably detained and couldn't meet at their arranged time. Alternatively, he wrote, he would visit her at her home after he'd concluded his business. Mary would understand. Satisfied he'd averted a disaster, he hailed a Hansom cab and paid the driver to deliver the message with some urgency.

Small waves lapped against the mostly gravelly beach of Oriental Bay. A few families with young children, taking advantage of a pleasant Sunday, walked and played along the narrow shoreline. It was too chilly to swim or splash in the waves. Others just sat on the beach enjoying the sunshine, a welcome respite from the recent storm. Seagulls loitered near those eating, and those more adventurous, noisily intimidated fishermen, who, with lines cast, stood in reflective, peaceful solitude on the handful of rocks at the edges of the bay. Farther out, in Lambton Harbour, a scattering of ships sat at anchor, providing a lovely backdrop to a splendid and picturesque *vista*.

Leonard was already seated at the tea rooms anxiously waiting for Miss Gringle to arrive. He watched the children playing and wondered, wistfully, if he would ever be a father. He didn't see her arrive and he sat up with a start when she sat down across from him.

In his eagerness to greet her, he stood too quickly, clumsily knocking the chair over. He felt foolish and laughed.

"Good morning, Mr Hardy," she said. A small smile played across her face. "Did I startle you?"

"I apologise, I'm still a little agitated after yesterday's encounter with that monster, that brute at the Victoria Hotel," he said while righting the chair.

She looked down at her lap.

Leonard guessed she was fidgeting with her ring beneath the table. "Would you like a cup of tea and something to eat?"

She raised her head. "A tea would be lovely, thank you, Mr Hardy."

Leonard could see the strain on her face. Her skin pallor and sunken cheeks—all side effects of opium use. But if anything, she was more present and alert today. "Please, call me Leo," he said.

She smiled in acknowledgement, and he saw again the glimpse of the beauty that once was. He wondered if she would ever fully recover and restore the vitality, health, and mind, that had slipped away into the dark abyss of a euphoric, opium-enhanced lifestyle. He excused himself, walked to the counter to place his order, and returned to his seat.

It felt a little awkward. He noticed that she had made an attempt to dress appropriately and, by all casual appearances, thankfully, gave no outward suggestion of her immoral trade.

"Father and Mother used to bring me here," she suddenly said.

Again, her voice was sultry and mellow, with no trace of the hardness he had heard from the previous day at the hotel.

"They were good times…" She turned and watched the children playing near the small waves that folded gently on the stony beach. Sand used as ballast in ships had once been deposited on the beach, but most of it had been washed away.

"You were close to your father and mother?" he asked.

She nodded. "When Mother passed, everything changed, and Father couldn't cope. He never recovered from her death, and he took solace in liquor." She turned to face Leonard. "The alcohol should have killed him, but it didn't. It was a soldier, a military man that took his life. Do you believe that to be fair, Leonard?"

Leonard considered his response. "I don't believe death through abuse of alcohol, or certainly from the hand of another, is equitable at all, do you?"

They made eye contact, and she didn't look away. "Or death through opium." She leaned forward, and he saw her eyes looked slightly glazed. "I have a fondness for laudanum[3], and I compulsively seek its company and infinite pleasure. It has an unnatural firm grasp on my soul. It won't release me — I know it will eventually gain the upper hand and see me succumb." Her lip quivered. "I shall welcome death, for only then may I free myself from its ceaseless torment." She took a deep breath as she leaned back in her chair. "But I do wonder … do you doubt that even in death, I will be liberated of its desire and need?"

Leonard held her bold stare. *Laudanum, opium!* He exhaled. "Then to be sure, and with absolute certainty, you need to unbind yourself and break that unnatural union with opium before your soul yields. Death through natural causes is certainly a preferred choice."

"If only…" she sighed wistfully and turned away.

The tea arrived and they waited in reflective silence for it to steep. Leonard knew it was time to change the subject. "This soldier you spoke of, what can you tell me about him?"

"Not much. Whomever he is, he is associated with horses."

Leonard rubbed his chin. "Horses … horses," he repeated. "I suppose he could be associated with cavalry. Anything else?"

3   *Laudanum – A tincture of opium that contains morphine and codeine.*

"I believe he is with the Permanent Militia. Is that helpful?"

"That isn't a surprise, and yes, I expect that narrows things a bit," he replied. He leaned forward. "Miss Gringle, have you ever had occasion to meet Harold Bedingfield?"

She nodded, "Twice, I believe. Why do you ask?"

"Because I have never met him and haven't the foggiest notion of his appearance."

"He is ordinary in all respects." She paused briefly. "I keep thinking there is more, but for the life of me, I cannot recall. My memory isn't the best these days." She looked embarrassed and began toying with her ring.

He poured tea for them both, and they sipped quietly.

"How did you come by this information of the soldier, and are the police aware?" he asked.

She held the cup to her lips and shrugged. After taking a sip, she carefully set it on the saucer; he noticed the slight tremor of her hand.

"The Victoria Hotel is patronised by many men," she began. "Most are happy to talk about things that they wouldn't normally share, not even to their wives. Some are willing to quietly ask questions on my behalf and even bring me answers."

Leonard raised his eyebrows at the revelation.

She saw his response. "Oh, as long as their enquiries preserve their dignity and marriage."

"Uh, of course," Leonard replied. He felt his face begin to redden.

"But those favours only extend so far." She laughed.

Leonard felt she didn't laugh at the humour, but at the irony. "If I have need to contact you again, how can I do this without incurring the wrath of that brute at the door, that guard?"

She smiled. "You mean, Russell."

"Russell?"

"He is a friend and looks after me."

"I declare that he is not a friend. I saw the way he manhandled you back inside the hotel yesterday."

Agatha giggled. "That was for the benefit of Sophronia, the madam. Did you not see her looking through one of the upstairs windows at us?"

Leonard shook his head. "No."

"I am required to … uh, be available … six and a half days a week. During that time, I am at her beck and call and she prefers I do not liaise with men outside the confines of the Victoria Hotel. I have no choice, Leonard. I am afforded a few hours on Sunday to rest, that is all."

Leonard's mouth opened. He had questions, but none seemed befitting. He closed his mouth and swallowed.

"You wish to ask, why?"

He could only nod.

"Because Sophronia provides me with all the laudanum I need."

Leonards mouth tightened. He wanted to shout, grab her by the shoulders and shake her, make her see reason, make her see common sense, make her see how the evil potion she consumed had ruined her life and would eventually kill her. He couldn't. He just stared at her in mute rage. If she saw his reaction, she didn't acknowledge it.

"If you need to contact me, go to the hotel, Russell will greet you at the door as he does all our patrons and you can give him a message, either written or verbal. He will not hurt you, I will ensure he knows we are friends," she smiled apologetically, "…er, professional acquaintances."

"I feel somewhat relieved." He regretted his response as it sounded more sarcastic than he intended.

With a trembling hand she emptied the last of her tea. "I must go. Thank you, Leonard. I hope we can find this man who killed my father, he was a good man who deserved better."

He stood, and moved to help her to her feet. She gave him her hand. It was cold.

As he watched her walk away he felt moved by her sad and despairing predicament.

Chapter Eight

"What do you want from me, Leonard? Where do I fit into your plans?" Mary stood with arms folded, facing him as he sat in an armchair in her home in Newtown. "What was it about your meeting with… with… this woman that was so important and couldn't wait?"

After watching Agatha Gringle leave, he'd immediately caught a Hansom cab and made his way to Mary's home to apologise profusely for cancelling their planned luncheon. However, his apology wasn't accepted in the way he'd initially envisioned.

"She is the daughter of the man who died at Courtenay Place, er, you recall our discussion about that with Tim?"

"You mean the hobo?"

"Yes, but not–"

"The one who disappeared?"

"No, Mary, the other."

Mary unfolded her arms and raised them both in exasperation. "Leonard …" She took a step closer and sat down in a chair facing him. "I know who you are. You have a natural curiosity that leads you astray. You are an honourable, good-hearted man who wants to help people…" She paused and shook her head. When she spoke again, her voice was again calm. "But your willingness to help others has taken a convenient priority over our relationship. Don't you see?"

He couldn't meet the intensity of her gaze and looked guiltily away.

In the ensuing silence the ticking clock seemed unnaturally loud.

"You are focusing on others and not on us."

He knew she spoke the truth and it hurt.

"And meeting this woman, was it worth it?" she asked.

He was in a quandary. He didn't think she would be quite so understanding if she knew more about Agatha Gringle and her questionable virtue. He thought it pertinent not to detail her background information and carnal skills; in fear that this would create further disharmony when he only sought peace and calmness — he just wouldn't divulge all. Not that he'd lie to her, he couldn't.

She sat quietly as he told her what he learned about Balthazar Gringle and the soldier. When he finished, he stood to stretch his legs and ease the tension in his body. Mary remained seated and silent as he walked to the window and looked outside. He waited for another verbal outburst.

"You said the hobo who died was an animal doctor?" she eventually asked.

He turned in surprise at the question. "He was murdered, and yes, Balthazar Gringle was a veterinarian."

"Do you know the trade of the missing man?"

"Why do you ask?"

"Leonard, you said the murderer is a military man, and possibly involved with horses …"

"Yes, conceivably cavalry with the Permanent Militia, and Mr Bedingfield is a saddler," he replied, still wondering where she was going with the questions.

"And what do all three men have in common?"

"Horses!" they replied in unison.

Leonard raised a hand to his forehead. "Why did that not occur to me?" He stepped closer to Mary who stood and pulled her easily into his embrace.

He felt her warmth but was not warmed by her. His own inability to dedicate himself to their relationship created a barrier that weighed heavily on his shoulders. He loved Mary Worthington; he didn't question that, he just couldn't commit to her and the marriage she wanted until he could release Mae from his consciousness—from his past life and the present. Poor Mae. There wasn't a day when he didn't think of her, and there wasn't a moment that he didn't miss her. Pledging himself to Mary seemed disloyal and improper, and while he could rationalise his misgivings, emotionally he was as inexplicably tied to Mae as Agatha was to laudanum.

Mary must have sensed his thoughts. She pried herself from his arms and pushed away to better look up and see his face. "When will you let Mae go?" she whispered.

He didn't know how to reply, so didn't.

She sighed and walked into the kitchen. "What will you do with this information you learned?"

Leonard felt the chill of shame descend over him.

"Leo?"

"Uh? Oh, uh, I shall discuss this with Tim, if he is forthcoming and willing to share any information he has with me. There can't be that many Permanent Militia in Wellington that are linked to horses."

"You hope," Mary added from the kitchen where she was preparing dinner.

Returning to the sofa, Leonard stretched out his legs and thought about all he'd learned. Did Mrs Bedingfield have an association with horses that would link her in some way to her husband's disappearance and Agatha's father's death? He thought back to when she first barged in to the bullpen at the newspaper's offices, and when he questioned her about Mr Bedingfield. She was so distracted and stared at the wall … *Stared*, he thought.

He sat up. Mrs Bedingfield had been staring at a painting of a horse on the wall of their conference room. He remembered now. Whatever was going on, horses were the centre of it all and she was linked. He was sure of it. He smiled and rose from the sofa.

"Can I help you with anything?" he asked as he walked into the kitchen.

"Mr Hardy," began Mr Pembroke who'd only just taken his seat in the bullpen. "How fruitful was your visit with Mrs Bedsworth — was it productive?"

Leonard grimaced. He had yet to visit her. He turned around to face the senior reporter and saw him unfold a letter and begin reading. "Mrs Bedingfield, sir," he corrected. "And no, I was intending to go on Monday, this afternoon."

Mr Pembroke slowly raised his head and removed his reading glasses. "Pray tell, please do not keep me in suspense. As you are so keen to point out my error, then I am equally anxious to learn of your reason for disobeying my instructions?"

"It was the weather, sir. I stepped into a puddle and felt that it would be inappropriate, if not rude to visit her and slosh around her home in wet footwear."

Mr Pembroke held Leonard's gaze for a moment or two, then raised his hand with the letter he'd been reading. "Perhaps it is fortuitous you did not visit with her, as this," he waved his hand that still held the missive, "is in response to our brief story and may prove useful to Mrs *Bed-ing-field* and aid her in discovering the locus of her estranged spouse." He held out his hand with the document and its envelope.

Leonard rose from his seat to retrieve it.

"This will be of use to her, perhaps you *could* deliver it, *if* — the weather is agreeable for you?"

"Of course, sir. I will do it this afternoon."

"See that you do."

Leonard returned to his desk to read the letter.

17 Bell Road,
Gracefield.

Dear Sir,

In response to the appeal by the Evening Standard for information regarding the whereabouts of Mr Harold Bedingfield. I can verify that I identified him at approximately 10:00 a.m., on August, 1st, whilst walking my dog. He is known to me through the Wellington Racing Club, and I witnessed his arrival at the race club premises, in Moera, that morn. He appeared somewhat dishevelled, which first drew my attention to him.

If I can be of further assistance...

Yours, respectfully,
Dr Dorian S. Andrews

He carefully folded the letter, returned it to the envelope and placed it in his satchel. His mind was working furiously. A turn of luck. *Another link to horses*, he thought. *But why*? He looked up at the clock on the wall. He had a number of calls to make this morning and needed to visit the coroner's office to retrieve a list of the newly departed. Then, wander to the Harbour Master's office for an updated list of shipping arrivals and departures, and finally, call on an advertiser to have their advertisement approved before tomorrow's deadline. Later, after seeing Mrs Bedingfield, he and Mary would have dinner together at the Hotel St. George. Hopefully this would smooth out any remaining tension between the two of them.

Leonard cleaned his desk, grabbed his satchel and prepared to leave for the day.

"I do not wish to see her darken our doorway again," growled Mr Pembroke.

"Sir?" Leonard paused and turned to his superior.

"That woman, Mrs Bed … Beda …"

"Oh, Mrs Bedingfield."

"I do not want her here disrupting this office, do I make myself clear, Mr Hardy?"

"Very, sir," Leonard replied. "Uh, good day, Mr Pembroke."

Mr Pembroke grunted without looking up.

Leonard exited the bullpen, passed the receptionist, offices, and down the stairs onto Willis Street, and wondered why Mr Pembroke was in such a disagreeable mood. While often grumpy, Leonard knew most of the time it was a charade, a theatrical act. But today he was truly waspish. He shrugged and stepped outside into the sunshine.

The morning passed without any problems, except he was made to wait at the Harbour Master's office longer than normal. It was always a battle to obtain the shipping list, and try as he might, the employees there always found a way to make him wait. One day, they would come to him with need, and he would enjoy turning the table on them.

While waiting, he thought about the letter from Dr Andrews, and about Agatha Gringle. He wished he could help her in some way. But opium was indeed evil; it required some dedication and commitment to rid one's self from dependency. He wondered if Agatha wanted to be truly free of it.

After receiving the latest shipping updates, he walked through Wellington towards Ellice Street where Mrs Bedingfield lived and realised he could either detour around Frederick Street, or pass through it. He had a question for Miss Gringle and pondered his chance of surviving the ordeal if he asked the brute at the door for Agatha to contact him. With some trepidation, he decided to risk an encounter and briefly visit the Victoria Hotel.

Chapter Nine

With Uncle Jun's shop front just ahead, he moved to the side of the footpath and paused. A thought came to mind and he reflected. Coming to a decision, he turned and entered the store, passing beneath the sign *Chen Jun Qiang, Purveyor of Medicaments and Chinese Herbal Remedies.*

Of unknown age, Uncle Jun was an energetic and enthusiastic Chinese immigrant who had taken care of Mae when she first arrived in New Zealand. She had always referred to him as her *uncle,* and the name stuck with Leonard. His knowledge of Chinese remedies, herbs and treatments were legendary. If anyone could provide help to Agatha, then surely, he could. *If she wanted it*, he thought.

Uncle Jun was perched high on a ladder, putting some mysterious substances away into a drawer when he entered the shop. As always, the medley of smells was astonishing and powerful. Not unpleasant by any means, but potent all the same. Hemp sacks, crates and casks lay haphazardly on the floor; some open, their obscure mysterious contents spilling out. On shelves jars with tinctures, tonics and remedies were displayed; their labels in graphic Chinese script, meticulously detailed their purpose and origin.

Uncle Jun looked down and his face broke into a huge smile. "Leo, where you been, why you no come to see me?" Uncle Jun nimbly scrambled down the ladder.

Leonard couldn't help but reciprocate, his own smile equally broad. He was fond of Uncle Jun, it was just sad that he reminded him of Mae.

"Where is Ming?" Leonard asked. He saw no sign of Uncle Jun's wife in the shop.

"She gone to help daughter," Jun smiled. "Baby."

"Ah, I see," Leonard responded. He was disappointed Ming wasn't here.

They chatted for a short while, catching up on news and developments before the astute proprietor nodded thoughtfully and looked at Leonard more closely. "You need help, Leo?"

He couldn't explain why he wanted to help Agatha, but deep down inside he felt she needed support and encouragement to rid her of her craving, and perhaps even return to a normal way of life, if that was even possible. "Perhaps, Uncle Jun. Is there a way to help someone who is a routine user of opium to minimise the effects of prolonged use and reduce dependency?"

Uncle Jun leaned closer to Leonard, and squinted as he peered at his face and into his eyes. Even prodding and pinching the skin on the back of Leonard's hand. "Not you Leo, I see you not use opium. Who for?"

"It's for a woman, she takes laudanum. She isn't really a friend, but someone I met because of my work," Leonard quickly added.

"Ahhh, I see." Uncle Jun shook his head; his expression stern. "Leo, opium very bad." He tapped his head with a bony finger. "Is here, opium is thief, it steal the mind." He tapped again. "She need much strength for this." He frowned and nodded a few times. His head bobbed comically up and down. "If she want, then I help. For you Leo, eh?"

"Thank you, thank you very much. But tell me, how do you do

this? Give her a tincture, a potion?"

"No, no, Leo, you silly boy. She must come here and we look after her ... take time."

"How much time?"

He shrugged. "How old?"

"About twenty-five years old."

"Young, is good. Everyone different. One week for first part, then body want more and sometime they become very sick. Your friend on laudanum, maybe not so bad, eh?"

"How much will this cost, Uncle Jun?"

The aging Chinaman, again looked into Leonard's eyes. "This friend ... she important to you, yes?"

Leonard looked away, "No, a business acquaintance, nothing more."

Uncle Jun gave a toothless smile. "But still important or you not come to me, eh." He laughed. "For you, Leo, I do this, no money, I help."

Leonard felt relief. Uncle Jun was remarkable. "I don't know what to say. Again, thank you, Uncle Jun. Her name is Agatha, if she comes here ..."

"If she come here, I will know." Uncle Jun looked serious. "Worry not, Leo."

Leonard said his goodbyes, promised to visit more often, and feeling remarkably better for the visit, he departed the shop and walked towards the Victoria Hotel. When he saw the entrance just ahead, he felt his chest tighten in anticipation of a possible confrontation with the burly guard. He stopped, took a deep breath and walked purposely towards the door hoping Agatha had spoken to him.

Uncle Jun stood unseen in the shadowed doorway of his shop and watched Leonard. His brows furrowed as he stepped towards the entrance.

The Victoria Hotel's door opened and the space was immediately filled by the hulking brute. Leonard stopped. The guard gave no impression he recognized him and without pause began to approach. Leonard took an involuntary step back.

The man was formidable, unusually large, as emphasized by his jacket that tested the workmanship of the seams and fabric strength. He looked like he could shred the garment by just flexing his muscles. The monster's arms were thicker than his own thighs. His fists were clenched causing Leonard to prudently decide to turn and flee.

"Mr Hardy." It wasn't a question, just a statement, almost lost through his gravelly unemotional tone.

Leonard froze, then slowly turned his head back. The guard had stopped and loomed over him from a single yard away.

"I wasn't sure if you remembered me," Leonard said with a forced smile as he turned.

The guard said nothing and looked at him blankly.

"Ur, I, um need to give Agatha a message."

This time Leonard saw a miniscule reaction.

"Can you ask her if we can meet? Same place and time where we met yesterday?"

The brute nodded slightly.

"And uh, I need to know if she has knowledge if her father ever went to the Hutt Park race course, to the horse races, and if so, where did he go when there? It is important."

The guard shifted position and took half a step closer. Leonard fought the temptation to take a cautionary step back.

"Where do you live?" he asked. The raspy voice almost a heavy grunt.

"Uh, well …" Leonard was reluctant to give the man his address, but quickly realised if he needed answers to his questions he needed to know where to contact him. "Ninety-one, Marjoribanks Street, on Mount Victoria," he replied with some reluctance.

Leonard felt someone watching, the guard must have sensed it too. Suddenly the brute reached an arm out and grabbed his elbow, then stepped close behind him.

"The madam watches. Struggle a little, I won't hurt you," he whispered.

Leonard understood and immediately tried to pull his arm free. The guard roughly pushed him forward, then a final shove sent him onto the footpath where he nearly fell. He looked up at a second story window and saw the curtains move. He guessed that Madam Sophronia had been observing. The astute guard had been vigilant too. Feigning indignation, Leonard made a show of straightening his coat and uncharacteristically, he raised a clenched fist and shook it in mock anger at the broad back of the guard as he returned inside. Leonard turned away and smiled. It felt good to demonstrate some bravado.

Leonard admitted the guard's attitude was actually quite clever. Anyone watching his mannerisms and body language would have believed the brief encounter was quite hostile. With his heart returning to a safe tempo, he trudged towards Ellice Street for an unpleasant rendezvous with Mrs Bedingfield.

Uncle Jun returned inside his shop with a head shake. He'd witnessed the entire exchange and wasn't happy at all.

Chapter Ten

It had been quite a Monday afternoon, and it wasn't over yet. With some trepidation, he approached Mrs Bedingfield's door. Before he could knock, it opened and she loomed in the entrance glowering at him with arms folded. "I certainly hope that you've come here to explain yourself to me?"

"Good afternoon, Mrs Bedingfield, lovely day isn't it?"

Her lips were compressed into a bloodless thin line.

Leonard surmised she wasn't interested in discussing Wellington's weather. "I, uh, Mr Pembroke suggested that I visit you on the way home and ask if there had been any developments with locating your husband." He tried to look behind her into the house without making it obvious. She shifted her weight and leaned against the door post, an invitation inside for a friendly chat, a cup of tea and biscuit seemed highly unlikely.

"How the *Evening Standard* can operate as a profitable business astounds me, Mr Hardy. The article you penned was not only unsatisfactory, it was incomplete, and far from the calibre of journalistic excellence I would expect from a city newspaper." She raised her eyebrows and waited for his response.

"Mrs Bedingfield, I suffer at the whim of the publisher and editor. They dictate to me their wishes, and as a lowly employee, I have little or no voice. I do as I'm told or risk censure and reprimand."

"That's a poor excuse and totally unacceptable." She harrumphed and paused a moment. "I suppose you'll want to come in?" She moved aside so he could enter. "Shoes off first."

This was a turn. He undid his laces, kicked off his footwear and stepped into her home. He wasn't sure what to expect, but at one time she must have been affluent. The furnishings were all of exceptional quality, but were now old, worn and had seen better days. If she once had wealth, she had none now.

She led him to a sitting room, picked up a glossy green cardboard file folder that sat on her chair and slid it, out of sight, beneath a newspaper that sat on a low table. She sat down and looked up at him expectantly. "I'm presuming you have news for me, as I am no closer to learning where Mr Bedingfield might be."

She hadn't invited him to sit. He stood awkwardly while she sat primly. "I just want to …" He raised his satchel to his chest, undid the buckle of the leather flap and reached inside. He saw the letter from Dr Andrews he was required to deliver to her and froze.

"I'm waiting … I don't have all day," she said, testily.

He'd been given clear instructions by Mr Pembroke to deliver the letter. But he couldn't. He didn't believe Mr Bedingfield wanted to be found by his wife and he felt a measure of sympathy for him. Coming to a quick decision, he grabbed his notepad instead. "…ask you a few questions, if that is acceptable, Mrs Bedingfield?"

"Hurry then," she sighed loudly in displeasure. "What questions?"

"Uh, can you tell me who Mr Bedingfield's closest friends or associates are?" he waited with his pencil poised above a blank page.

"You've asked me that before," she snapped.

"Yes, and you didn't answer. It would be most helpful."

Instead of another rebuke, she paused and appeared to give the matter some thought. "I don't believe I can," she said. "I never approved of his association with the men he chose to socialise with.

Their names are unknown to me."

"Are you familiar with Mr Balthazar Gringle?"

He saw her reaction.

"No," she said rather quickly, "should I be?"

Her eyes gave her away—she lied and did know of him. Leonard glanced around the room. There were small wooden carvings of horses, and a couple of paintings of horses graced the walls. He could see that horses played an important part of her life.

"I can see that you have a love of horses and –"

"Frankly, that is none of your concern, Mr –"

"Hardy, Leon –"

"Hardy," she interrupted. "If you have no pertinent information as to the location of my husband, then I suggest this meeting is over. You've overstayed your welcome." She stood. "I have better things to do than sit here and idly chit-chat with you about personal matters." She waved him to the door.

Leonard returned his notebook to his satchel and walked to the door, opened it and stepped outside onto the porch to put on his shoes. He turned around to face her. "One last question, Mrs Bedingfield. Do you or Mr Bedingfield have friends in the military?"

He winced as the door slammed shut.

It wasn't what she said, because she never really answered his questions. It was what she didn't say. With total conviction he believed she was aware of, or involved, somehow, in the murder of Balthazar Gringle. *Is Harold Bedingfield's disappearance related to Balthazar's death*? He believed it was, and most certainly, he believed Mr Bedingfield was in hiding, and, if he guessed correctly, most likely in some jeopardy.

Disobeying Mr Pembroke may have saved Mr Bedingfield's life. The letter written by Dr. Andrews clearly indicated Mr Bedingfield to be somewhere in the vicinity of the Hutt Park Race Course, and if he'd handed the letter to her, as instructed, then within days, he imagined the body of her husband would be found floating face down somewhere near the Petone foreshore.

Leonard walked home to freshen up and change his clothes before meeting Mary at the Hotel St. George for dinner, something he was looking forward to. As he climbed Marjoribanks Street towards home, he realised Mr Pembroke would be absolutely livid if he found out he'd been disobeyed and not delivered the letter to Mrs Bedingfield as instructed. Should he be forthright and explain his reasonings and concerns to him? Mr Pembroke would require genuine evidence and facts, not unsupported theories, and as yet, he had nothing but presentiments to show for his efforts.

He quickly washed, changed clothes and headed back down the street to catch a Hansom cab. It was too far to walk to the Hotel St. George and he was at risk of being tardy. After determining that the Hansom cab driver was sober, he climbed aboard for the journey across town. The cab safely deposited him outside the landmark hotel and Leonard rushed in. Thankfully Mary had not arrived. Relieved, Leonard could finally relax and look forward to a pleasant evening with her. He was shown to a table, where he ordered a beverage while he waited.

His glass was empty and Mary had still not arrived. Rising from his table he looked around the dining room in case she had been seated elsewhere. She wasn't to be seen. Puzzled, he walked to the *Maître d'* and enquired after her.

"I apologise, sir, the lady you seek has not yet arrived. Perhaps soon, eh?" he replied with an insincere smile.

"Has there been any message?"

"No, sir."

"Thank you." Leonard walked back to his table and waited. He ordered another refreshment, then another. He stared down at his empty glass and realised she wasn't coming. *Something must be wrong—a mishap*? he thought. After waiting for an hour and a half, he paid the bill, and hurriedly caught a Hansom cab to Newtown.

There were no lights on in the house, it was empty, and no one was home. Where was she?

It had been a long day and he was tired. Normally he'd walk, but tonight, feeling despair and worry he caught another cab home.

After a restless night, Leonard hoped a missive would arrive in the morning that would explain her absence, but nothing came. If something untoward had happened to her, then he knew either Bridgette or Meredith would send word to him, but they hadn't, and that was of concern. He arrived at work earlier than usual hoping a message would be waiting for him. There wasn't.

Mary had vanished before. But then, her aunt had been stricken with an illness and she left a note for him at the hospital when she went to be with her. The note had been kept from him by an unscrupulous doctor, but there was no valid reason that would happen this time.

He was seated at his desk, staring at the wall, when Neil Flanagan entered. He was whistling and appeared to be in a joyful mood.

"Oh, good morning Leo," Neil greeted cheerily. "You are here bright and early this fine morn."

Leonard didn't feel like engaging in a lengthy discourse about his personal life. "Good morning, Neil. I have some work to catch up on. Thought I'd make an early start."

"Yes, very good, then," Neil replied.

Thankfully, to Leonard's relief, he didn't push the matter and turned away to begin softly humming. The other reporters arrived soon after and were talking amongst themselves when they heard the mechanical noise of the doorknob. The chatter ceased immediately and all heads were down, creating the appearance that all staff were positively engaged when Mr Pembroke arrived. Without saying a word, he placed his satchel on his desk, removed his coat, arranged his pillow, and slowly scanned the room.

"I detect the detestable signs of inactivity and slothfulness. Both of which I abhor. For here, we have come to learn that diligence and assiduity, and not indolence, will promote a long and prosperous relationship with the *Evening Standard.* Is this not so, Mr Hardy?"

Leonard's head was down, and despite his dour mood, he grinned. Mr Pembroke was in fine form this morning. "I concur, sir."

"Very good, Mr Hardy. You are indeed learning, and making progress. But others are not. Perhaps, Mr Flanagan, you could share with me why the story on Housing Affordability is not on my desk? Was I remiss, did I not make myself clear to you?"

Leonard slowly turned to look at Neil. He was grimacing. Failure to turn in a completed assignment on time was an unforgivable, cardinal sin.

"I'm just reviewing some last-minute edits, sir," Neil replied without turning around.

"Re-view-ing ed-its? Shouldn't this elementary task have been completed prior to your arrival at work and the deadline, or are you still feeling the effects of your weekend's debauchery, Mr Flanagan?"

"I'll have the story on your desk promptly, sir."

"I understand you had time earlier, but devoted it to bragging of your conquests with the fairer sex. While your sordid private life is entirely your business, it is my concern when one affects the other. Do I make myself understood, Mr Flanagan?!"

Leonard felt a tiny measure of sympathy for Neil. Normally *he* was at the receiving end of one of Mr Pembroke's tirades. However, today, Mr Pembroke was quite abrupt. No doubt as a result of being away from the office all day yesterday.

"Yes, sir."

"Mr Hardy?"

And here it comes, thought Leonard. "Yes, sir?" he raised his head and turned to face Mr Pembroke.

"I presume the weather was to your liking on Monday?"

"It was a lovely day, sir. Thank you for asking."

"Then I can make the assumption you visited Mrs Bedington and you brought with you the letter?"

Leonard felt his heart rate increase. He didn't want to lie. "Yes, I visited Mrs Beding-field yesterday, and had the letter with me."

"Then we all have cause to celebrate, as there is no reason, Mrs Beda... Bedingfield need visit us here, and grace us all with her objectional presence again. Is that not so, Mr Hardy?"

Leonard felt the relief and exhaled slowly. "It is highly improbable she will visit us again, Mr Pembroke. However, in the unlikely event she does, I will ensure that as Senior Reporter, and editor, you will have opportunity to speak with her, sir." Leonard grinned and hoped he didn't overstep his bounds.

As all heads were facing the front of the room, no one saw the corners of Mr Pembroke's mouth twitch slightly. The reporter, Milton Camden, who sat immediately behind Leonard, supressed a laugh with a cough.

"That's enough of that, Mr Hardy," admonished Mr Pembroke. "Carry on, we have a newspaper to publish."

Time seemed to pass with agonising slowness. Each time the door to the bullpen opened, Leonard hoped it would be someone delivering a message for him. It wasn't to be, and he was beside himself with worry. He knew something awful had befallen Mary.

Chapter Eleven

He saw the letter when he arrived home and stepped inside. Someone had pushed it beneath the door. He scooped it up, immediately recognising Mary's distinctive penmanship. Without removing his coat, he threw himself into his chair and tore open the envelope.

250 Adelaide Road,
Newtown, Wellington.

Dear Leonard,

It causes me indescribable pain and heartache to write to you, but correspond to you I must. My three previous attempts now lay on the floor, crumpled, discarded, and forgotten. Oh, Leonard, where do I begin?

My tears fall freely and drain my soul of the love I feel. The agony of your deception, so real, so damming; as if a knife was cruelly driven into my aching heart.

The realisation you are not the man I thought you were has brought me grief and hurt me terribly. Simple words on paper cannot accurately portray how I feel. My disappointment in you is profound, the sadness, like a burden I shoulder alone, for I was gullible and seduced by your false charm and insincere affections.

That you seek companionship from an immoral, licentious woman outside the confines of our relationship is both astounding and unforgivable. That you did so, brazenly, in daylight, demonstrates how callous you are. The disrespect you afforded our relationship only heightens my revulsion. Did you truly believe that I would never discover the truth?

To preserve my dignity and virtue, I insist you do not contact me or make any appearance at my home or place of work. Any attempt by you to do so will be met unkindly and without sympathy or warmth.

Mary Worthington

The letter fell to the floor as he raised both hands to his face and groaned. He felt the searing pain of heartache, and the desolate agony of frustration as the sun slowly descended behind the Tinakori Hills. He sat alone in the shadows and descending darkness and contemplated how to respond.

He wasn't sure what time it was when he rose from the chair, lit a lamp and sat behind his writing bureau where he began to compose a sincere reply. Mary had made it very clear she didn't want contact with him, but how could he explain to her the truth? She didn't want him to visit. A letter was his own viable option, and he only hoped she would read it.

He put pen to paper and began to write. Again and again, he

crumpled his attempts, tossing them to the floor in anger. He tried to explain the nature of his meeting with Agatha Gringle and how he met with her only to seek answers in relation to the disappearance of Mr Bedingfield, but his penned words seemed fabricated and insincere—how could he convince her that there wasn't a romantic liaison or a carnal tryst between Miss Gringle and himself as she suggested? He didn't feel guilty for meeting her. The only reason he never told her about Agatha's questionable virtue and her fondness for opium was because he didn't want her to worry about him or risk any unpleasantness.

He stared at the paper and what he'd written, and for the umpteenth time, wondered how she came to learn of his meeting. Had someone seen him enter the Victoria Hotel, or had he been recognized with her at Ivy's Tea Room on Oriental Bay?

It had to have been the former. Agatha was dressed appropriately at the tea rooms. Who would have known she was a dolly-mop[4], unless, of course, she was identified by a previous customer. Leonard shook his head. *Had to be the Victoria Hotel*, he thought grimly.

It was late in the evening. He'd written a truthful and unfeigned explanation to Mary and he fervently hoped it would be enough for her to agree to meet him where he could elaborate further. He'd addressed and sealed the envelope when he heard a firm rap on his door.

Puzzled as to the identity of the late night caller, he carried a candle and opened the door to reveal the hulking guard from the Victoria Hotel. Leonard was taken aback.

"Mr Hardy," he croaked.

4   *Dolly-Mop. Old slang for prostitute.*

Leonard peeked outside to see if anyone was with him. Although it was difficult to tell, he appeared to be alone.

"It's late," Leonard said.

The man didn't reply.

Realising it was best if he came inside and away from prying eyes, he invited him in. The man dipped his head as he entered and filled the hallway. Leonard led him to his sitting room. If he appeared to be a large man standing outside the Victoria Hotel, he was positively huge inside Leonard's cottage.

"I, uh, know you're trying to help Miss Gringle… she'd be a good woman … is the poison she consumes, Mr Hardy." The man shook his head. "She doesn't need to be working at the hotel, she's too kindly a lady, she is. I, uh, appreciate someone of the likes of you doing all you can to help her." His rasping voice was deep-toned and gravelly.

Leonard was shocked. It was the most he'd heard the man speak. "Please, be seated." He waved to an arm-chair and held his breath as the man eased himself down. It protested loudly. "I'd like to help her too," he replied. "I agree, she deserves better."

The man nodded.

"Uh, how can I help you?"

"Miss Gringle said she'll meet you at the same place and time as you met on Sunday last."

In light of Mary's missive, Leonard had a fleeting thought that perhaps it wasn't a good idea. "That's good, thank you."

"She also told me to say that her father did go to the Hutt Park Race Course, to a stable. But she don't know where it is, only that she knows what it looks like, and can recognise it."

Leonard's eyebrows raised at the revelation. "That's very helpful. Again, you have my gratitude. Especially for coming out this late."

"Russell."

"Pardon me?" Leonard questioned.

"Russell, my name. It's Russell."

"Oh, uh, it's a pleasure to meet you Russell. Please call me Leonard, my friends call me Leo."

"Very well, Mr Hardy. But, if I may say…" Russell paused.

"Carry on."

"If you're looking for that bloke, the one who may have done her father in, then you need go to the racecourse with Miss Gringle. Find that stable, eh?"

Leonard scratched the back of his head. "I was thinking similar thoughts, Russell."

"Is hard for me to talk, Mr Hardy. My throat, you see." He pointed to his neck with a hand the size of a ham-hock. "Had me a stoush[5] and my throat was damaged."

Leonard grimaced. "Ah, I see, yes." That explained the way he sounded when he spoke.

Russell put considerable weight on the armrests of the chair and rose. The chair complained and creaked. He towered over Leonard who remained seated. "Sir, Miss Gringle told me you're a good honest sort. That's good enough for me. I want to help, can I?"

"I'd like that Russell, thank you. Tell me, how is it you're not working?"

"Because I knock off at ten o'clock."

"Oh." Leonard had a thought. "If we were to go to the Hutt Park Race Course, could we go on Sunday? Would Miss Gringle be able

5 *Stoush – Slang for fight*

to … uh, have free time from her … employer?"

Russell smiled for the first time. "She said you'd ask. She arranged to have all day available, so, Sunday is good."

"How did she manage that?"

"She told the madam, she'd work all of next Sunday." Russell looked thoughtful. "I can't go with you, have to work."

Leonard felt pity for Agatha. He looked up at the face of the large man. In spite of his brutish appearance, he was kind and considerate. He was warming to him. "Thank you again for your help, Russell."

"I like to help those who need it, sir."

Me too, thought Leonard. *A shame Mary thinks otherwise.*

They discussed the details of meeting Agatha on Sunday morning and then Russell departed. In the moonlight, Leonard watched him lope down the street. His thoughts returned to Mary, and he felt the evening chill, damp and despair descend over him.

He'd been foolish. He should have been more forthcoming and willing to share with Mary. Procrastinating over the date of their marriage was childish and insensitive. And now … he felt remorse and guilt. Mary's anguish was unnecessary and could have been avoided if he'd been more considerate and behaved in a mature and loving way. He shivered and returned inside.

He didn't sleep well. For most of the night, he tossed and turned, and felt terrible for how he'd treated Mary. He had taken advantage of her love, failed to talk and openly share, and as a painful result, she had lost trust and faith in him. The only consolation was that he hadn't done the things she'd accused him of. However, that did little good when she didn't want to communicate.

He devoted some time to thinking about Harold Bedingfield and his friend, Balthazar Gringle, now deceased, and of course, Miss Agatha Gringle. Sunday's outing to the Hutt Park Race Course could prove interesting and could provide an opportunity to learn more about why Mr Bedingfield chooses to remain at large. They'd have to find him first, and would he be willing to talk?

He walked to the *Evening Standard* offices and mailed Mary's letter on the way. He passed by the hobo's on Courtenay Place but spared them only a passing glance. Nothing appeared to have changed — the same disaffected men still shivered in abject misery, begging for coins to soak in poison they called relief.

The bullpen was empty when Leonard arrived at work. Distracted, he stared at the wall in front of his desk where company notices were pinned. Their yellowed, curled corners, reminders of past social gatherings. He never heard the door open and jumped when he was greeted by one of the reporters.

"Good thing it wasn't his lordship, eh, Leo. You'd be in a spot of bother," said Milton Camden with a laugh.

"I could tell it wasn't Mr Pembroke. He always turns the handle one way, then the other," Leonard grinned. "Gives us more warning."

Milton hung his coat and hat on the stand and sat wearily down at his desk. Leonard turned around to face him. "When are the next races at Hutt Park?"

Milton Camden covered recreation and entertainment for the *Evening Standard* and was the self-proclaimed expert on all sports. He opened his diary and flicked through a few pages. "Here it is, uh, that'll be, Saturday, twenty-seventh of November. Going to place a wager or two, Leo?"

"Oh, no. I was just curious that's all. Are the horses still training?"

"They're always training. If you want to go to the races, the Island Bay Race Club is holding their Spring Meeting very soon and it's a bit closer than Hutt Park."

"I may consider going," Leonard replied distractedly, "and uh, thank you."

"Perhaps I will see you there. Mr Beaumont invited me to have lunch at the members dining room with him and a customer on that day."

"Lucky you," Leonard grinned.

"I wouldn't be so sure," Milton added with a frown. "I think he wants to put me out to pasture."

"Oh, why is that?"

Before Milton could reply, the sound of the turning doorknob alerted them, and in unison, both men immediately faced the front and lowered their heads as Mr Pembroke entered. Unusually, he said nothing as he fussed with his pillow and sorted through some papers on his desk. After a few moments the noise stopped; there wasn't a sound to be heard. It was deathly quiet.

"Mr Hardy?"

Leonard tensed and then twisted in his chair to face his superior. His expression almost saintly. "Sir?"

"Come this way, lad. Mr Beaumont wants a word."

Leonard felt his stomach tighten as he stood. "Did he say why?"

Mr Pembroke looked as if he wanted to say something, then changed his mind, walked to the bullpen's door and held it open.

Leonard looked down at Milton who raised his head. His eyebrows knitted together in puzzlement. Being called to the publisher's office was not a common occurrence and certainly didn't bode well.

Chapter Twelve

Mr Beaumont's secretary appeared discomfited but still greeted him with an awkward smile as he walked to the publisher's office with Mr Pembroke leading the way. The senior reporter knocked once.

"Enter!"

With some curiosity, Leonard walked into the office. Mr Beaumont was shuffling some documents on his desk. "Sit, Mr Hardy," he instructed without a glance or salutation.

Mr Pembroke closed the door and took a seat against a window, crossed his legs and brushed lint from his trousers. He didn't look up.

Leonard wondered if this meeting was about the advancement he'd been hoping for. The promotion denied him when Neil Flanagan was hired. He sat more upright and looked at the publisher and smiled with expectancy. Mr Pembroke raised a hand and coughed into it. *A subtle warning*? Leonard glanced around the room as the *Evening Standard*'s publisher completed his paperwork.

Mr Beaumont finally raised his head and sighed loudly. "Mr Hardy," he began, "this wonderful newspaper depends on advertisers for its survival. Those customers pay our salary—yours and mine. Without advertisers, the *Evening Standard* is nothing, we don't exist."

Leonard wondered where this conversation was going and spared a quick glance at Mr Pembroke for a clue, but his expression was unreadable. *This meeting isn't about career advancement*, he thought grimly and focused his attention on Mr Beaumont.

"Our reputation is paramount," continued the publisher. "While we pride ourselves on unbiased reporting, we do offer editorial opinions, and those opinions are often relevant to topical, social issues. Frequently we take a moral stance. Is this not so, Mr Pembroke."

"Indeed," he replied.

"When our employees become immoral, then this reflects badly on the paper …"

The word *immoral* struck him like a blow to the gut, and Leonard knew what the publisher was referring to. He felt his face begin to flush as his stomach tightened in knots.

"It was brought to my attention that an employee of the *Evening Standard* was seen entering a, uh–" Mr Beaumont cleared his throat. "A house of ill repute, and during daytime, what's more, and, made a foolhardy spectacle of himself."

"I, I can explain," Leonard interjected.

Mr Beaumont raised a hand. "Wait." He took a breath. "Further, you were also seen, uh, merrymaking with a woman, known about town to be a fallen woman of dubious character at tea rooms in Oriental Bay."

"Mr Beaum–"

"Leonard!" snapped Mr Pembroke. He shook his head in admonition.

Mr Beaumont chewed his bottom lip a moment. "Mr Hardy, your private life is of no concern to me or the *Evening Standard*. However, when your private life has an adverse effect on the income of this newspaper and when our advertisers are offended, then it becomes my business and I have a duty—I must—intercede!" He banged a clenched fist on the table. His anger palpable. "Your career for, for, ten shillings!" He shook his head in obvious disgust. "Do you understand, Mr Hardy!" He paused.

Leonard was overcome and didn't know how to respond.

"Do you understand Mr Hardy?" repeated the publisher.

Numbed, Leonard mutely nodded.

"Effective immediately, your employment and relationship with this newspaper, and its customers, is over — terminated. You are relieved of all your responsibilities, and I'm instructing you to vacate these premises — forthwith!"

Leonard couldn't believe what he just heard. *Terminated*? It took a moment to clear the fog and compose himself. "Mr Beaumont, these accusations are untrue, I was…"

Mr Beaumont stood, placed both hands on the desk and leaned forward. "Do you deny that you were in Frederick Street and entered the Victoria Hotel? What about your carousing in Oriental Bay with a … with a tart?"

A tart? "May I be permitted to account for my actions?" He turned from the publisher and appealed to Mr Pembroke.

"Yes, I think it's only fair —" replied Mr Pembroke before he was cut off.

"Answer my questions, Mr Hardy!" Mr Beaumont ignored the recommendation of his senior reporter.

Leonard shook his head in frustration. "I was not merrymaking nor did I pay for the services of an immoral woman, or a tart, sir! I am investigating a —"

"Goodbye, Mr Hardy, thank you for your service. Mr Pembroke will allow you to gather your personal items and show you to the street. That will be all."

Leonard rose from his seat and turned to Mr Pembroke. His expression revealed nothing.

He walked from the office in a haze of uncertainty and confusion. Who could have been watching him and then exaggerated the nature of his meeting with Agatha Gringle? First Mary, and now Mr Beaumont …

Once he'd collected and boxed his personal items, Mr Pembroke silently escorted him to the street. At the main entrance, Mr Pembroke placed a hand on his shoulder. "I defended you Leonard, I tried, but …" He shook his head. "At least he agreed to be circumspect about the reason for your dismissal. It serves both our purposes, does it not?"

Leonard nodded glumly.

"No one will know the reason."

"Mr Pembroke, these allegations made against me are untrue," Leonard implored.

Mr Pembroke's expression softened and he lowered his voice. "I believe you, Leonard, but Mr Beaumont …" He rubbed the bridge of his nose and sighed, "You're a naturally gifted investigative reporter. Before you submit your story, what is the golden rule?"

Leonard was puzzled and looked at the senior reporter. "Uh, check and confirm the facts?"

"How do you accomplish that, Leonard?"

"Evidence, Mr Pembroke. Evidence," he replied with a measure of confidence. He understood what Mr Pembroke was suggesting.

"Bring me the evidence, Leonard." With that, Mr Pembroke patted him on the shoulder, turned and slowly walked back upstairs to the hallowed, inner sanctum of the *Evening Standard*.

The walk home was slow and painful. Never had he felt so humiliated and misunderstood in his entire life. His job, the work he enjoyed, the woman he loved—all gone. *Who would do this to me and why*? he fumed.

His evening was spent in the company of a bottle of whiskey, and in the morning he was reminded why alcohol wasn't a good companion. It took a while for his dignity to resurface as he cleaned his home and pondered the vagrancies of life. When the sun began its slow descent over the western Tinakori hills, he began to think more clearly. His reasoning, once again, logical and practical.

He knew Mary received his letter yesterday and presumed she'd read it. Now it was time for him to visit her, explain in person and allay her concerns and dispel any misunderstandings. It was important to clear the air. Her letter had been succinct, she didn't want him to see him. But that was before his letter, and how he'd explained the truth.

Instead of catching a cab, he walked — it cleared his head and helped him focus.

With immense relief he saw light seeping from behind closed drapes as he neared her home. At least she was there. At the gate he smoothed his hair, hitched up his trousers, and walked up the path towards the door as his heartbeat quickened in anxiety.

He rapped on the door, took a step back and waited. He thought he heard voices … perhaps Bridgette was home, although he understood that she was working night-shift this week.

The door swung open and he saw her. She didn't smile, nor did she express any surprise at seeing him. "Mary …" he began.

"Leonard, I asked you not to call on me."

"My letter … did you receive my letter?" He thought she looked flustered.

"I, I did, but, I confess, I could not read it." She looked away.

"Why? I explained everything to you in my letter. I have done nothing dishonourable or to be ashamed of. Why did you not read my letter?" He was puzzled and looked at her expectantly waiting for an answer.

"Because I told her not too and destroyed it. More falsehoods and untruths!"

Leonard's mouth opened in shock. *Neil*? "Wh…what are you doing here?" He turned to her. "Mary? Explain this."

Neil Flanigan loomed in the hallway, and moved quickly to stand close behind her. "She doesn't want you here. See yourself off!" He stepped around her to stand in the doorway.

"The reason for me being here is not your regard, she and I are betrothed, and you are interfering and meddlesome."

"I told you to leave, and I will not ask you again, on your way!" Neil took a step closer with fists clenched. His threat very clear.

"Leonard!" she cried. "Please go. He will hurt you!"

He tried to peer around Neil, but he took a step to the side, shielding her. "Mary!" he pleaded. "Why is he here? This man has nothing to do with our relationship."

Neil took a threatening step closer.

Leonard remembered how he deftly handled himself at the Southern Cross Hotel when the two young men were creating havoc.

"Leave!" Neil shouted. His temper flared. "We don't want your sort here!"

"Mary! Stop this nonsense!" It was too dark to see her clearly.

"I want you to leave, now!" he heard her yell.

Neil took another step closer, and not wanting to be struck by a larger and very capable man, Leonard hastily retreated and almost fell on wet moss growing on the path. He scrambled to safety on the street; most fortunately, Neil stopped his pursuit at the gate.

There was nothing to be achieved by confronting Neil Flanagan and risking a physical altercation, so he reluctantly walked away, occasionally looking over his shoulder in case he was pursued. He was saddened and hurt. As the pounding in his chest settled, he wondered why Neil was involved. More disturbing were Mary's words he kept hearing over and over again, when she yelled, I want you to leave! *Was she speaking to Flanagan or me*?

Why was Neil Flanagan at Bridgette and Mary's home? What business did he have there? He recalled how charming he'd been to her when they met for a beverage at the Southern Cross a couple of times. Was it nothing more than jealousy, or was he trying to make inappropriate advances on her?

He stopped suddenly on the footpath. Who told Mary and Mr Beaumont about his meetings with Agatha Gringle? Someone had deliberately lied in an attempt to discredit him. Could it have been Neil Flanagan?

Barely in control of his simmering anger and frustrations, he continued walking.

"Dear boy, you've got yourself into a bit of a pickle haven't you?" stated Tim Yates.

They sat in Tim's cramped and cluttered sitting room where Leonard had just finished explaining about his dismissal from the *Evening Standard*, Mary's letter, and the unexpected appearance of Neil Flanagan at Mary and Bridgette's home.

Tim leaned forward slightly. "But Leo, do be forthcoming, we are close friends, are we not?"

Leonard raised an eyebrow.

"It matters not to me if you've frequented a *bordello* from time to time … and it's entirely your affair if you have. But, in this case, were you not just, er, caught with your pants down?" He grinned.

"No, Tim! Not you, too!" cried Leonard in exasperation. "I was there to see Agatha Gringle. All I did was talk to her in a parlour at the Victoria Hotel. We spoke for precisely thirty minutes before I was told to leave."

Tim leaned back in his chair, smirking.

"And again at Ivy's in Oriental Bay, but nothing untoward," he added.

"And now, Mary found out about your secret little rendezvous and you got caught. Did you learn anything of interest?"

Leonard rolled his eyes. "It wasn't a secret … rendezvous." He sighed. "Agatha's father, the chap who was murdered in Courtenay Place, was a veterinarian. I believe the common association between he and Mr Bedingfield has to do with horses. Would people resort to murder over horses?"

"When it comes to money, people will do anything. Certainly, horse breeding is a jealously guarded industry, and who knows what lengths people will go to protect or breed their animals. I will ask around and see if there are any rumours circulating around horse breeding and the death of Mr Gringle."

"Thank you, Tim."

"But this does not help you with that scoundrel, Neil Flanagan, does it?"

Leonard shook his head.

"I never took to him. I found him a little too, er, servile. And now he's cosying up to Mary. I can't say I approve, or of his heavy-handed and threatening tactics. Not at all sporting. What will you do, Leo?"

"I will persist. What else?"

"Write another letter and I will give it to Meredith and she can personally deliver it to Mary. Hopefully, without the presence of Mr Flanagan."

Chapter Thirteen

It was a peculiar feeling to be unwaged. He couldn't remember the last time he had time on his hands to do as he pleased. He had savings and wasn't concerned about money, but he questioned his desire to continue to search for Harold Bedingfield when he was no longer employed by the newspaper. After some reflection he decided he just enjoyed the sleuthing, especially if he could help someone, and Agatha Gringle needed help, and in more ways than one.

The quandary of his personal life was another matter. Mary Worthington was a remarkable woman and his feelings for her ran deep. He did love her and wanted her to be his wife, however, marriage involved making a commitment, and he still strongly felt love for his deceased wife, Mae. Making a marriage vow at this time felt wrong — to do so would dishonour Mae. It wasn't fair to Mary if his heart was divided between two women when Mary deserved all of him.

He'd tried to rationalise it. Mae was dead, and while his memories and love still lingered, and were as strong as when she was alive, it was also time to move forward. He knew he could be a wonderful husband for Mary and still retain his love for Mae. But how could he release himself from her and devote himself to Mary? "I am so confused!" he yelled aloud to the four walls.

He sat in an armchair in his sitting room and laughed at the irony. Here he was making a presumption about his relationship with Mary Worthington when in fact her last communication with him couldn't have been more succinct. She wanted nothing more to do with him. It was over.

But is it? he questioned.

She made a decision about their relationship based on information that was incorrect—she'd been lied to. Someone set out to deliberately deceive her. So far, everything pointed to Neil Flanagan. He was also the common denominator between his employer—or rather, ex-employer and his ex-fiancé. What was motivating Neil to be so guileful and duplicitous? It was time to find out. But first he needed to rewrite his letter to Mary and then deliver it to Tim at the Mount Cook Police Depot.

Wellington's library was located in Athenaeum Hall on Lambton Quay, a short distance from the *Evening Standard* offices. His intention was to read through any publications and find any information or references to the Bedingfields, and Neil Flanagan. Although he didn't have much hope of finding anything on Neil, as he was only a recent arrival to New Zealand. Then afterwards, go to the City Council offices and search through public records and do the same.

The library was largely in disarray. *Shameful*, thought Leonard, as he searched through mountains of periodicals, newspapers and bulletins that lay haphazardly in uncategorized piles. The bulk of the afternoon was spent reading. He avoided the *Evening Standard* newspapers as he knew what was written in each edition, but there were others publications, and he pored through as many as he could. He scanned the Police Court, and the Wellington Magistrate Court reports and found nothing of interest.

He was rearranging the newspapers prior to leaving when the

pile fell from the table onto the floor. As he picked them up, he saw a newspaper, a weekly publication called *The New Zealand Mail*. On landing on the floor, a few pages slid out and revealed a brief column on court appearances. He almost missed it. He picked up the page and read the article carefully. There was no mistake.

Resident Magistrate's Court, Wellington.
(Before D.H. Havell, Esq., R.M.)

ASSAULT.– Neil Euan Flanigan was charged by Alston Morgan with having committed a violent assault upon the plaintiff on Saturday last. It appeared that the assault arose out of a betting account between the parties. The defendant, who had won £2.00 from the plaintiff at the Island Bay races, called on the plaintiff for a settlement, which the plaintiff was quite willing to agree to; but there was a business account between the parties which left a balance to the plaintiff, which the defendant refused to recognise. It was stated that the defendant seized the plaintiff by the beard, and committed the assault complained of. The defendant denied the assault, but the Magistrate found the assault proved, and inflicted a fine of a guinea and costs.

He checked when the edition was published and did a quick calculation. The assault happened just over two weeks before Neil began his employment at the newspaper. Was Mr Pembroke aware of the conviction? Why had it not been reported by the *Evening Standard*? More importantly, Neil was also involved in horse racing. A mere coincidence? And, is he also involved in the disappearance of

Mr Bedingfield and the death of Balthazar Gringle? This discovery was telling and he could have leapt for joy. Additionally, and worth remembering, the criminal assault charge and subsequent conviction only confirmed that he had a predisposition to violence. *I must exercise caution*, he affirmed.

Leonard quickly glanced around the room to ensure no one was watching and folded the page from the newspaper, hurriedly put it in his pocket and departed for the City Council offices.

The only relevant information he learned from the council's public records was that Mrs Fannie L. Bedingfield was the registered ratepayer on her Ellice Street property, and she had no dues outstanding. On an impulse, he searched for records on the aggrieved Mr Alston Morgan and learned he was the proprietor of, *A. Morgan & Co, Construction*, with premises in Kilbirnie. He saw no benefit in approaching the man.

It was late afternoon when he departed the City Council offices and realised that if he took a cab to Wellington Hospital, he would arrive around the time Mary was scheduled to finish work. He could walk with her to her home on Adelaide Road and give her the letter without any interference from Neil Flanagan. A better option than having Tim give the letter to Meredith, he surmised.

He waited near the hospital's entrance, but Mary never walked past. After a while, he went inside, greeted the porter and walked to the enquiries counter. The women there were of little help, and disappointed, he waited outside a while longer, then dejectedly walked home.

Normally he and Mary would get together on a Friday night, but this evening, he ate alone. After dinner, and once he'd cleaned up, he settled down to read before bed. It was approaching 9:00 p.m. when he heard a knock at the door. Immediately his thoughts turned to Russell, the brute from the Victoria Hotel, and he hoped, wasn't visiting to inform him that Agatha had cancelled their Sunday journey to the Hutt Park Race Course.

With a candle lighting the way, he opened the door expecting to see Russell, and in his stead, saw the unsmiling face of Neil Flanigan. Leonard opened his mouth to speak when Neil stepped up, and Leonard found himself lying on the wooden decking of his porch with blood streaming from his nose. He never saw him cock his arm or throw the punch. It was totally unexpected and came without warning. The candle, laying near him, and on its side, was in danger of setting his porch alight.

"You were cautioned—stay away from Mary!" yelled Neil as he strode away into the darkness.

Leonard groaned, his nose painful. He righted the candle, sat up and scooted himself against the wall and tried to stem the blood flow.

His nose eventually stopped bleeding, although it was still painful, and within a short time, his eye had almost swollen shut. Sleep didn't come — he spent most of the night in bed, propped against a pillow feeling sorry for himself. In the morning, he would go to the police and lodge a complaint of assault against Flanigan. It was plainly obvious, he was a volatile and dangerous man with a quick temper. What did Mary see in him? His violence, and silky charm was nothing more than a charade, and yet why was he so obsessed with her? He couldn't fathom any of it. Men like this, Leonard knew, could also be brutal and violent towards women. Mary was certainly in some peril.

He wasted no time in hailing a cab and instructed the driver to take him directly to the Mount Cook Police Depot. He would file a complaint against Flanagan, and leave his letter for Mary there for Tim.

Leonard was no stranger to the Mount Cook Depot. He'd been here many times with varying results. Ahead of him, a few people stood in line waiting patiently for their turn to be called, while Leonard sat on a bench seat that ran along the length of the far wall. Out-of-date notices hung from bulletin boards, and the building was typically, institutionally dull and uninspiring. On the left side of the room, a sign pointed to a public urinal and Leonard wondered if he should avail himself of its use.

The man in line before him was called to the counter, and Leonard changed his mind, deciding instead to wait for his turn. It didn't take long; the gentleman was reporting a missing cat and the constable had little time and even less patience to acknowledge and accept the complaint.

"Next!" bellowed the aging constable.

Leonard stepped up to the counter and waited while the constable finished scribbling an entry onto the daily log sheet. He sighed loudly when finished. "Now, then…" and looked up and saw Leonard's swollen nose and black eye. "Oh dear, had a spot of bother, eh?"

"You might say that," Leonard replied. "I'm here to report an assault." He didn't ask if Tim Yates was available, because he knew

Tim was currently assigned to patrol the wharves to stem excessive pilfering.

"As you would," replied the constable as he reached for the appropriate form.

Leonard explained the details as the constable took notes. After a short while the constable paused. "Eh, you said this alleged assault took place at 9:00 p.m.?"

Leonard nodded.

"At this address?" The constable pointed to the address Leonard had given him.

"Yes, why, is it important?" he asked.

"Ah, well, you see, sir ..." The constable reached for a clipboard that hung on the wall and began flipping pages. "... yes, as I thought," he said, and turned back to Leonard.

Leonard looked puzzled.

"A complaint was made by a Mr ... ah, let me see ... oh, here it is. A Mr Neil Flanagan, the same name of the gentleman who you allegedly claim committed the assault. He asserts that you provoked and threatened him with physical bodily harm and went to strike at him with a fence batten. In order to defend himself, he struck you. Is this correct sir?"

Leonard felt the blood rush to his head. "No, absolutely not! What is this? The man is fabricating a falsehood. He's lying, he is..."

"Sir, I wasn't there, so I don't know what happened," he smiled. "But either way, it's your word against his and as you stated there were no witnesses to corroborate your version of events."

"Or his version!" Leonard fumed and shook his head. "Then I presume you're suggesting that since I cannot prove what happened, and since he can't either, then its best to drop the entire complaint, is that correct?"

"No, sir. I can't tell you what you should or shouldn't do, that's for you to decide. I'm advising you that if you wish to continue with this assault complaint against Mr Flanigan, that nothing may come of it." He shrugged.

"I should have known. I should have …"

"Sir?"

"Eh, never mind. The incident is logged regardless of what I choose to do, is that correct?"

"Indeed it is, sir," said the constable.

"Good, then that is a start. If he attacks me again, then the prior incident becomes relevant, does it not?"

"Possibly, sir."

The next person in line coughed.

Leonard reached into his coat and extracted the letter for Mary. He'd put it in a second envelope and addressed it to Constable Tim Yates. "Can you please ensure Constable Tim Yates receives this? It is important."

The constable took the envelope from Leonard, turned it over to read the sender's address. "Very well, sir. I will do this."

"Thank you," replied Leonard. It hurt to smile.

"Next!"

Chapter Fourteen

It was 8:15 a.m. on Sunday morning, as Leonard stood outside the plain and unpretentious Lambton Railway Station waiting for the arrival of Agatha Gringle. Part of him doubted she would even show, but Russell, her rather brutish friend, assured him she would be there promptly at 8:00 a.m.

The weather had changed for the worse and a biting southerly wind raced through the streets of Wellington. Leonard turned up the collar of his coat, and with hands buried deep in his pockets, paced anxiously back and forth outside the station's entrance. A few people gave him a second look—his black eye creating some unwelcome attention. Thankfully the pain from his nose had subsided to a dull ache and wasn't really bothersome unless he accidentally knocked it.

He'd almost given up waiting when a Hansom cab pulled up, and to his relief, Agatha stepped out.

When she saw him, she smiled warmly. "I apologise for dawdling; I had some difficulty arranging my hair. The wind ..."

Leonard relaxed; he knew women were always concerned about their hair and keeping it in check while the wind threatened to liberate their hat and set their tresses adrift. He walked towards the cab.

"Oh my, your eye," she gasped, and placed her hand to her mouth. "What happened? Surely it wasn't Russell, I..."

"No, it wasn't him. A minor disagreement and of no concern," he added, hoping she wouldn't push the matter.

She looked at him more intensely. "Has this anything to do with Father and Mr Bedingfield?"

"No, I, er, don't believe so, but I'm not sure. We, er, we shouldn't dilly-dally, the train is scheduled to depart soon," he said, changing the topic of their conversation.

She said nothing more, slid her arm through his as they entered Lambton Station and boarded the Hutt Valley Train.

Once inside and seated, Agatha again questioned him about his eye. She was relentless, and eventually, he gave in and explained everything to her about his relationship with Mary Worthington and the ensuing problems with Neil Flanagan. Normally he was reticent about disclosing personal information about himself, but this time it felt good, almost therapeutic.

It surprised him when she asked about his work, connecting together Mary, the *Evening Standard*, and Flanagan. *She'd make a fine investigator*, he thought. When he finished explaining, she sat quietly staring out the window at the white caps in Wellington's harbour as the train chugged away. He noticed how she trembled; the effects of laudanum, so saddening and apparent. Yet today, she was more alert and lucid than when he saw her last.

Petone Junction was just ahead when she turned to him with tears welling. "I'm so sorry, Leonard. I always seem to cause misery and heartache for those who get close to me. I don't know why, I... I just seem to bring about calamity."

He was surprised by her outburst and as he sought the right words to offer comfort she continued.

"What can I do? Please, Mr Hardy, I can understand how your fiancé would be upset with me. Can I write her a letter, visit her, what can I do to reassure her you've done nothing to be ashamed of?

And your employer, surely I can vouch and speak on your behalf?"

"Thank you so much. I'm hoping that won't be necessary when we locate Mr Bedingfield and learn more about the death of your father.

"You are a dear man, thank you for all you are doing." She placed her hand on his and squeezed.

Her hand felt cold and clammy, another effect of opium. It was a little awkward and he stood as the train screeched into Petone Junction. "Let's see what the day brings, eh," he said, hoping to lighten the mood.

As he assisted her from the carriage they were greeted by a bitterly cold, howling southerly wind that raced over the harbour and slammed into Petone. Leonard shivered. They were some distance from the race course, and trains only travelled along the privately owned railway towards the racecourse on race days. Walking was out of the question; they needed to find a Hansom cab.

As instructed, the cab deposited them outside the main entrance to the Hutt Park Race Course. They entered the grounds and sought shelter from the chill behind a grandstand and looked out over the huge expanse of the circuit. A few horses with their trainers were out on the track. Some cantered, others galloped as they went through various training regimes. It was all very structured and orderly without the throngs of the race day crowds, and other than the weather, it was actually quite pleasant.

"Where to begin?" Leonard asked Agatha after three thoroughbreds, side by side, thundered past. "What are we looking for?"

"Stables, blue stables, with red doors," she replied. "The stables are over there." She pointed in an easterly direction.

Leonard could see a cluster of outbuildings in the distance where she indicated. "Then let's wander over, shall we?"

They attracted no unwelcome attention as they walked around the racecourse perimeter. They weren't alone, others stood in small groups talking, and all appeared to be involved with horses in some way. They passed by owners and trainers leaning on fence rails discussing tactics and training. Riders led sweaty horses to stables so they could be rubbed down after a strenuous workout. There were wagons delivering sacks of feed, and oblivious to the chilly wind, even a few children played. Leonard observed two gentlemen standing near the grandstand watching horses exercise. One of them struggled to keep his lightweight fedora hat from blowing away. He gave up and held it under his arm. No one spared Leonard and Agatha a second look.

When they approached the outbuildings, they saw stables, but not as Agatha described.

"Could they have been recently painted?" he asked.

"No, I don't believe so," she replied, although, to Leonard, she didn't seem certain.

Just ahead, she saw a man grooming a horse. She pulled Leonard's arm, and they casually strolled towards him.

"Good morning," Leonard greeted the strapper[6], who was bent over and digging dirt from his horse's front hoof with a small metal hook.

He turned, released the horse's leg and straightened. "How are ya?" He gave Agatha a long look.

"We are looking for stables, blue, with red doors," Leonard stated.

6   *Strapper– A racehorse groom or stableman.*

"Oh, let me see," said the groom, while stretching his back. "Uh, I think, over the other side, ya might find 'em. Don't go that way much me'self." He removed his hands from his back and gestured to indistinct shapes in the distance.

Leonard couldn't see much other than a stand of trees.

Seeing Leonard's confusion, the strapper added, "Some train in paddocks on the north side of the course. Is more secluded and cheaper than coming here."

"Ah, thank you kindly. Can we walk there?"

"Yep, bloody cold though," he looked guiltily at Agatha for his profanity. "Sorry Miss."

The horse stamped a foot and snorted.

"Again, many thanks," said Leonard as the strapper slid his hand down the horse's leg and attended to the next hoof.

With the wind at their back, Leonard and Agatha continued to walk around the course towards the trees. As they approached, they could see more stables, smaller and run-down. Leonard was relieved to see a little activity there.

"This is beginning to look familiar," Agatha said. "But which stable, which stall?"

"Let's ask him," Leonard suggested.

An older man, somewhere in his mid-sixties, appeared carrying a bucket of water. He entered a stall, emptied the bucket into a trough and walked back outside. He set the pail on the ground and pulling a pipe and a tobacco pouch from his pocket, began filling the bowl. "Bit chilly today," he exclaimed in greeting. He looked unkempt, his clothes soiled and worn.

"Very. Nothing like a Wellington southerly," Leonard added as he and Agatha stopped near him.

"You look like you need help, are ya lost?" the man asked, then placed the pipe stem in his mouth and began sucking loudly.

"Perhaps you can help us," Leonard began.

The man, in the shelter of the stable, struck a match, then expertly shielded it as he held it over the tobacco-filled bowl. The flame sucked down into the bowl, and the tobacco began to smoulder. He flicked the match away and released a mouthful of smoke which rose, caught the wind, then blew away. Eminently pleased with his effort, he again turned back to Leonard.

"My name is Leonard Hardy, and this is Agatha Gringle; she is the daughter of Balthazar Gringle."

The man nodded in acknowledgement and remained silent.

"Were you acquainted with Mr Gringle?"

"I have yet to meet a finer veterinarian," said the man. He removed the pipe from his mouth and pointed the stem at Agatha. "You look like him. Your eyes. I'm sorry for his passing; he was a good man."

Agatha smiled. "Thank you."

Leonard felt relief. Finally, he was getting somewhere. But now came the tricky part. "Are you also acquainted with Harold Bedingfield?"

"Now, why would someone like you, and I can see you ain't a horsey bloke, be wanting Harry for?" His expression changed, and he casually looked around before turning back to Leonard with some suspicion.

Leonard took a deep breath and took a half step closer to the man. "It's personal, and I seek Mr Bedingfield because I have information I wish to share with him, and he might be able to answer some questions."

"Sir," appealed Agatha. "My father died by the hand of another. We believe his death and the disappearance of Mr Bedingfield may be related. We want to find the man who killed my father, can you help us, please?"

A cloud of blue smoke momentarily shrouded the man's face before dissipating. He looked thoughtful before nodding. "He ain't here no more. He was—he's with Sweet Hazel. They went to Island Bay in preparation for the spring meeting."

Leonard's eyebrows furrowed. "He's with Hazel? Is she his mistress, who is this Hazel?"

The man laughed, coughed and then laughed again before wiping his eyes. "I *had* you pegged for a city bloke. Not Hazel, Sweet Hazel. That's his horse!" He laughed again and shook his head before hawking over his shoulder.

Leonard felt foolish. "Do you know where I can find him in Island Bay? It is important."

The man glanced around them. "Look," he said in almost a whisper, "there are some bad people around, they want to do horrible things to Sweet Hazel and Harry and he doesn't want to be found."

"What do these bad men want?"

The man shook his head. "I can't tell ya. But the both of you are at risk, too. You can't go meddling in this."

Leonard was becoming frustrated. "We want to help Mr Bedingfield, but we need to talk to him first. Please, where can we find him?" Leonard pleaded.

"I'll tell ya this, and it's all I know." He looked around to ensure no one could overhear. "There's a farmer in Island Bay, up on the hills near the race course. I forget his name, it might be Dennis or Derris … something like that. Be careful, make sure no one follows you or see's you go there." He shook his head. "I don't know any-thing more."

"Can you tell us what this is all about, why the secrecy and what danger?" Leonard asked.

The man ignored his question and looked over Agatha's shoulder at something that caught his interest. Leonard turned and followed his gaze. In the distance, two men approached. One looked famil-iar, and he recalled seeing him struggling with his fedora near the grandstand earlier, and now they were here.

"You'd better go, those men … them, they're troublemakers," said the man. He took a step away from the stable. "Come this way, don't tarry, come, come." He motioned Leonard and Agatha to fol-low.

Once around the corner and out of sight from the two approach-ing men, he gestured to the path ahead. "Go that way; it will lead you to Woburn. Hurry, for these men are hoodlums, and they seek Harry as you do, but methinks their motives are different. They will hurt you."

Leonard looked puzzled but understood the urgency in his voice. "Come," he held out his hand to Agatha. "Time to leave."

They hurried as quickly as they dared. The path wound between fenced paddocks and was obviously used by horses to either train or as a thoroughfare. The track was quite wide, but mud, rocks and puddles were obstacles to avoid and slowed them down. Agatha had been wise and dressed appropriately for the day—her footwear was sturdy and laced boots offered good support. However, her poor physical condition and skirts prevented her from moving at any-thing faster than a brisk walk.

Leonard risked a quick look behind and saw the two men round the corner and begin to follow. "They're coming, we must hasten."

Although the two men were a considerable distance behind, Leonard knew he and Agatha would be easily caught. Agatha was tiring. She was unfit and unhealthy, her body not used to this type of physical exertion. She was breathing hard and he knew she couldn't continue for much longer. Ahead a narrow but solid bridge crossed a stream, on the other side, a few trees on a rise hid what lay beyond.

He urged her on with kind words and encouragement, but it did little good. She stopped at the bridge, exhausted. Unable to continue, he could only stand at her side and feel pity. Laudanum had taken her vitality and drained her of life. In the cold wind, he'd expected to see rosy cheeks, but all he saw was pale skin and watery eyes.

"Go, Leonard," she gasped between breaths. "I will stay. They won't hurt me."

"We have done no wrong, committed no foul or taken part in any illicit activity. We have nothing to fear from those men," he told her, feeling foolishly brave.

"They must have recognised one of us." She shook her head, smoothed her dress and repositioned her handbag. "Do you think they'll offer you a cup of tea? I expect they will want to know why you were talking to that man earlier, and if you refuse to answer, they will resort to violence and persuade you to talk." She took a few deep lungfuls of air. "I know what men like that are capable of." In spite of her physical condition, her face hardened.

Leonard saw two men run around the corner, and to his chagrin, they weren't even fatigued.

One of them pulled a cudgel from his belt. The other, a much larger fellow, puffed out his chest and, with fists clenched, slowly advanced.

"Whom do you seek?" Leonard challenged.

They didn't respond and strode aggressively towards them.

Chapter Fifteen

Leonard eased himself protectively in front of Agatha, who was now breathing more easily. The two men swaggered closer, and without pause or thought, the larger fellow stepped up and drove a fist firmly into his stomach. It was delivered with force, felling Leonard to his knees, retching. They weren't finished with him yet. The larger man bent down, grabbed him by his coat lapels and hauled him roughly back to his feet, only to be struck by the cudgel wielded by the smaller man. Leonard felt the jarring brutal impact across his forehead and nose, and his vision exploded into a bright searing flash of light. He collapsed back onto the track with a groan as blood streamed from his nose. Through the haze of pain and confusion, he thought he heard the sound of a woman's scream.

He tried to focus his thoughts on Agatha. Fighting dizziness and fear, he struggled to his hands and knees.

He heard one of his assailants laugh, but the sound was abruptly cut off by the loud retort of a gunshot. It was unbearably loud, and his ears rang. Leonard blinked his eyes open to see the larger man who'd beat him, lying prostrate and twitching on the ground. A spreading red stain expanded greedily across his chest.

In shock, dazed, and in disbelief, Leonard swung his head to look at Agatha.

She stood motionless. Smoke wafted from the barrel of a handgun that she still held in both hands. Her eyes narrowed, and with bloodless compressed lips, stared at the corpse. "That's for Father," she hissed.

"You bitch!" screamed the smaller man, who bent down to assist his fallen accomplice. There was little he could do; the man was dead. "You killed him!"

Leonard tried to clear the ringing that impaired his hearing and shook his head to clear the fog. Blood sprayed from his nose. Agatha began fumbling with the handgun, it had jammed and she tried to eject the offending cartridge so she could shoot the second man.

"Agatha, no!" Leonard yelled, as he attempted to stand. His voice sounded muffled.

Suddenly realising that he was going to be shot, the remaining thug rose quickly to his feet and ran off, back down the path from where he'd come.

He stood precariously and swayed, then lurched for the bridge hand-rail for support before he fell. "Agatha, wh-what have you done?" he finally managed to say.

She seemed to be in a trance and compulsively struggled with the handgun's mechanism to no avail.

"Agatha!" he yelled again and reached for the weapon. She didn't react or pull away and stood frozen, staring at the lifeless corpse. He took the pistol from her as she returned to the present and rationality.

She turned to face him, her eyes wet and glistening, and spoke softly. "Leonard, for your safety, we must leave now."

He spat out some blood. "We have to report this to the Police … we must, Agatha."

"No!"

"Agatha, a man is dead," he pleaded, as blood dripped from his nose.

"Not yet, Leonard. I need to return home and compose myself first. You, uh … we can report it to the police in the morning. But we should leave here before others come, you are in danger." She reached up and began to wipe blood from his face with a handkerchief.

Leonard was in a stupor. He tried to comprehend what had happened, but his mind wasn't functioning properly. He was in no condition to argue. His ears rang, his head hurt, and the blow he received to his head addled his thinking. He meekly complied.

She gently took him by the arm to lead him away. In a moment of clarity, he suddenly pulled free from her and stumbled back to the body and looked for the man's pocketbook. He found it easily and placed it in the inside pocket of his coat. Agatha helped him to his feet, and together they slowly walked along the path into Woburn.

The journey home was a muddle, and he couldn't remember much. He had a knot on his head the size of an egg, and he felt poorly. With surprising patience and compassion, Agatha helped him the entire way back to Wellington, and from her demeanour, you wouldn't have known she'd shot and killed a man only hours before. She took him home, undressed and tenderly cleaned him before quietly leaving after helping him to his bed. After a fitful sleep he arose in the morning feeling remarkably better. The incessant ringing in his ears finally stopped, but his head still ached. His poor nose had taken a beating.

It seemed like a dream as he began to recall and process the events of the previous day. For a while, he wondered if it had just been an opium-fuelled fantasy—had Agatha slipped him a potion? But then he found the handgun lying like a paperweight on top of a note she left. With a groan, he sat down to read.

My dearest Leonard,

I apologise for my deceit. You are an honourable, kind-hearted man and deserve so much better than how I misused you. The disappearance of Mr Bedingfield and the death of my father led you to me, and I sought advantage of our amity because I knew you would help.

From our discussions, I have learned how your mind functions, how you think, and even now, as you read my missive, you are planning to report the death of Leon Barrow and claim to the police that he was shot in self-defence. He wasn't. Without coercion or duress, I freely admit, that I killed him with the weapon at your fingertips to avenge the death of my father. I deeply regret that you were hurt and fervently pray that you will quickly recover.

I hope that your fiancé can accept how you were always a perfect gentleman to

me and accounted for yourself with dignity and virtue. She is indeed a fortunate woman to have you. That your employer understands that the accusations made against you are false, you never sought to take advantage of my distasteful and immoral lifestyle, and you always behaved appropriately, as a gentleman should.

The solace and relief afforded to me through opium diminished the pain, but not the reality. I've become a servant, a slave to its vile grip. Its potent legacy, lasting, permanent and indelible. Please forgive me, Leonard. I have no choice.

I am, Ever your friend,
Agatha Gringle

She knew the name of the man she killed, and now plainly obvious, she knew far more than she'd disclosed. He let the letter drop to his lap and stared blankly at the far wall of his sitting room. Thoughts and abstract notions coursed through his mind as he sought to make sense of it all. One thing was certain; he had to report the shooting and death to the police immediately. Failing to do so would be irresponsible and only aid the police in assuming he was culpable. What it would do to Agatha, he didn't know. Perhaps self-defence was still a viable plea for her vindication. That the opium had affected her rationale? Nonetheless, he was still a witness and could testify on her behalf.

He decided to locate his friend Constable Tim Yates and report the shooting to him. Then at least, he would be heard and treated fairly. He slowly eased himself from the chair and prepared to leave the house.

With the handgun in a paper bag, and Agatha's letter in his pocket, he walked to the wharves where he knew Tim would be patrolling. The wind had abated somewhat, and while still chilly, it was at least sunny. Walking made him feel better, and before long, he felt reasonably sharp of mind and alert again. The bump on his head still hurt, and his nose was painful, but in a day or so, they would improve. Poor Agatha. He pictured the police arriving at the Victoria Hotel and marching her away. *If only there was another option.*

He never found Tim, it was Tim who tapped him on the shoulder from behind. "What are you doing skulking around here … My God! Leo, your face, what happened?"

Leonard grimaced. "Tim, we need to talk, and with some urgency. Is there somewhere close we can go?"

"Leo, I'm working, perhaps after at the Southern Cross, later?"

"Tim, this is about work. I need a constable."

Tim nodded, his expression serious. "Looks like you need a doctor. Very well, come."

Leonard sat on a bench in front of the vacant offices of a shipping company while Tim, with hands clasped behind his back, paced back and forth. Leonard had just explained all that happened to him yesterday.

"Leo, you could be charged as an accessory to murder!"

"I have this. It's a missive I found this morning." He extracted Agatha's letter and handed it over.

Tim nodded after reading it. "This helps considerably, Leo. Do you still have the handgun she mentions?"

Leonard pulled the paper bag with the pistol inside from his coat pocket.

"And you can put that thing away—I hope it isn't loaded? But as long as you have it, that's the main thing." Tim resumed his pacing. "I need to think on this."

"What shall we do?" Leonard asked. "I do not wish to become a fugitive. With everything else that's happened to me recently, being wanted by the police for murder wouldn't sit well."

Tim stopped and faced him. "Let's go to the Mount Cook Depot. I will discuss this with a superior and take your report. That will be a start. Beyond that … I really don't know if you'll be charged as an accessory, an accomplice, or just treated as a witness."

"At least we have the weapon, we know she had a motive, and she confesses to the killing. I don't see this as a problem."

Tim nodded. "I hope not. I think we should go now."

Rather than wait in the public waiting room, Tim escorted Leonard to a small, sparsely furnished interview room with a small desk and two chairs, where he was required to write a statement detailing the events of the previous day at the Hutt Park Race Course.

It took an eternity before Tim reappeared with two men. Leonard recognised Inspector Gibbard immediately, the other man was unknown to him. He'd had dealings with the inspector before and knew him to be tough and frequently abrasive, but above all, he was honest and fair.

Inspector Gibbard hadn't changed much since Leonard had seen him last. His rather generous whiskers did little to hide his pock-marked face and an almost lipless mouth. He stood with hands on hips and stared coldly, a moment longer than was deemed polite.

Under his scrutiny, Leonard felt uncomfortable and his hands began to feel clammy. He wiped them on his trousers and nervously shifted his feet. He knew Inspector Gibbard was a very astute and capable investigator, and in the past, had accounted himself well, but …

"Mr Hardy, a pleasure to see you again, although, this time, under more, rather troubling circumstances." He reached out a hand.

Leonard stood. He wasn't sure if the inspector smiled or grimaced. "I wish it were different, Inspector," Leonard replied as they shook.

"Er, your face, do you need anything? It looks dreadful. Have you received medical treatment?"

"No, not as yet, thank you." Leonard raised his hand and touched the sensitive knot on the side of his head.

"This is Senior Constable Hale, and he is here at my request."

Leonard greeted the senior constable but did not shake hands.

Tim stood against the far wall and remained silent.

"Let's get to the bottom of this, shall we," said Inspector Gibbard. He shared a quick glance with the senior constable, and Leonard wondered what the secretive look was all about.

"Please, sit."

Senior Constable Hale handed some documents to the inspector.

He recognised the written statement, a declaration, that he'd completed with Tim earlier.

"I understand you have a missive?" asked the inspector, as he lowered himself onto the other chair.

Leonard retrieved the letter and gun from his pocket and handed them over.

Inspector Gibbard ensured the handgun wasn't loaded and then slowly read the letter. Once finished, he handed it to Senior Constable Hale who stood at his side and waited for him to finish reading it. Leonard opened his mouth to speak but the inspector raised a hand. Leonard obediently paused.

Senior Constable Hale folded the letter and returned it to the inspector. He nodded, and again, Leonard saw them make eye contact.

Inspector Gibbard briefly consulted Leonard's statement. "Now then, who is Harold Bedingfield?"

"Ah, if I may, sir," replied Senior Constable Hale. "He is an intemperate vagrant who has gone missing. His wife has filed a missing person's report with us, but as of today, we've not been able to locate the, em, gentleman."

Leonard surmised the police hadn't even begun to search for Mr Bedingfield.

"And what is his involvement in all this?" asked Inspector Gibbard.

Leonard wasn't sure what to say. Unusually he kept his mouth shut and waited to hear what the police knew, or didn't know.

There was a brief moment of silence. "Up until today, sir, we didn't believe he had any involvement," answered the senior constable.

The Inspector focused his attention on Leonard. "And what do you believe?"

Leonard took a breath. "Horses."

Gibbard raised his eyebrows. "Horses?"

"The man who was killed on Courtenay Place, Balthazar Gringle was an animal doctor, a veterinarian, and apparently he was a specialist with horses, sir. Mr Bedingfield was a saddler and ..." Leonard looked at each of the faces in the room. "Uh, that's all, that's the only link I have confirmed."

"I see," stated the inspector. "Horses ... not much to go on, is there?" He looked at Leonard closely. "When did you last see Miss Gringle, approximately what time?"

He thought about it carefully. "Not sure, Inspector. Yesterday late afternoon or early evening sometime at my home."

"Did you see or visit her since then?" Inspector Gibbard leaned forward. His eyes probed.

"No, I was poorly and in bed and remained there until this morning."

The inspector kept his gaze firmly on Leonard's face. "Let me confirm. Did you leave your home, at any time after you returned from the Hutt Park Race Course yesterday?"

Leonard shook his head. "The only time I left my house was this morning, and that was to locate Tim, er, Constable Yates at the wharves."

Inspector Gibbard seemed satisfied with his response. "Mr Hardy, why did you or Miss Gringle not report the shooting immediately after it happened yesterday?"

"I was rather unwell, and not thinking rationally, sir. I don't recall travelling back to Wellington or arriving home. Miss Gringle took care of me and suggested I report the incident on Monday, which I have done, have I not?"

"Then why do you think she asked you to report it, and not do it herself?"

Leonard's eyebrows furrowed. *A good question.* "I have no idea, sir. I haven't really given it any thought."

"Had you previously made the acquaintance of the man who was killed by Miss Gringle? Uh, what was his name? Ah, yes, Mr Leon Barrow."

Leonard shook his head. "No, never. I saw him earlier in the day and remembered him because he was having difficulty with his hat in the wind. Those two times are the only occasions I've seen him."

This seemed to satisfy Inspector Gibbard. He grimaced and referred back to the statement. "Uh, the other fellow, the smaller man who ran off, what do you know of him?"

Leonard thought about it, there was something about the way he spoke, but he couldn't hear properly. "Uh, I can't be sure ..." Slowly, he remembered, the events becoming clearer. "I'm not sure, but believe he may have had an accent, perhaps American, but I'm not positive."

"But the only words you think you heard were … let me see …" The Inspector consulted Leonard's written statement again. "Here it is, uh, 'You bitch, you killed him.' But your hearing was affected because of the close proximity to the gun when discharged, yes?"

Leonard shrugged. "I believe that was what he said."

"And have you seen *him* before?"

"No, never."

Inspector Gibbard slid back his chair and stood. "Thank you for your cooperation, Mr Hardy. If we have further questions, we know where to find you. You are free to go."

"But what about Miss Gringle? Will I be required to testify on her behalf? Are you charging her?" Leonard asked as he rose from his chair.

Leonard saw a vein pulse on the Inspector's neck as his jaw tightened. "No, we will not be charging her."

Leonard felt relief.

The inspector took a step closer to Leonard. "Mr Hardy, Agatha Gringle is deceased."

Chapter Sixteen

Leonard suddenly felt light-headed and slowly lowered himself back onto the chair. He looked up at the inspector in disbelief.

"Self-immolation, suicide, Mr Hardy. It appears she drank enough laudanum to knock out a herd of elephants. Her death was reported to us early this morning."

Leonard leaned back and covered his face with his hands. *It can't be, it can't.*

"And we will not be making any charges against you at this time," added the inspector. "Go to the hospital and have your head seen to and then return home and stay in bed," he advised.

Leonard pried his hands from his face. "Why, why are you not charging me? Is her missive alone enough evidence?"

"Her letter supports a credible eyewitness account. Someone saw the entire incident near the bridge at the race course. Good day, Mr Hardy."

"I need that letter, Inspector. Miss Gringle's letter, I need it to show my employer and my fiancé."

Inspector Gibbard talked quietly with Senior Constable Hale for a moment. "Return in two days, and you can retrieve it, meanwhile, we will have it copied." He picked up Agatha's hand gun and letter, then exited the room with the senior constable following.

Leonard shook his head. *Poor, poor Agatha.* Such was the hold opium had on her—the misery and endless dependence. The last paragraph in her missive made sense to him now. She'd intended to commit suicide after avenging her father's murder, and she did exactly that, hence her note.

"How did she know who killed her father?" asked Tim suddenly.

Leonard looked over at him. "I was wondering the same thing. She even knew his name. Leon Barrow."

"And an American?" Tim clarified.

Leonard nodded. "Inspector Gibbard doesn't believe me, but I know what I heard, ringing ears and all. He spoke with an American accent, I'm sure of it. Oh my, poor Agatha."

Tim straightened from the wall and walked over. "I'm so sorry, Leo. Is so tragic." He placed a comforting hand on his shoulder as Leonard lowered his head to his arms on the table.

Leonard had a mild headache and wanted to rest. After kicking off his shoes and arranging pillows on his settee, he eased himself down and closed his eyes. Constable Tim Yates ensured he arrived home safely and then returned to his assigned patrol at the wharf.

His thoughts returned to Agatha, and the internal pain and turmoil she must have endured. Why she had chosen such a lifestyle, he couldn't fathom. The hold opium had on her was fatal, its grasp permanent and unforgiving. Yet her trade and dependence on opium were enduringly linked. One couldn't exist without the other. She had been conscious of that fact, and she knew the outcome would always lead to death.

She had killed that man in cold blood without remorse and she'd fully understood the consequences of her actions. She'd taken the handgun with her, believing she may encounter her father's killer, and if their paths crossed, then she planned to shoot him dead. She knew his name, and she knew more, a lot more than she'd divulged.

From where had she obtained that information?

She had been very eager to go to Hutt Park Race Course, and encouraged him to go with her. Despite the headache and sadness he felt, he smiled. Agatha had used him, and he never suspected—he'd underestimated her—she was a very clever woman.

He suddenly sat up. The man she killed, Leon Barrow. *His pocketbook.* Leonard walked to his bedroom and found his coat hanging behind the door where Agatha had placed it after thoughtfully cleaning the blood from it. He reached inside and found the pocketbook. He grimaced when he realised he'd forgotten to tell Inspector Gibbard about taking it. *Oh well.*

Sitting at his writing bureau, Leonard began to look through its contents and discovered a great deal of money. He counted eighty-six pounds—a significant amount. There was even a folded United States one hundred dollar bill. There were business cards that contained names and addresses that were from overseas locations. Some old scraps of grimy, well-used paper, notes of some sort were slid into a partition. With care, he pried them apart and leaned lower to read them better. He saw two names, the first, Balthazar Gringle, but a line had been drawn through the name. *Because he was killed,* Leonard reasoned. At the bottom of the note, a single word had been written, four letters that spelled *dope.*

Without thinking, and more from force of habit, he copied the names to a separate piece of paper as he contemplated the mystery. He had no idea what the word *dope* meant. He'd never encountered it before and determined it must be an abbreviation of some sort. The last note contained a business name, *Tyne, Lewis & Chatswood,* and beneath was written *Rhodes* and *Newcastle.* All seemingly innocuous and meant nothing, but he still felt it was important somehow. He returned the scraps of paper back to the pocketbook and placed everything on his bureau where he'd look at them again later.

Leonard spent the remainder of the day napping and thinking about two women, Agatha Gringle, who was now dead, and Mary Worthington, who wished he was. The irony didn't sit well with him. He hoped that Tim had received his letter and passed it to Meredith.

The answer to his question came later, as the sun was setting when Tim arrived to check on him. They sat in Leonard's living room with Tim sprawled on the settee, and Leonard in an armchair.

"Meredith has your letter, Leo. As yet, she hasn't seen Mary, but she will give it to her when she does."

Leonard scowled.

"Look, old boy, she promised she would."

"It isn't that, Tim. It's the mere fact I must resort to writing a letter to explain myself when I can't even have a private discourse with her without fear of being assaulted."

"Well, you've certainly put yourself in the thick of it, eh?"

Leonard stared out the window at the colourful sunset. Orange clouds, ringed by violet, dominated the early evening winter sky. "I'm tempted to return to Mary and Bridgette's house — he might not be there this time."

"Do you think that is wise? Look, Leo, give her time, let her read your letter, and digest and mull over it the way women tend to do. Then you can arrange to meet her somewhere, a nice place. Perhaps dinner?"

"What of Neil Flanagan? What is his interest in Mary?" Leonard asked, ignoring Tim's advice.

"It might not be about her at all."

Leonard's head shot around. "What do you mean?"

"Perhaps this sordid business is about you. It's plainly obvious, isn't it? He's discredited you to your fiancé, and who else informed the management of the paper about your so-called immoral pursuits? I'll tell you. Someone who had access to your employer and had the opportunity, that's who."

Leonard's eyebrows knitted together. "And why do I deserve such attention?"

"What work have you been assigned that is different from your normal scheduled tasks?"

"I don't know." He shrugged. "Just the normal menial duties a junior is required to do."

"And the work you were doing on the misplaced hobo?" Tim sat up and smiled.

"But that is nothing, just an incident of a missing person. Is routine and of no consequence."

"I dare say it isn't routine. Look what's happened. Two deaths so far..."

"Three! Agatha, her father, Balthazar, and Leon Barrow, that's three," Leonard corrected.

Tim leaned back. "And that, dear Leo, is my point."

"According to your reasoning, Neil Flanagan is targeting me?"

Tim nodded.

"Because of Harold Bedingfield or Balthazar Gringle?"

"Why not? It has worked for him. You are no longer employed by the *Evening Standard* and cannot investigate or publish anything that draws attention to either man. Having your fiancé distance herself from you only adds credence and validates the claims he's made to the newspaper about you." Tim looked smug.

Leonard rubbed his chin. "This whole affair is quite extraordinary, isn't it?"

"Indeed it is, Leo."

They sat in companionable silence for a while before Leonard rose from the chair. "I think I need to dwell on this. If what you say is true, then, going to Mary first is unlikely to change anything. My efforts will be thwarted by Flanagan. Then I need to speak to someone else, and in confidence. I need to learn more about Neil Flanagan and, sadly, there isn't much here about him because he's a new immigrant. Other than the assault in Island Bay I informed you about, I have nothing to use to help dispute the claims he's made, until Agatha's letter is returned to me."

"I wish I could help you there, Leo." Tim stood. "I must be off."

"You *can* help."

"Pardon?"

"Are you familiar with the word, *dope*, d, o, p, e, dope?"

Tim looked puzzled. "Never heard of it before. In what context?

Leonard thought quickly, he didn't want Tim to know of the billfold where he found the note. "I'm not sure, and I haven't heard of it either, but, er, Agatha mentioned it, I don't know anything about it but I feel it is important."

"Dope, eh? Alright, Leo, I will sniff around for you."

The headache eased, the pain from his nose dissolved to a familiar dull, throbbing ache and even the swelling had diminished a little when he woke the next morning. The blackness around his eye had turned yellowish, but overall he considered he physically felt better. Emotionally, unfortunate circumstances of Agatha's tragic suicide were still upsetting. He knew it was also compounded by anxiety over his tenuous relationship with Mary.

He wanted to go to her, be with her, and explain candidly his feelings and thoughts. However, he knew the sensible course of action was to wait, until she read his letter, and then approach her.

With a sigh he dressed and stepped outside into a grey, overcast day to visit the markets and purchase food.

The markets were located on Tory Street. He would need to walk quickly past the offensive Wellington waste collection site with its vile, toxic odours, and inadequate and over-worked incinerators spewing oily black smoke from labouring, wheezing chimneys. Then onwards, past the city morgue that was unfortunately and conveniently located next door. People were still making their way to work, and he greeted a few he recognised with a polite head nod as he approached the morgue. A Hansom cab pulled up near him, and the coroner alighted. He was familiar with the coroner, as part of his responsibilities at the *Evening Standard* required him to visit the morgue and receive a list of the newly deceased for the death notices he compiled.

The medical examiner, or coroner, Dr Milliken-Brown was a diminutive man, short in stature, but not in pomposity. He was burdened with a ruddy complexion and a short temper and took enormous pride in his prodigious moustache that curved endlessly around his mouth.

He saw Leonard and cordially greeted him with a smile, easily recognizable by the exaggerated upward movement of his walrus whiskers. "Oh dear, Mr Hardy, I dare say, you've had a spot of bother, I see."

"Morning, Doctor. Yes, but all is well now, thank you," Leonard replied, hoping the cause of his black eye wouldn't require a lengthy explanation.

"Enjoy your day," added the doctor as Leonard passed him by. "Oh, forgive me, I really must apologise …"

Leonard stopped and looked back.

"My most sincere condolences for the loss of your associate."

"Thank you, her death was most unfortunate," Leonard replied.

Dr Milliken-Brown's eyebrows furrowed together. "Her?"

Leonard was equally flummoxed. "Miss Agatha Gringle."

The doctor's face relaxed and his moustache returned to its normal position. "No, no, your colleague from the newspaper."

"I beg your pardon!" Leonard exclaimed and took a step back towards the doctor. "Who do you mean?"

"Again, I must plead your forgiveness, I assumed you would know."

Leonard was confused.

"Mr Camden, your associate and colleague from the newspaper." Dr Milliken-Brown lowered his voice. "He was found deceased in his home last evening by a neighbour."

Leonard looked down at the coroner in shock. "Milton Camden? He's dead?"

"Very much so."

"For what reason? I mean, what was the cause of death, do you know?"

"I will be performing a forensic investigation this morning to determine the cause of death. All I know at this point is that he had seizures."

147

"But he was so healthy and young. He was a gentleman of moderation without vices or afflictions."

"The Lord moves in mysterious ways, eh? Good day, Mr Hardy. This fair city has immediate need of my clinical expertise." He made to walk away.

Leonard was dumbfounded. "Doctor?" he asked. "Er, would you be able to share with me the results of your investigation … if I, uh, returned later in the day?"

"Good heavens no, that would be highly irregular and most inappropriate." He frowned disapprovingly. "That just won't do."

Despite the shock, Leonard thought quickly. "My turn to apologise, Dr Milliken-Brown. He and I were very closely acquainted, and, of course, we were associates for quite some time. His unexpected death has left me a little bewildered and distressed, and I, uh, I just wish to know why he died, that is all. Personal reasons."

The coroner's look softened. "I shouldn't really…" He raised a hand and smoothed his whiskers. "I will be here until four-thirty this afternoon," he whispered. "If you happen to be standing here, I will give you a brief summation. Cheerio." The moustache travelled upwards as he smiled and then he continued on towards his office.

Leonard stood frozen in the middle of the footpath. *Milton Camden dead? How can this be?*

Milton reported on entertainment and recreation and was well suited to his role. He was a popular and well-liked employee of the *Evening Standard*, and loved reporting on the events he covered. He was a fan of most sports, loved cricket, was an authority on horse racing, and knew just about anything to do with recreational sporting activities. For years, he'd sat at his desk immediately behind

Leonard and become a mentor of sorts. Certainly they weren't close, as he'd intimated to Dr Milliken-Brown, but Milton was a likeable and jolly fellow, all the same. He knew Mr Pembroke would be in a state of disbelief and despair.

Chapter Seventeen

Leonard was impatient and eager to learn why Milton Camden suddenly passed away. When he saw him last, less than a week ago, he was in fine form, sturdy and seemingly in healthy spirits.

Milton lived alone, and to some, he was considered a dallier, a ladies' man. Previously married, his wife had an illicit affair with a Type-Setter and fled to Australia some years earlier. Since then, and when opportunity availed, which by most accounts was quite frequent, Milton took advantage of his entertainment and recreation portfolio to always enjoy the pleasures of having female company at his side. Mr Pembroke was fully aware of where Milton's amorous passions lay, and Milton had explained to the senior reporter how a delightful woman with a coquettish smile would help grant him access and loosen tongues, when otherwise denied, to the events he covered for the newspaper.

It was only natural curiosity that led Leonard to ask the coroner about the cause of Milton's death, and keen to learn more, he approached the city morgue at the time Dr Milliken-Brown suggested. The coroner was not waiting outside, but his assistant, Lambert Souter was.

"Oh Leonard, is a pleasure to see you again," greeted Lambert with a grin. He grimaced when he saw Leonard's black eye. "Ouch," was his only comment.

"Don't ask, is a long story," replied Leonard with his own smile.

He always liked the young man who assisted the coroner with his morbid tasks. He was a jolly chap with a friendly and outgoing disposition. "Good afternoon Lambert and where is the good doctor, he promised to meet me outside?"

"He asked me to come in his stead," answered Lambert. He leaned forward. "His lordship asked me to greet you, and he requests the pleasure of your company inside."

Leonard was perplexed as to why the coroner wanted to see *him*. "A busy man, eh? Best we not keep him waiting."

Lambert led the way into the morgue and medical examiner's clinic, and found the Coroner in his tiny office. Leonard had been here many times when his friend had been the medical examiner, until he was killed. Being here always made him feel a little melancholy.

"Mr Hardy, thank you for dropping by. Er, I wonder if I may ask you a question or two? This is unofficial, of course, and is just to satisfy my own inquisitiveness." He smiled and the walrus whiskers rose considerably. "Please, sit." He waved to an empty chair. The only chair. There wasn't room for another in the cramped office.

Leonard wondered whether if the moustache became any bushier it would obscure the doctor's vision when he smiled.

"Uh, now then … this is a delicate matter and I won't keep you, I'm sure you have more important things to do." The coroner shuffled some papers. "Uh, your associate, Mr Camden … were you aware if he favoured any artificial stimulants?"

"I know he liked a drop from time to time, but no, he was certainly not an inebriate or a drunkard." Leonard was puzzled. "Why? Is this important, Doctor?"

"Er, perhaps. Although I'm not referring to alcoholic beverages, but rather other forms of stimulation."

"Like opium?" Leonard felt a chill.

"Or others," added the doctor.

Leonard thought about all those people he'd met who'd suffered from prolonged opium use. He scratched his chin. "I don't recall, Doctor. Uh, I'm no authority, sir, but Mr Camden never displayed any typical manifestations that I recognise."

Dr Milliken-Brown leaned back in his chair. It squeaked loudly. "I found nothing to suggest he had a habitual fondness for such immoral pursuits."

"May I enquire, sir? What was the cause of his death?"

The coroner was deep in thought.

"Sir?"

His eyes shifted to focus on Leonard. "Oh yes, forgive me."

"What was the cause of his death?"

"The deceased suffered a myocardial infarction, Mr Hardy."

Leonard didn't understand and looked puzzled.

"Additionally, he sustained a cerebral vascular accident …"

"Forgive me, doctor, can you explain in simple terms?"

The coroner took a deep breath and exhaled slowly before continuing. "He had a cardiac arrest which was compounded by apoplexy[7]."

Leonard wasn't any wiser.

"Mr Hardy, as far as I can ascertain, the deceased suffered a catastrophic coronary artery spasm that led to cardiac arrest. Additionally, through my findings, I conclude he then endured apoplexy immediately after."

Leonard looked down at the floor as he tried to make sense of

7   *Apoplexy – Stroke.*

what the coroner told him. After a moment he looked up. "Then why enquire about artificial stimulants?"

"Now there is a question worth consideration. I believe his body had an adverse reaction to an artificial stimulant, which triggered a series of medical events that proved fatal."

"Like poison?"

"In a manner, yes."

"Then he was murdered!"

"Mr Hardy, please curb your assumptions! It is not my role to speculate, I deal in facts. I gather information, and it is for the police to make informed decisions on how they wish to proceed."

Leonard looked contrite. "Do you believe it was opium?"

"Simply put, no!" replied the coroner. "What your associate ingested was a veritable cocktail of potent analeptics[8]."

"Which could lead the police to conclude that he may have been poisoned. Although I find it peculiar that Milton Camden would willingly consume a mixture of powerful drugs to the extent it would prove fatal," finished Leonard.

Dr Milliken-Brown rose from his seat. "Mr Hardy, I thank you for your time and contribution. Now I must complete my report. I have informed the police that the cause of Mr Camden's death is highly irregular. I'm sure your wonderful newspaper will be reporting the details as they arise and become public. Good day."

"Thank you for sharing your insights, Doctor, I know the way out."

The coroner's moustache travelled upwards, then settled as he returned to his paperwork.

Leonard departed the office and walked to the door that led out-

8   *Analeptic – medication, potion.*

side and reached for the handle, only for the door to open suddenly leaving him staring into the pock-marked face of Inspector Gibbard.

"Well then, Mr Hardy. I dare say, I'm somewhat astonished to find you here." He stepped aside so Leonard could exit.

"I was just leaving, Inspector. Farewell." Leonard did not feel any compunction to share with him the reason for his visit and hurriedly departed the building.

The Inspector turned and watched Leonard walk away.

He didn't remember the walk home as he considered what the Coroner had divulged about poor Milton. *An aggrieved lover seeking retribution*, Leonard surmised. Milton must have offended someone's honour, and they sought revenge and poisoned him. Based on what the coroner said, it was a traumatic death, and Milton must have suffered terribly. Out of respect for his colleague, he decided to attend the funeral service and pay his respects.

Leonard sat in his armchair with an open book in his lap, but he couldn't read. His mind drifted to Mary. He felt self-reproach for his churlish behaviour towards her and decided that committing to a wedding date would be a positive step towards reconciling their differences. A door knock interrupted his introspective musings and gave him a start. He rose from his chair, hoping it was Tim with news.

"Uh, Inspector Gibbard," greeted Leonard with some surprise.

"Mr Hardy, I am somewhat relieved to find you at home. The thought of having to trudge up that confounded steep street again is not appealing," remarked the Inspector.

"How may I assist you?" Leonard asked rather brusquely. He didn't intend for his response to appear so harsh, but the appearance of the inspector at his door was a little disquieting.

"I think the prudent course of action would be to invite me in, out of the cold so we can have a little chat, eh?"

Leonard didn't really have any other option and invited him inside, and once seated, Leonard apologised.

The Inspector's features were hard and cold. The pock-marked skin and the large sideburns, which extended down his face and ended at a lipless mouth, made him seem severe and almost vulgar. Anyone could be forgiven for thinking he was unrefined and a malefactor. However, Leonard knew from his own past experiences that the man was far from uncouth or a villain. He had demonstrated astuteness, a quick wit and was unbiased, beyond reproach. This is what made Leonard feel uncomfortable in his presence because anything the inspector said, or intimated, was done so with purpose and reason, and if the inspector chose to visit him this evening, then there was a rationale. Leonard was on guard.

The inspector didn't disappoint.

"Mr Hardy, you are no doubt aware of the disturbing death of Milton Camden?"

Leonard nodded. "I find it difficult to believe."

"Let me make this succinctly clear to you. I know you are not involved in these unfortunate deaths, caused Mr Camden's death, or are responsible for the death of others."

Leonard opened his mouth to speak.

"Let me finish. Balthazar Gringle, Agatha Gringle, and the murder at the Hutt Park Race Course, the Barrows chap, and now Milton Camden … these are the deaths that I am aware of, are there more?" It was rhetorical and didn't require an answer. "I do believe you have a perspective on this that I am very eager to hear. I know you weren't totally forthcoming with me when we last spoke. But, my visit here today is not just for a pleasant chat and to hear your theories, but sadly about something more sinister."

Leonard swallowed. *Sinister?*

Gibbard leaned forward. "Now, why is it," continued the Inspector, "that these people all died?"

Leonard knew the inspector sought help in solving the mystery around the deaths. It was his duty to be forthcoming. "Tea or whisky?"

Chapter Eighteen

Inspector Gibbard sat comfortably back against the sofa and sipped from his glass. He'd listened, without interrupting, as Leonard explained and detailed all he knew.

"I do believe you may be wrong, Inspector, the death of Milton Camden is no more than a jilted lover seeking revenge and has nothing whatsoever to do with the other cases."

Gibbard nodded and looked thoughtful. "You may be correct, however …" He rose from the sofa and stepped closer to Leonard's writing bureau. "Who stands to benefit from Mr Camden's death?"

"The person seeking revenge?"

"No, discard that reasoning. There is more."

Leonard gave the matter some consideration.

"Everything that has happened so far has, by your calculations, involved horses, yes?"

"That's what I believe," Leonard replied.

"How does his death tie into horses, then?" The inspector took a healthy pull from his glass.

The ticking clock broke the silence. Its measured cadence, loud, reassuring and predictable.

Leonard's eyes opened wide, and he shot up from his chair. "I know!"

Inspector Gibbard's lipless mouth broke into a smile before he spoke. "Don't keep me in suspense."

He returned to the sofa.   "Milton was the *Evening Standard*'s reporter on recreation and entertainment.

That includes reporting on horse racing."

"Continue," encouraged the inspector.

"An opening now exists to find a new reporter. Neil Flanagan told me that he originally wanted to have the Recreation and Entertainment portfolio. It seems plausible that Mr Pembroke will now assign him to that position."

Inspector Gibbard nodded. "Very well, but why? For what purpose? What does a reporter write about horse racing?"

"In all honesty, I don't pay a great deal of attention to horse racing," Leonard replied.

Again the ticking clock seemed loud during a pause in their conversation.

"Does a sports reporter comment on horses favoured to win a race?" asked Gibbard whilst scratching his face.

"Of course he does. Milton would frequently write his predictions on whom he believed would win."

"And would this affect wagering, the pay-out, odds?"

"I expect it would," Leonard replied. "If Milton favoured a horse, then betting on that horse would most likely increase."

"That is what I believe, too," Inspector Gibbard added. "If the death of Milton Camden is related to the other deaths, as you suggest …"

Leonard nodded.

"Then your safety is of concern. These perpetrators have no compunction about removing any obstacles that stand in their way. They've proven that and they will kill again Mr Hardy, and I believe *you* represent a clear threat to them."

"They tried already," said Leonard, remembering the incident at Hutt Park Race Course. He had another thought. "Inspector Gibbard, was Miss Gringle's death really a suicide, or may she have been poisoned in the same way as Milton?"

The Inspector hadn't considered that prospect. He raised his eyes and stared at Leonard. "Ah, a valid question. And I wonder …" He turned his head and stared at the writing bureau, the sentence unfinished.

"You wonder?" asked Leonard.

"There is something else, and highly unusual. Dr Milliken-Brown found some minor skin abrasions on the wrists and ankles of Mr Camden."

"Rope? Was he restrained?"

"Perhaps, but not with rope, the coroner believes a fabric like silk was used that wouldn't damage the skin."

"Then as far as the police are concerned could this now become a murder investigation?" Leonard asked.

"Possibly, I will speak to the superintendent and make that recommendation tomorrow." Inspector Gibbard inhaled deeply. "Your safety is of concern, and you should look at spending a few days away from here, or at least until such time as it is safe to return."

Leonard shuddered at the thought of dying in a similar fashion to Milton. "Yes, not a silly suggestion."

Inspector Gibbard placed his empty glass on the table. "It is late and I must be getting home. One thing, though ..."

Leonard looked expectantly at the inspector as he rose from his seat.

"I was somewhat remiss. When we last spoke at the Mount Cook Depot, I failed to ask if you retrieved any possessions from the body at Hutt Park. Do you, er, have something for me? We found it most unusual that the body contained no identification or pocketbook."

Leonard's face reddened. "Er, I ah, it slipped my mind, and was going to bring it to you." He stepped to the bureau and retrieved Leon Barrow's pocketbook and handed it to Inspector Gibbard. "Everything is there."

Inspector Gibbard smiled. "You'd make a fine policeman, Mr Hardy. If you are considering a new vocation, please come and see me. He glanced through the pocketbook. "Leon Barrow ... What did you learn about him?"

It seemed the good inspector was more than a step ahead of him. He'd come here this evening and interrogated him successfully in his own home, retrieved the pocketbook he probably didn't know was missing and enjoyed a glass of his finest whiskey. "I think he is an American," Leonard replied, feeling miffed. "As I told you."

"Thank you for your cooperation, Mr Hardy."

"But, but, what about Neil Flanagan?" he asked.

"What about him?"

"Surely you'll arrest him?"

"For what?" Inspector Gibbard glanced around the sitting room. "Keep safe and consider an alternative place to stay for a while. If you learn of any new details, please keep me informed. Thank you for the, er, refreshment." He strode into the hallway.

Leonard stood transfixed and frustrated for a few heartbeats. "Of course, Inspector, have a pleasant evening." He rushed past him and quickly opened the door.

"Good evening, Mr Hardy," said the inspector as he departed.

Leonard closed the door and returned to the sitting room and his chair. *Inspector Gibbard is indeed a wily character.* He lifted his glass and drained it with a grimace.

If he'd learned anything from his talk with the inspector, Harold Bedingfield had disappeared in fear for his life. *But why*? What had he done or witnessed that would cause him to flee from his wife and those who sought him?

Mrs Bedingfield was not a pleasant woman, but was that reason enough for her husband to run and hide? Perhaps she was somehow involved with the recent spate of deaths. If that were so, he concluded, then concealing his whereabouts from her made logical sense. She must be involved, and therefore, could she and Neil Flanagan also be acquainted?

The next morning Leonard headed towards Mary and Bridgette's home in Newtown. He arrived early and walked anxiously up the path. The curtains were still drawn and when he knocked on the door, there was no response. He considered leaving a note, but the thought of Neil Flanagan finding it left him feeling somewhat reluctant. He tried knocking again, but still no answer.

He had turned to leave when the neighbour's window slid up, and a head poked out. "Who you looking for?" the woman asked.

Leonard turned to face her.

"Oh, it's you," she stated emphatically.

Leonard had greeted the woman in passing, once or twice, but didn't know her name. He wasn't sure if her last statement was a good omen. "Have you seen Mrs Worthington, or Mrs Leyton?"

The neighbour shook her head, "Not for a few days."

"Oh, it's important I contact Mrs Worthington." He had an idea. "If I left a missive with you, could you see she receives it?"

"Well, er, I suppose."

Leonard reached for his notebook and scratched a few lines, tore it from the book and folded it. In large text he wrote Mary Worthington, then took a step closer to the window and handed the note to the woman. "You are most kind. But it is important she receives it as soon as possible. Not to anyone but Mary."

The woman murmured something that sounded like she was too busy, then said, "I'll see she gets it."

Leonard felt relief. "Thank you."

The head withdrew and the window slammed down.

Feeling somewhat relieved for not encountering Neil Flanagan and for finding someone to deliver a note to Mary, there was little else he could do so he returned home.

Chapter Nineteen

Even though the sun shone, a cool, moderate breeze rippled through the large trees surrounding the Bolton Street cemetery. Branches swayed to an unheard rhythm and leaves rustled, casting strange moving shadows over headstones and sombre burial spots. About two dozen people stood huddled together as a reverend intoned a dull monologue extolling the virtues of a wholesome Christian life and the bleakness of death. Leonard buried his hands a little deeper into his pockets and fought off the chill as he wondered why death was seen as such a dark forlorn place to be feared. How did anyone know? As far as he was aware, no one had ever returned from where the deceased departed to and explained about the sights and experiences of what they'd witnessed or endured.

If they were surprised at seeing Leonard, they didn't show it. Mr Pembroke stood opposite him on the other side of the grave and returned a friendly greeting, as did most of the other employees of the *Evening Standard*. Mr Beaumont, however, did not acknowledge him and coldly turned away. Neil Flanagan stood near the publisher and scowled repeatedly. His mannerisms and furtive glances delivered like silent threats—a foreboding of things to come? Leonard felt fearful that the man, so easily provoked, would break from decorum and shout an obscenity or, worse, rush over and assail him. It seemed provident to maintain a safe distance and avoid antagonising him rather than risk an unnecessary outburst or an unpleasant encounter that could easily cause embarrassment or distress.

Apparently, Milton Camden did not want a traditional funeral Church service; instead, he'd requested in his last Will and Testament that Mr Pembroke speak for him at the cemetery. Leonard admitted that Mr Pembroke was a skilled orator and would honour Milton with deserved eloquence.

With some reluctance, the minister completed his lengthy parlance and paused briefly as if he'd forgotten something. Most everyone in attendance raised their heads and turned to the venerable reverend and held their collective breath, hoping his homily had indeed run its full course. To everyone's relief, he finally introduced Frederick Pembroke as an esteemed colleague and dear friend of Milton.

Mr Pembroke shuffled forward to stand beside the coffin. With hands clasped, he looked down and mouthed a few silent words before raising his head to regard the faces of those who'd come to pay Milton Camden their last respects. "I am reminded of the sharp-witted philosopher Ralph Emerson, who penned these introspective words," he began in a loud clear voice. "It is the secret of the world that all things subsist and do not die, but only retire a little from sight and afterwards return again…"

Leonard looked up to find Neil Flanagan staring at him—his baleful expression unsettling and malevolent. He felt uneasy. Inspector Gibbard's warning rang loudly.

"Nothing is dead; men feign themselves dead, and endure mock funerals and mournful obituaries, and there they stand looking out of the window, sound and well, in some new strange disguise ..."

Flanagan continued to stare. The hair on Leonard's neck stood upright, and he knew then, that Neil Flanagan would come for him. *Time to leave.* Silently he stepped back, pivoted, and walked down the path. Mr Pembroke's words faded at his back.

"Jesus is not dead; he is very well alive, nor John, nor Paul, nor Mahomet, nor Aristotle; at times we believe we have seen them all, and could easily tell the names under which they go..."

It was a long walk, and Leonard utilized that time wisely as he considered all his options carefully. He knew many people in Wellington, and they would gladly open their doors and welcome him into their homes for a day or two, or for however long he needed. But would he feel safe, and would Flanagan and his people find him? More importantly, would he be unfairly putting those who aided him at risk? His mind was made up. Resolutely, he quickened his step and detoured to Frederick Street.

He paused a moment, gathered himself, then entered Uncle Jun's shop. The familiar smells assaulted him immediately, and he breathed them in. The shop was in its usual state of disarray. Open sacks, crates, and glass jars with mysterious innards lined the walls and filled all the available space. And as he should, Uncle Jun stood behind his counter, facing his realm and dispensing potent herbs, tonics and remedies to the ailing and needy. Two customers waited to be served, so Leonard wandered around, marvelling at the multitude of products and their uses.

One customer departed, and Uncle Jun looked up giving him a toothless smile before enquiring to the next.

Early gold discoveries in the 1860s brought Chen Jun Qiang, 'Jun,' to New Zealand from China, and a short time later, his wife Ming and their young family arrived. Most Chinese gold miners came to New Zealand alone, their wives not permitted to join them, but Jun had no intention of returning back to his homeland.

Before restrictions through government legislation were devised to discourage Chinese immigration, he sent for his family. With moderate success in gold mining, Jun and family slowly travelled up the southern island to eventually settle in Wellington. With pockets bulging money from hard-earned gold, he bought property and fulfilled his lifelong dream of establishing a business in *Zhongyao Xue,* or Chinese herbal medicine, that he was formally trained in. His five grown children now lived locally in the Wellington region with their own young families.

Uncle Jun maintained strong links with the Chinese community, and Leonard knew those ties extended to the Chee Kung Tong Society. Some would call them a secretive gang, a *Tong*, but Uncle Jun had previously told him the Chee Kung Tong Society were like Free Masons, organised, with many members who help each other and benefit the local community.

"Leo! Is good to see you again!" exhorted Uncle Jun as the last customer departed.

Leonard walked towards the counter and smiled.

Uncle Jun saw the damage to his face and his smile disappeared. While Jun appeared diminutive and frail, he was far from weak or of ill health. His cheeks were hollow, his teeth were gone, and wisps of grey hair poked out from beneath the traditional *jin* cap he wore. Yet his clear eyes radiated energy and spirit, and his skin glowed in youthful vitality. He stared back at Leonard intently and knowingly with the wisdom of experience and the patience of age.

"You are busy this afternoon," said Leonard.

"Always busy," he grinned. His eyes scanned Leonard carefully.

Scrutinizing and assessing the black eye, his skin pallor and eyes. He didn't comment on what he observed and waited for Leonard to explain. "Come, we have tea."

Leonard followed the old man towards the rear of the shop where a curtain separated the shop from his private quarters. A table and chairs sat amongst stored merchandise, and a lit stove fumed. He didn't see Uncle Jun's wife. "Has Ming returned?" he asked

"She still no here. Gone to help daughter; new baby," he grinned.

"Congratulations. How many grandchildren do you have now?"

Uncle Jun thought a moment. "Eighteen," he grinned again.

Just as quickly, his face changed, and his expression showed concern. "Leo, you in trouble. What have you done?" He placed a kettle on the stove to boil water. "Sit."

Leonard sat as ordered, and began to tell Uncle Jun a shortened account of all that happened, including the death of Agatha Perkins and her association with the Victoria Hotel. When the water boiled, Uncle Jun filled the teapot, then a short time later, after the tea had drawn, poured his special blend of green tea into each of the cups, as Leonard finished speaking.

Uncle Jun was silent as he digested what he'd been told. Finally, he looked up. "You silly boy, why you no come and tell me?"

"I didn't want to intrude or inconvenience you, that's all."

"That place, Victoria Hotel, no good. I see you go there. Then I hear of death of girl. I know you involve in this somehow."

"But now some bad men want to hurt me. Do you remember Inspector Gibbard?"

Uncle Jun nodded. "His face," he tut-tutted, "I have something to help face."

Leonard laughed. "Yes, his complexion certainly needs attention." His expression changed to a more sombre look. "The inspector says men will come, possibly to kill me and that I shouldn't be at home. He thinks it best I move somewhere else for a little while, at least until it is proven safe for me to return."

Uncle Jun nodded. He sat cross-legged on a chair and rubbed his chin thoughtfully. "You want to stay here where safe?" he raised a single eyebrow in question.

"Perhaps for a week or two, if it's not an inconvenience."

Uncle Jun refilled both tea cups and remained silent.

Leonard sat back and enjoyed the mild Chinese green tea. He knew better than to hurry Uncle Jun into talking or making a decision.

"You say men involve with horse and from America?" Uncle Jun asked.

"Yes, possibly. I think two of them are Americans, but do not know how many more. And everything connects to horses and possibly horse racing."

"And gamble?"

He knew the Chinese were fond of gambling and wouldn't like it if someone was manipulating the outcome of racing, but he wasn't completely sure if gambling was what the Americans were trying to control. "Possibly," Leonard answered truthfully.

"Ahh. I see." Uncle Jun fiddled in his pocket and extracted a pencil and scrap of paper which he placed on the table. With a bony finger he tapped the paper. "You write name. Name of bad men." He tapped again.

Leonard slid the paper closer and wrote down the names of the people he believed were implicit, beginning with Mrs Bedingfield, then Neil Flanigan and finally Leon Barrow. "That's all I know." He slid the paper back, curious to the reason why he wanted the names.

Uncle Jun shook his head. "Why you find trouble Leo? You foolish."

Leonard shrugged. "I ask myself that question all too frequently, Uncle Jun."

"And now you in danger." Uncle Jun uncrossed his legs, and leaned forward over the table. "Leo, you not stay here—no good." He shook his head again to emphasize his point.

"Oh?" Leonard felt his heart sink.

"Not good to hide here or anywhere, in any house. Bad men will always look and they will find you. Best you stay home, then they come to you."

"And kill me?"

"Silly boy," admonished the aging man. "We help and watch, eh?"

"You mean I'm the bait?"

Uncle Jun laughed, it sounded like a cackle. "You good for something, Leo. You no worry."

It was early evening when Leonard walked from Frederick Street towards home. He thought about Uncle Jun's logic and proposal and it did seem sensible. If he stayed anywhere, it wasn't possible to remain locked up indoors all day long, he couldn't hide every waking moment and expose others to danger and possible harm.

What Uncle Jun proposed required considerable resources; no doubt he felt he had access to them, and certainly enough to keep watch over him. It was a generous offer and showed the warmth and spirit of the man. He felt fortunate to have such friends that cared.

Leonard returned home and lit the fire. It now blazed, providing much needed warmth and with it the assurance of comfort and security. He settled into his chair and watched in reflection as slender flames danced this way and that. Hot and delicate leaping tendrils, like sinuous fingers extending repeatedly outwards, fuelled by the wood that provided them life.

Melancholic thoughts filled his head, along with repeated haunting visions of Neil Flanagan's face. His countenance, so hate-filled and malevolent. Why Neil resented him so much, he couldn't fathom. What had he done to provoke such rancour from the man? Initially when he'd first come to the *Evening Standard*, Flanagan had sought his companionship under the guise of friendship that so quickly turned toxic.

The fire spat and crackled contentedly. Leonard stretched out placing his hands behind his head, and gave thought to Mr and Mrs Bedingfield and how his life and theirs had now become entwined. Then his living room door crashed open.

Chapter Twenty

Leonard shot to his feet as two men barged into his sitting room. Neil Flanagan entered first, followed closely by a smaller man, who he recognised from the Hutt Park Race Course —the associate of the deceased, Leon Barrow.

In abject fear, he took an involuntary step back, tripped against his chair and fell to the floor. He heard Flanagan laugh before he stepped up and kicked him hard in the stomach. He felt sick as he curled protectively into a ball gasping for air.

"Whoa, easy," said the smaller man with a distinctive American drawl. "We can't leave impressions."

"That was for Leon," Flanagan snarled, and prepared to launch another boot at Leonard's midriff.

"The son of a bitch will suffer enough," said the American as he scanned the room. "There! We'll use that chair."

Flanagan kicked again, this time striking Leonard's knee that now protected his stomach.

It hurt, but thankfully not as much as the first kick.

Temporarily satisfied, Flanagan stomped around him, picked up the chair and repositioned it to his liking.

Leonard risked opening his eyes and saw the American extract some lengths of ribbon from his pocket and then a small, clear glass bottle of liquid. It was difficult to see but the liquid had a slight pinkish hue. In terror, he realised they were going to poison him, and in a moment of absurd clarity, he guessed they had killed Milton in a similar way. He panicked, and in desperation tried to scramble on hands and knees towards the open living room door but Neil grabbed a handful of his hair and cruelly yanked his head back. Leonard yelled as tears of pain filled his eyes.

Neil Flanagan was a large muscular man, broad across the shoulders with a a thick neck, yet it required considerable effort to hoist Leonard up and onto the chair. He struggled, kicked, and flailed his arms but it did little good against Neil's superior strength. Before he knew it, he was forcibly placed onto the seat. The American walked over as Flanagan held him immobile, and using the ribbons, attempted to carefully tie Leonard's wrists, and bind them securely to the chair's armrests.

"The bastard hit me," said Flanagan, breathing hard from the exertion.

The American laughed. "Ya probably deserved it."

Leonard continued trying to fight Flanagan and the American off. It accomplished little, and only evoked more anger from Flanagan, while the American was beginning to lose patience.

"Hold him still!" cried the American as he again attempted to wrap the ribbon around Leonard's wrist and the armrest.

It was inevitable, Leonard couldn't fight both men, and eventually one arm was secured, then the other. Flanagan was now binding Leonard's ankles to the chair's legs.

"Who gave you the shiner?" the American asked Leonard, as he stepped away from the chair to retrieve the bottle.

"It was me, from a well-delivered jab, if I dare say so myself," said Neil, rising to his feet.

Leonard was finally secured and couldn't move. "Why are you doing this, what have I done to offend you, or … or him?" he yelled in protest.

"You take everything personally Leo," Neil laughed, then thrust a handkerchief into his mouth.

"You see, Leo, you've been such a busy-body. If you'd left well-enough alone, all would be as it should. But you couldn't, eh. You had to persist and dig for more information. Even when you lost everything — your employment, your woman, friends and your re-spectability — you wouldn't stop. And now you find yourself in a bind," Neil laughed at his humour. "And, you leave us with no alternative."

Leonard fought the bindings and tried to spit out the handker-chief to no avail. *Where was Uncle Jun's help?*

The American stood beside the chair and shook the bottle near Leonard's face so he could see it. "What we're going to do is give you a little tonic. You'll open your mouth and drink, just like your friend, Milton Camden. In case you're wondering, he was a very obliging gentleman." He smirked. "If you want to make it more dif-ficult for yourself, we'll just force your mouth open, tilt your head back and pour. Makes no difference to me."

This was it, the moment he feared. Leonard knew he would die from a series of drug induced spasms. The coroner had explained to him in enough detail to know how his body would react. His graphic elaboration only made it worse. He imagined his body convulsing violently as it reacted to the powerful drugs they'd force him to in-gest. He'd never felt so frightened in his entire life. In panic, he tried to pull against the bindings and topple the chair.

Flanagan bent down and held the chair steady. "However, please enlighten me, Leo, who have you been sharing your fanciful theo-ries with? Who have you told?' Flanagan asked, and prodded him in the chest with a finger.

Leonard's eyes were wide open in terror. He shook his head and tried to speak but couldn't.

"If I remove the rag, you'll be agreeable, won't you Leo?"

Leonard nodded. He needed time to think of a way out. Anything to delay what these men would do to him.

Neil removed the handkerchief.

"I haven't told anyone," he spluttered. "No one would believe me."

Neil drove a fist into Leonard's stomach."

Leonard yelled as loudly as he could, hoping a neighbour, or anyone would hear. He wanted to vomit.

"Do that again and you'll get another," said Neil as he drew his arm back.

"Careful," warned the American. "Don't leave marks on the body."

"Leo just requires a little incentive to be truthful. Isn't that so?"

Leonard was trying to regain his breath and was gasping for air. He couldn't speak.

"With whom have you been discussing your presumptions about Harold Bedingfield's disappearance?" Neil asked, his voice containing an edge.

"Do ya know where he is?" asked the American. "You do know something, tell me!"

"I don't—believe me—I don't know where he is," Leonard said wide-eyed, between breaths.

"And our dear friend Constable Tim Yates. You mean you haven't spoken with him about all this?" Neil asked.

Leonard shook his head. "No!"

"Let's get this over with," said the small American impatiently.,

"He ain't telling and doesn't know where Bedingfield is."

"I don't believe you, Leo." Neil turned to the American. "We need to find a way to silence the constable, I know Leo has spoken with him."

"Then it has to be through an accident, we can't use this concoction again, we don't have enough and someone may begin connecting these deaths. Now let's get this over with," said the smaller man, turning back to face Leonard.

Leonard caught a movement from his peripheral vision at the same time he heard a floorboard creak. Neil Flanagan and the American heard it too and both turned simultaneously to see what created the unexpected noise. What they saw caused them both to pause briefly. Their inaction was long enough for Russell to take two quick steps into the room.

Before the American could react, Russell grabbed him by the coat and heaved him backwards, overturning a coffee table, to crash against the wall by the door. He lay winded and gasping.

Neil straightened, turned to the threat and immediately assumed the stance of a boxer with raised, clenched fists protecting his face. He advanced cautiously, with one foot leading the other, towards the imposing brutish figure of Russell.

Russell was undisputedly the larger and stronger man, and with his own fists raised, he swung powerfully at Flanagan. He missed and received a bloody nose for his effort. He never saw the left-handed punch that hit him. Russell shook his head and grinned, then successfully fended a right uppercut.

Neil's head weaved and bobbed. He ducked under another haymaker from Russell and landed a flurry of hard blows to Russell's unprotected stomach.

Leonard could only watch in fear. "He boxes!" was all he could manage to yell, hoping Russell would heed his warning. His living room was small, and there was little space for two men to brawl. Neil brushed against him time and time again as he dodged and swayed, while Russell kept missing, his fists gliding past Neil's constantly moving upper body.

Leonard could only watch helplessly as Russell lumbered after his lithe opponent, either a step behind or just too slow, while Neil side-stepped and probed with accurate jabs. Russell couldn't match Neil's speed, however, if Flanagan stepped into one of his powerful punches, the fight would end immediately, and Neil was only too aware of it.

Again, Neil landed another combination to Russell's gut and then dodged a roundhouse swing in return. Russell staggered, and looked like he would fall, but then catching Neil off-guard with a nimble sidestep, he quickly regained his footing and drove a fist squarely into Neil's midriff. It was a powerful punch, delivered with his full weight behind it, and it connected solidly. Neil grunted loudly and doubled over only to collide with a well-timed uppercut to the jaw. He tumbled backwards and hit the back of his head on the bookshelf before sliding to the floor in a heap.

Russell bent over, resting his hands on his thighs, breathing hard.

"The other one!" Leonard yelled in warning and twisted his head to see where the American was. But he'd gone. Other than Russell, and Neil lying unconscious on the floor, there was no sign of the American. It was the second time the small man had escaped.

Russell slowly straightened, wiped the back of his hand across his bloodied nose and scanned the room. He hadn't said a word.

"He's vanished." Leonard could feel his body trembling. He was so frightened having come so close to death!

Neil groaned.

"Tie him, quick, before he wakes," Leonard advised.

Russell rubbed his knuckles and began fumbling with the ribbons securing Leonard. Eventually they loosened and Leonard began untying his legs that were still strapped to the chair while Russell secured Neil.

"Thank you so much ... I, uh, I believed they would succeed and were only moments away from poisoning me." Leonard looked at Russell who held a handkerchief to his nose. "You came at the right time. I am so grateful."

Russell grunted. "I saw you at Frederick Street today. Uh, I wanted to have a word about what I saw. But then you'd scarpered." He shrugged his massive shoulders." So I thought I'd come visit and heard a yell," he said quietly and then wiped more blood from his nose. "The door was open and I heard something."

It was difficult to understand him through his hoarseness.

Russell nodded. "Good thing I came, eh?" he smiled and looked at his handkerchief. His nose had stopped bleeding.

"I owe you my life and am in your debt, but," Leonard turned to face Neil, "I do believe I need to contact the police."

They both stared at Flanagan for a moment.

"I'll go, you should stay here," Russell volunteered. He took a step towards Neil and looked down at him. "If you touch Mr Hardy again, I'll kill you. Do you understand?"

Neil slowly raised his head and looked at Russell and sneered. "Bugger off, we'll meet again, and you'll be mine." He laughed as blood dripped from his face. He slowly moved his head towards Leonard. "The police can't detain me, and you've not seen the last of me, either. You've got no idea of the predicament you're in."

Leonard thought Russell was going to attack Flanagan, instead, he checked the ribbons that bound him. Satisfied, he turned away and walked towards the door.

"Have the police send for Inspector Gibbard, Inspector Gibbard!" Leonard repeated.

Russell raised a hand in acknowledgement.

"Wait!" Leonard yelled after him. "You said you saw something. What did you see?"

Russell turned, looked over Leonard's shoulder at Neil lying on the floor. "Outside, might be best, Mr Hardy."

They stepped onto Leonard's front porch where they could talk without being overheard.

"The night Miss Gringle was … uh … when she died." Russell paused and placed both hands on his hips, and took a deep breath.

Leonard could see that the large man was fighting his emotions, and he guessed that Russell had a strong affection for Agatha. "Continue, please," he gently coaxed.

"I'd seen a bloke, and he'd been loitering around the Victoria Hotel for a day or two. I easily recognized him and thought he was up to no good. On the day, I, uh … found her … I'd seen a man leave the hotel after she returned from her day with you at the racecourse— he was a soldier. I didn't think anything of it at the time. But then I sees him again, following you this afternoon, but this time he ain't in uniform."

"Do you have any notion to his identity? Would you recognise him again?

Russell nodded. "It was him."

"Who?"

"The other chappie who ran away when I came here."

"The American?"

Russell shrugged. "I didn't hear 'im speak. But t'was him, I'd seen his mug a few times now, so I knows."

"He must have changed his clothes." Leonard looked thoughtful. "You miss her, don't you?"

Russell looked down at the wooden decking of Leonard's porch. "I, uh, should fetch the police." He turned and was gone.

Leonard went back inside to wait.

Chapter Twenty-One

$\mathcal{A}$ horse snickered outside, and Leonard rose from his chair, sparing a quick look at Neil who still sat morosely against the bookshelf, and went to see if the police had arrived. He opened the door as a constable clomped onto his porch. He looked for Russell, but saw only the dark outline of the policeman's horse securely tied to the gate post. To ward off the evening chill, the constable wore a black greatcoat, riding breeches and knee-high riding boots. He politely removed his shako cap when he saw Leonard at the door.

"Evening, sir. I understand there's been a disturbance?"

"Thank goodness you came," Leonard replied, grateful that Russell had kept his word and fetched the police. "Didn't take you long." He looked again for any sign of Russell, but couldn't see him.

The constable remained quiet.

"Where is Russell?" Leonard asked.

"Russell?"

"The man who reported the incident to you."

"Oh, uh, I believe the gentleman went on his way, I believe he had other matters to attend too, sir."

Peculiar. "Yes, there's been an attempt on my life, but we need to notify Inspector Gibbard, he needs to be here."

"Inspector Gibbard has been alerted, sir, and should arrive shortly. Er, I believe you have a man inside?"

"He and an accomplice tried to poison me."

The constable looked concerned. "And the other gentleman, sir?"

"He's gone, ran away."

He inclined his head and raised an eyebrow.

"Uh, you'd better come in," Leonard invited.

The constable glanced over his shoulder, back towards the street, before stepping inside.

"An accomplice, eh?" stated the constable as he stood looking at the pitiful sight of Neil Flanagan.

Leonard observed Neil looking at the constable with equal intensity. If he was concerned about being arrested, he didn't show it. "The other man ran off, when he saw him being beaten. But I don't know his name and he," Leonard pointed to Neil, "isn't talking."

The constable bent down, untied the ribbon around his ankles, leaving his wrists bound, then grabbed Flanagan by the elbow and helped him to his feet. "Don't make this difficult for me," cautioned the constable as Neil made a weak attempt to pull away. He began to lead him to the door.

"What are you doing? You need to ask details, uh, for your report. Shouldn't we wait for the Inspector!"

"In this instance, we need to remove him and take him to the Mount Cook Depot for immediate questioning. Orders from the Inspector." He pushed Neil in the back and encouraged him to walk to the door.

Leonard was puzzled and followed the constable outside onto the porch. "If the Inspector is coming, surely he needs to talk to him here, and, and, a wagon has yet to arrive. How can you take him to the depot?"

"Best if you return to the safety of indoors, sir," the constable instructed.

"Your name, Constable, may I have your name?" Leonard tried to look at the constable's identification number attached to the collar of his coat, the darkness made it difficult to see.

The policeman turned quickly, and suddenly thrust out both hands and shoved Leonard hard in the chest. Caught completely unaware, he lost his balance and with a cry, fell across the threshold of the door. With horror, he saw the constable extract his truncheon. It appeared to be about three feet in length, and with a snarl, the policeman drew his arm back to strike.

Leonard wasn't having any of it. He'd been nearly killed earlier and he wasn't going to allow this man any opportunity. In reflex, he drew his knees to his chest, reached for the door, rolled inside, and slammed it closed before the constable could bludgeon him. He heard a muffled voice urging Flanagan to flee.

With knees drawn to his chin, Leonard sat on the floor of his hallway in terror. His body shook as he waited for his front door to crash open and the violent ordeal of a beating to begin anew. The sight of the unusually long baton used by mounted constables was horrifying and he had no doubt the weapon could inflict serious damage and snap bones with ease. He had no strength to stand, and even if he could, there wasn't anywhere he could run. He was hopelessly trapped.

But his door remained closed and thankfully no one attempted to forcibly enter. Eventually he eased himself to his feet, stood unsteadily, and returned to the living room where he pondered his next move. He righted the overturned coffee table and immediately saw the bottle of poison the American had threatened him with. *He must have dropped it when Russell threw him,* he thought. Holding the unlabelled bottle near the light of a candle, he stared at its contents and shuddered.

He was told to wait. Again he found himself in the public waiting room of the Mount Cook Depot. His valise sat between his feet as he stared at the institutionally dull interior. The same yellowed posters graced the walls, some brochures sat on a counter and troubled people came and went, reporting misdeeds, some minor, inconsequential and others astounding. Inspector Gibbard would attend to him as soon as conveniently possible, he was told. There was nothing to do but sit and patiently bide his time.

After finding the bottle of poison the previous evening he knew they, whomever the group was that Flanagan was associated with, would return for it. As quickly as he could, he packed a valise and cautiously walked down his street and spent the remainder of the evening in a hotel. Where were the Chinese that Uncle Jun promised would protect him? They weren't anywhere to be seen. He didn't sleep, and at every noise tensed, believing the door would be kicked in and the grinning face of Neil Flanagan would reappear. Morning couldn't come quick enough and after eating breakfast, he caught a Hansom cab to Mount Cook Depot.

A door opened and a fresh-faced and youthful constable appeared. "Mr Hardy?"

Leonard stood.

"If you'd come this way, sir."

Leonard hoisted his bag and followed the young man to a sparsely furnished interview room.

The room was small—only large enough for a table and two chairs. The interior brickwork had been painted cream, and was now stained, chipped and scarred, while two barred windows provided light.

"Wait here, sir," suggested the young constable. "The inspector will see you soon." Thankfully he left the door ajar.

Leonard was alone again and brooding over his tenuous future. After his experience with the constable last night he didn't feel safe, not even here. Thankfully, the wait wasn't long and the Inspector entered, and to his immense relief, so did Tim Yates.

"Good morning, Mr Hardy," greeted the inspector. He carried some documents and placed them on the small table before taking a seat.

"Morning, Leo," said Tim with a smile. The inspector indicated Tim should also take a seat.

"Now, what is so important that brings you up and about this early?" He looked down at Leonard's valise. "Do you intend on sleeping here?"

Leonard took a deep breath, and looked at his hands. They still trembled and he moved them out of sight beneath the table.

Inspector Gibbard and Tim shared a look. "What happened?" asked the Inspector seeing the state of Leonard. "Do you need assistance?"

"I don't know where to begin … they tried to kill me last night," Leonard gushed, then looked at Tim, "and you are in danger, they want to kill you, too!"

Inspector Gibbard raised a hand, "Mr Hardy, please take a moment, collect yourself, and why don't you start by telling us what happened."

The Inspector scribbled notes and asked questions to clarify a few points, allowing Leonard to talk freely. Finally, Leonard finished recounting the incident and the room was quiet as the Inspector finished detailing the events. He looked up at Leonard. "That's quite a story. I have more questions, so let me begin with them one at a time."

Leonard nodded.

"Let's discuss the small man with the American accent. Can you confirm he was at the Hutt Park Race course?"

Leonard nodded. "With absolute certainty and he is American."

"Now this man, Russell, do you have his family name, and other details?"

"No, sir. That's all I know, other than where he works."

"I'm familiar with him, sir," said Tim. "There's been some complaints made against him for assault, but nothing more. I will get his details."

The Inspector nodded. "See to it." He turned back to Leonard. "This bottle that you claim contains poison, any idea what it is? Did they suggest to you what it contains?"

"They only referred to it as a tonic. Oh, yes, I almost forgot, in his haste to leave, the American left it behind." Leonard bent down to his valise and retrieved the bottle and placed it on the table.

The Inspector's face tightened. "This evidence changes things considerably. I will need this," he informed Leonard as he held the bottle to the light. The slightly pink hue of the liquid looked innocuous. "I think we need to confirm if the contents of this bottle match what was in Mr Camden's stomach."

"And in Agatha Gringle's," Leonard added. "I don't believe she committed suicide, she was murdered, just like Milton Camden.

"Let's wait and see what the coroner says before we make assumptions, eh." The inspector referred back to his notes. "I admit to being perplexed about this constable that came to your home last evening. Can you describe his general appearance?" asked the inspector.

"He was at least six feet tall, lean, black hair, with a moustache. His uniform was normal in all respects, sir."

"You've described half the constables on the force, Mr Hardy. By any chance did you see and recall his badge number?"

Leonard scratched his head. "It was dark and difficult to see … the first number was definitely a nine, the last number is either a one or seven, inspector."

"Bring me the register and also the file on that Russell chap," the inspector asked Tim. "Don't tell anyone why you want them."

"Yes, sir." Tim slid his chair back and departed the room.

"How credible is the threat to Constable Yates?" Inspector Gibbard asked, once they were alone.

"I never took the threats against me seriously, but in light of what transpired at the race course, and then last evening, I believe Tim is in imminent danger, as am I."

Inspector Gibbard nodded and looked thoughtful. "The reason I was delayed in seeing you this morning was because I went to visit your ex-employer, Mr Pembroke …"

"Oh? About Flanagan?"

"Yes, after we spoke, I thought it wouldn't hurt to get the measure of the man and have a chat with him."

Leonard listened intently.

"Seems he never appeared for work this morning and left no

word for his unexcused absence. I have sent a constable to his place of residence and am awaiting word on that."

Leonard glanced down at the table and thought of Mary and Bridgette. *Could Neil be at their home?*

"You wish to say something, Mr Hardy?"

Leonard looked up. "Perhaps, Inspector, if he is not at his residence, he may be at the home of Bridgette Leyton, in Newtown. My fiancé lives with her, and she seems to have disappeared as well. Flanagan was spending considerable time over there after he discredited me to her."

"Yes, Constable Yates informed me of that. In light of these new developments, I am quite eager to talk to this Mr Flanagan."

Tim returned carrying more documents. "Inspector, Constable Raines returned, and he said the woman who runs the boarding house where Neil Flanagan was living informed him that he absconded, his possessions have gone, and he didn't pay the outstanding rent."

"All right then." Gibbard threw the documents onto the table. "Constable Yates, take Constable Raines and visit the home of ..." he consulted his notes. "Uh, Mrs Bridgette Leyton, I believe you are acquainted and are familiar with her address?"

Tim spared a quick look at Leonard before focusing on his superior. "Yes, sir."

"With utmost caution, determine if our elusive Mr Flanagan is hiding there. If, by chance, you locate him, bring him here for questioning." Inspector Gibbard began to read the information handed to him.

"And find out where Mary is, Tim," Leonard volunteered, then shrugged as both the Inspector and Tim looked at him. "We need to locate her, too," he added.

"Dear God, what have you stumbled into, Mr Hardy?" said Inspector Gibbard with a head shake.

"Uh, I shall be off then, sir," said Tim. He gave a quick head nod to his friend before leaving.

"Mr Hardy, I'm going to have to discuss this with my superiors. I don't have the resources available to begin a prolonged investigation into this case. We are looking at potentially four linked deaths, one attempted murder, two missing persons, including your fiancé and Mr Bedingfield." He sighed loudly. "And then … what unlawful activities are Neil Flanagan and his American associates actually involved in, what are they up to?" He shook his head and picked up the bottle of poison, looked at it closely and placed it back on the cluttered table. "Now, to add to this …" the Inspector grabbed a document, one that Tim had just given him and held it up, "we have an imposter posing as a constable."

Leonard's mouth dropped open.

"Yes, if your memory is accurate, and as I believed, there are no policemen with an identification number that high. Additionally, no mounted constables were assigned to be patrolling near your residence, or in the vicinity, last evening."

Leonard swallowed. "What do we do now?"

"*We* do nothing. Mr Hardy. *You* need to find somewhere safe to hide and allow me to do my job without encumbrance or hindrance. Is that understood?"

Leonard mutely nodded.

"I didn't hear you, Mr Hardy."

"Yes, Inspector."

"Good. Make sure you leave details with Constable Yates as to where you will be residing until this thing blows over. I will have more questions for you, so please make yourself available for when I have need." Inspector Gibbard rose and scooped up his documents, and placed the bottle of tonic into his pocket. He looked over at Leonard who was standing with his valise. "Be careful, and most importantly, be heedful in whom you place your trust."

"Thank you, Inspector."

"Do you know where you will go?"

He gave the matter some thought. He hadn't yet spoken to Uncle Jun, but… "I will go to Uncle Jun, I believe you met him."

Inspector Gibbard smiled, the first one of the day. "Then you couldn't have chosen a safer place to be. Good day, Mr Hardy." He turned and exited the room.

Chapter Twenty-Two

Leonard didn't know how Uncle Jun managed to sleep at night. The incessant din from Frederick Street only worsened during the evening. Fuelled by alcohol, drunken revellers yelled, fought and laughed at all times of the night without consideration for those who preferred sleep or just sought peace and quiet. Sometimes he woke with a start at the sound of a bottle smashing or from a boisterous cry.

The days were worse, and the humdrum tediousness of doing nothing began to play on his mind. He could only read for so many hours each day. He'd asked Uncle Jun to give him something to do, but a lack of knowledge of herbs, potions and tonics made it near impossible. He swept the shop floor twice a day and then again, even when it didn't require sweeping. He stacked boxes, moved sacks and even dusted shelves. Boredom had set in and his worries about Mary only deepened. He was anxious, nervous and fearful, and each successive day made him feel worse. His only highlight was when Tim came to visit at the end of each day with news, or lack of news. Neil Flanagan was not at Bridgette's home, and neither was Mary, he informed Leonard. They had simply vanished.

Occasionally, he'd cautiously step from the safety of the shop and approach the Victoria Hotel hoping to see Russell, but there was no sign of him either. He, too seemed to have disappeared.

After four days he'd had enough of boredom and had just decided to return home to retrieve some items and his mail, when Uncle Jun parted the curtain and entered the private area at the rear of the shop where he sat. Uncle Jun was followed by another man whom he'd never seen or met before.

"Leo, this is Bohai, he old friend. Good man, but have problem with bottom," Uncle Jun patted his posterior and grinned. "He no speak English, but he have information."

Out of respect for the older gentleman, Leonard stood. Then with a straight back, bowed at the waist.

"He say, he happy to meet you," said Uncle Jun, translating for Bohai.

"Bohai has market on Tory Street," began Uncle Jun. "He some-time deliver vegetable to people."

Leonard nodded, curious where this conversation was going. He knew Uncle Jun all too well, and allowed him to continue.

"Bohai have new customer," added Uncle Jun. "Customer want food deliver to Cuba Street." He turned to Bohai, who in turn nod-ded even though he didn't understand a word of what Jun was say-ing. "Bohai deliver food and man pay with American dollar. Many American man in room."

"There are many Americans in Wellington," replied Leonard.

Uncle Jun nodded. "But American man cooking in office, not house. They no want people to see what they do."

Leonard looked sceptical.

"I have other friend, he keep watch on building, he listen care-fully. He say one man who live there is call Neil."

Leonard leaned forward. "He heard this? That someone living there is called Neil?"

Both Uncle Jun and Bohai nodded their heads vigorously.

"How do your friends obtain this information, and how did they know about Neil Flanagan? Many people are called Neil, doesn't mean it's him, even if he didn't misunderstand what he overheard."

"You gave me paper with name, remember, Leo? I talk to Chinese people, I say listen and watch."

Leonard grinned.

Both Jun and Bohai were smiling, and obviously waiting for Leonard to comment. "Is there a way I can observe this office without being seen?" he asked.

Uncle Jun and Bohai spoke together loudly in Chinese before Uncle Jun turned back to him. "He say, you can watch office from across road. No one will see you. But kitchen is in back of building."

"What type of place is it where I will watch?"

"Is laundry house. Bohai's cousin."

Leonard thought about it. He was dubious but certainly being proactive was better than sitting and doing nothing. "Can I go tonight, when it is dark?"

Again, Bohai and Jun conversed loudly.

"He say, someone will come here to take you when dark. Is this good, Leo?"

Leonard knew Cuba Street wasn't far from Frederick Street, and he considered that if he could watch this house for a couple of hours, then it would be better than doing nothing at Uncle Jun's. He'd take the risk. "Yes, I can watch." He turned to Bohai and bowed. "Thank you."

It had just become dark when a young and very beautiful Chinese woman entered Uncle Jun's shop. Immediately, Jun brought her to Leonard in the back. "Leo, this is Li Yan Yong, she take care of you. She ask you call her Yan. Be good to her, eh?"

Leonard was struck by her flawless skin and beauty and he estimated her to be about twenty to twenty-two years old. "A pleasure to meet you, Yan. Uncle Jun says you will take care of me," he smiled.

"A pleasure to meet you, Mr Hardy, Chen Jun has already told me much about you, and yes, I will help you all I can," she spoke almost flawless English. "Are you ready, we should go?"

Uncle Jun nodded and Leonard followed Yan outside onto Frederick Street. There were many people out, and immediately Yan followed behind a fairly large group of about a dozen adolescent Oriental youths.

Leonard stepped up beside her. "Are they your friends?" he asked, pointing to the group ahead.

"Yes, do not worry, no one will come near us," she looked up at him and reassured him with a smile. They crossed over Taranaki Street, continued up to Vivian Street, then ducked into a small alley that ran parallel to Cuba Street. No one said anything or looked at him suspiciously.

Suddenly Yan grabbed his arm and pulled him into a doorway. Ahead, the youths continued nonchalantly on. "We are here," she said quietly. "Come."

She pried open the door and stepped into the chaos of a huge laundry house. It was hot and noisy and filled with people, all Orientals. Some tended fires, and others stirred huge vats with wooden oars. People were ironing and folding clothes while a few sat at tables working with needle and thread to mend rents and tears. Yan turned a corner and began climbing a staircase up to the first floor. On entering, Leonard realised this was just like Uncle Jun's shop. Upstairs was where the sleeping quarters were, where entire extended families lived. Yan led him into a large unlit room with windows facing Cuba Street. She pulled over a rug and pillows and lowered herself down, onto her knees. "Come, sit," she said, inviting him to a pillow.

Yan pointed to a building almost opposite them. "That building is where the men you seek are," she said.

Leonard looked carefully and could see the offices were lit, but frosted glass made it impossible to see into. "What is written on the door? I can see writing but …"

"Accountant, General Commission Agent for the New York Contributionship Company," she recited.

"An American company, so yes, that may explain why Americans are working from that office, but does not preclude any wrongdoing," he said.

"We wait, get comfortable, Mr Hardy."

He eased himself down onto the pillow. "Please, call me, Leo or Leonard."

She smiled, and sat on her knees with her hands resting on her thighs. Her long, silken jet-black hair cascaded over her shoulders and he was suddenly reminded of Mae. He felt his heart flutter and then felt guilty as his thoughts turned to Mary. He looked down at his hands and tried to compose himself. After a moment, he gazed out the window and waited. Waiting is all he seemed to be doing these days, but this was better than doing nothing at Uncle Jun's shop.

An hour drifted into two, and he shifted position again and again, trying to get comfortable. They talked about a few things, polite small talk, then Yan asked him about Mae. His composure crumbled and he struggled to answer. She didn't apologise but turned to look at him with genuine interest. He understood, she wasn't being meddlesome, she was just simply curious.

And he did speak of Mae. He spoke lovingly of her, telling Yan of the years they spent together, how happy they were, the garden she tended with devotion and then he told her of her unfortunate passing; how she'd been pushed under a quickly moving Hansom cab. He surprised himself. This was the second time within a short period he had confided to a beautiful woman about his life. He talked about Mae openly without fear of judgement or criticism, and it felt good to share. It passed the time.

Yan asked him about how they'd met, but suddenly the sound of breaking glass stopped him in mid-sentence. "What was that?" he exclaimed.

They could only see the far side of the street, not the near side. Both Yan and Leonard swivelled their heads trying to identify where the sound originated. The window was open, but pinpointing the location was impossible. Leonard scooted closer to the window and listened.

"Someone is yelling — an argument," he stated.

Yan slid closer and listened. "It's from across the street," she said after cocking her head.

All thoughts of Mae disappeared as he focused on the offices of Accountant, General Commission Agent for the New York Contri-butionship Company.

Suddenly the door to the offices was thrust open and a man emerged. It was too dark to recognise faces, but Leonard immedi-ately recognised the physique of Neil Flanagan. He was obviously angry, slamming the door as he stormed from the building.

"That's him, it's Flanagan," he said quietly and leaned away from the window lest Neil look up and see his face.

"Don't move," said Yan. "Remain still or your movement may

draw his attention."

Leonard watched as Flanagan paced back and forth outside the offices, his agitation obvious. It seemed he was letting off steam.

Leonard's heart was thumping in his chest, it seemed loud and he wondered if Flanagan could hear it.

"Relax and breathe, Leo. He cannot harm you here, you are safe," she reassured him.

Leonard turned to face her. She was a remarkable young woman. For her years, she was wise and sensible. Not only that, but with dawning realisation he knew she understood him perfectly. A unique gift.

They watched as Flanagan slowed his pacing, then stopped and finally reached into his pocket and extracted a pipe. He went through the routine of packing the bowl with tobacco then lit a match. The flickering flame briefly illuminated his face confirming, without doubt, who it was.

"What will you do now?" Yan whispered.

"I will report this to the police. They are looking for him. I think he is responsible for many deaths."

"He sounds like a dangerous man, you must be careful, Leo."

He recalled how close he'd come to being poisoned. He sighed. "I am intimately aware of his violent nature."

Someone, a man he didn't recognise, opened the office door. "Best if you return inside!"

Through the open window, they could hear the conversation without difficulty.

Neil Flanagan turned to look at the man, then took the pipe from his mouth, reached down and lifted a foot and tapped the pipe against his heel, emptying the burnt tobacco and ash from the bowl.

With the pipe returned to his pocket, he about-turned and re-entered the offices, this time without slamming the door.

"Do you wish to stay longer?" Yan asked.

"No, I've seen more than enough, we can go."

They departed as they came, quietly and without fuss. As they walked down the alley towards Vivian Street, the same group of young men appeared. As before, they walked ahead and ensured no one would bother them. Leonard looked behind, another few men followed.

"Thank you so much for all you have done, and these young men helping me. I am astonished."

"Chen Jun Qiang is a respected elder in the Chinese community. He has much influence over our people. It is to him you should offer thanks," she said.

"And I will. I also thank you for your company. You are a delightful young woman. I hope we meet again."

She bowed her head.

Chapter Twenty-Three

Leonard arrived back at the Mount Cook Depot early the next morning and resigned himself to a long wait, but to his surprise he was escorted immediately into the interview room and found Inspector Gibbard already seated.

"A pleasant morning, Mr Hardy. I'm very perplexed why you've chosen to visit me, and can only assume you are hoping for an update or developments." He pointed to the vacant chair. "Be seated. Oh yes, your face is improving," he added.

"Is good to see you too, Inspector," replied Leonard as he slid the chair back and lowered himself onto it. "But you did tell me when we last met not to make assumptions," he grinned.

Inspector Gibbard grimaced. "What have you done?"

Leonard wasted no time. "Uncle Jun used his resources within the Oriental community and located the whereabouts of Mr Neil Flanagan, and perhaps others involved in his enterprise."

The Inspector sat a little straighter and leaned forward. "Details, Mr Hardy, I require details and facts, not suppositions and inuendo."

"Well, I, er, managed to verify it. I know where Flanagan is — I saw him."

Inspector Gibbard drummed his fingers on the table. "I distinctly recall telling you to go to ground and not become involved, did I not?" A vein on his neck pulsed. "Why put yourself at risk?" He saw the expression on Leonard's face. "Very well … don't keep me in suspense, enlighten me."

"You said you didn't want me to be an encumbrance, and I

wasn't. I have aided you," Leonard smiled. "There is an office on Cuba Street, and the tenant is listed as Offices of Accountant, General Commission Agent for the New York Contributionship Company." Leonard leaned back on his chair and folded his arms feeling pleased with himself. "That is where you will find Neil Flanagan."

Inspector Gibbard's eyes opened wide. "I, uh, I am somewhat familiar with this place. Are you sure, could you be in error?"

Leonard shook his head. "No, Inspector. I was there and observed and witnessed Flanagan walk from the premises, and then return inside the office."

"When?"

"Last evening, at approximately 9:30 p.m."

The Inspector rose from his chair, walked to a window and peered out through the bars and dust-covered glass.

"No doubt you'll be sending men to that building to arrest Flanagan and his accomplices?"

Leonard didn't see the Inspector grimace.

Gibbard remained silent as he stared through the dirty window.

"Inspector?"

The Inspector scratched his blemished face then turned. "This may not be quite so simple …"

Leonard looked perplexed. "How can it not be? I've identified the suspect and…"

"Mr Hardy," Inspector Gibbard returned to his seat. "The proprietors of the premises you have ascertained are Mr Elijah Riley and his brother Joshua Riley. Are you familiar with either of these two gentlemen?"

Leonard shook his head. "Not really, I've heard the Riley name, but nothing more."

"You should. Mr Joshua Riley headed the New Zealand Permanent Militia, or Armed Constabulary prior to the inception of the New Zealand Police Force. When the Constabulary was officially dissolved into the Militia, he retired and re-entered civilian life. He partnered with his brother Elijah whose wife, an American, had the contacts and credentials to establish the agency for the New York Contributionship Company. By all accounts, these premises you've identified are beyond reproach and any investigation into its activities will not be met kindly."

"But that doesn't alter what I witnessed, Inspector," Leonard appealed.

"Perhaps not, but the harsh reality is somewhat skewed. You see, Mr Hardy, Mr Joshua Riley is well connected. His circle of social influence extends far beyond cosy tea parties and croquet club committees. He is privileged to call the Prime Minister, Wellington's mayor, and other esteemed political and business leaders as his most intimate friends."

Leonard was confounded. "You are well informed, Inspector. How is it this information is so readily at your fingertips?"

Inspector Gibbard's cold façade cracked, and he slumped in his chair. "I attended a social gathering at that location earlier this year. I am mildly acquainted with Mr Joshua Riley because of my professional role in Wellington's Police. And no, before you ask, he and I are not personal friends."

Leonard rubbed his face with both hands. This was an interesting but problematic development. He was astute enough to know the politics behind any police investigation into respected businesses and civic leaders would create consequences that trickled down. "So may I ask, what will you do?"

"Before you accuse me of involvement in Flanagan's activities, may I also inform you that your ex-employer, Mr Beaumont, Mr Frederick Pembroke and his wife, were also in attendance at that social gathering."

Another interesting revelation. Leonard shook his head in exasperation. Mr Beaumont, Mr Pembroke? That didn't surprise him, but it did not preclude they were implicit in any criminal activities—or were they? He remembered his astonishment at being chosen to deal with Mrs Bedingfield about her missing husband, and Neil Flanagan's unexpected employment at the *Evening Standard*; were these decisions deliberate, and was there some ominous intent behind them? He glanced at the Inspector and saw he looked disconcerted. "As I asked, what will you do?"

Inspector Gibbard raised his head and met Leonard's inquisitive gaze. "I am sworn to uphold the law and have a duty to the Crown to ensure I do. In my capacity as a policeman I have a responsibility and obligation to investigate with impartiality and to the best of my ability—and I *will* do this, Mr Hardy. But before I do, I must ensure I have facts and corroborated evidence because if I fail, then rest assured, my career *will* be at an end." He stared into Leonard's eyes. "Can you tell me, without doubt or dispute, that the man you saw enter those premises was Neil Flanagan? Answer me simply, yes or no."

Leonard paused for half-a-dozen heartbeats. "Yes."

"I was hoping you'd say no," grizzled the inspector.

"What happens now and how will you proceed? I take it you will continue to investigate or does this become a conflict of interest?"

"I must again bring this to the attention of my superiors because they will, in all probability, receive complaints when I authorise an investigation. However — between you and I — my superior, Superintendent Taggett, was also in attendance at the Riley's social event, and this will test his integrity. I must act in accordance with the law but also proceed with the utmost caution, Mr Hardy."

"I'm in shock," Leonard stated.

Inspector Gibbard's expression was unreadable.

"Uh, one more thing, Inspector …"

Inspector Gibbard leaned forward.

"Did you learn anything after questioning Mrs Bedingfield?"

"Not much we didn't already know, and certainly nothing incriminating," Gibbard replied. "When we questioned her she claimed we were harassing her, and as we had no evidence linking her to any crime or wrongdoing, she wouldn't answer anything other than simple questions… and only then with reluctant hostility. A difficult, unpleasant woman, nonetheless." The Inspector's face soured.

Leonard smiled as he imagined Mrs Bedingfield being interrogated and how she would react.

In a confused daze, he chose to walk to his temporary home at Uncle Jun's shop on Frederick Street. What became more clear to him was that Harold Bedingfield's disappearance was inconsequential to a much larger and sinister criminal operation. Where Neil Flanagan's role is small, and undoubtedly, he is subservient to men with loftier goals and higher ambitions, Leonard affirmed. How far up the ladder of Wellington's gentry did this go, whom could he trust?

As he wandered back to Uncle Jun's shop, Leonard weighed up what he knew. Inspector Gibbard, while certainly cold and brusque, was beyond reproach and entirely trustworthy. What about his friends — Tim Yates, Uncle Jun, Russell, Bridgette, Meredith and Mary? *Mary*! He stopped walking, forcing people behind to suddenly step around him. *Mary*? Could he trust her, was she sharing information about him to Flanagan? He relaxed, of course he could trust her. And of Mr Pembroke? Now that was a question worthy of an answer.

He knew Mr Frederick Pembroke and his wife Louise had a time in their lives when they experienced pain and suffering. The death of their daughter had ultimately guided them to New Zealand, where they sought the man responsible for causing her death. They had their secrets, but were they complicit in some way, shape or form with Neil Flanagan and the Riley brothers?

While the elderly couple may have their secrets and faults, they were, for the most part, upstanding citizens and he was convinced the Pembroke's were not involved. What of Mr Beaumont? A dour, serious man, dedicated and focused entirely on the *Evening Standard* .

His thoughts were interrupted when he recognised the unmistakable form of Russell walking towards him. "Where have you been? I've been searching for you!" exclaimed Leonard and stepped to the side of the footpath to talk.

"Mr Hardy, you're looking no worse for wear after your stoush with those men," replied Russell. He turned and looked behind, in the direction of the Victoria Hotel. "I'm not working there no more — after the death of Miss Gringle, the madam saw no need of my services."

"I'm sorry, and hope you find, uh, gainful employment soon.

Why did you work at such a distasteful place?"

Russell shrugged, "What else am I to do? No one wants me to work for them unless they need a minder."

"Ah yes, I see your point." Leonard leaned closer to the large man. "But please tell me, the other night when you interceded and came to my aid, what happened when you went in search of a policeman?"

Russell looked perplexed. "Uh, there was a policeman on a horse at the bottom of your street. Convenient really." His raspy voice difficult to hear. "When I told him what happened, he told me to bugger off. Uh, thought it odd at the time, but he was insistent. All he says was, that if needed, someone would contact me."

"He was an imposter!"

Russell raised his eyebrows. "And the bloke who fought with me, what became of him?"

"Gone, taken by the imposter. He is still at large."

"Then you're still in a spot of bother, aren't you?"

"So it seems, and this is why I am currently living there." Leonard pointed to Uncle Jun's shop, a short distance away.

Russell nodded. "If I can help you, Mr Hardy, I've nothing better to do, and it would make me feel better to lend a hand in some way …"

Leonard thought about having Russell as a minder and smiled. "I'd enjoy that, Russell. Come, I want you to make the acquaintance of Uncle Jun."

Uncle Jun was at his counter, grinding away with his mortar and pestle. He was infusing some herbs that he believed would benefit Russell's throat. Russell and Leonard were seated behind the curtain at the rear of the shop, where Leonard had just explained his meeting with Inspector Gibbard and what he'd learned when Tim Yates entered. Uncle Jun greeted him warmly then directed him to go through to the rear of the shop.

After introductions, both Tim and Russell appraised each other warily—neither willing to fully trust the other. Hoping to ease the tension, Leonard asked about developments.

"Leo, you created a bit of a brouhaha. The inspector and the superintendent got into a bit of a scrap, and were screaming at each other," Tim laughed.

Leonard looked worried. "Is this because of my visit earlier today?"

Tim nodded. "Inspector Gibbard won the battle, and immediately sent a small force to that office on Cuba Street you identified."

Leonard sat straighter. "Did they find and arrest him? Please tell me they did."

"Not Flanagan, he got away, but they did apprehend a man, possibly the one masquerading as a mounted constable. Witnesses have identified him as being complicit in a number of crimes around Wellington. He also matches the description of a man seen loitering around the home of Milton Camden on the evening of his death. They found the uniform in addition to other military uniforms in a trunk he owned. However, to make life more complicated, two other men the Inspector questioned are actual soldiers of the Permanent Militia. This is causing us even more headaches."

Leonard nodded. "And what of the small man, the American?"

Tim shook his head. "We have not located him yet, but we will, be assured of that. Both of you may be required to positively identify the pseudo constable."

Russell shrugged and nodded.

"I will feel better when Flanagan and the American are in custody," said Leonard, leaning back in the chair as his thoughts turned to Mary and Tim's safety. "They are my main concern. And you need to be careful too."

"Thanks Leo, I'll be alright," he laughed. "Based on your assumptions, we are still waiting for a report from the Coroner hoping to match that mysterious tonic with the contents of Miss Gringle and Milton Camden's stomach." Tim was feeling quite pleased with himself for being able to provide an update. "And additionally, you may be required to make another statement if the Coroner's finding supports your theory she was poisoned by that tonic," he advised.

Leonard shrugged. "Was it worth it? Was the information I provided useful to the point where Inspector Gibbard isn't in danger of losing his job?" he asked.

"No need to be concerned, Leo," Tim replied.

Leonard felt relief. "And these men, what is it they are doing? What illicit activities are they actually involved in?"

Tim shook his head. "We are no closer to learning what their intentions are, as no one is talking. One thing they say repeatedly is that they will be freed soon."

"What did the Riley brothers have to say in defence of these men being in their offices?"

"They claimed they knew nothing of any wrongdoings and were overtly supportive of any police action that resulted in the prosecution of criminals. They said the men had been hired to perform some minor tasks for the company, and neither Joshua or Elijah Riley would elaborate further. Other than those men being on their property, inside their offices, the Riley brothers have done no wrong."

Leonard shook his head. "So they say ... and Tim, what of Mary and Bridgette?"

Tim's expression changed. "Meredith doesn't know where they are. And they haven't been home. No one has seen them in days. Like you, Leo, I am concerned for their welfare."

Leonard didn't say anything, but had an idea where they both might be.

"How much danger is Mr Hardy in?" Russell asked.

Tim looked at Leonard. "I'd say not as much as before, Neil Flanagan has enough to worry about without devoting time to you, or me, but until all these men have been apprehended, then Leo, you still need to be cautious." He turned back to Russell. "Are you going to keep an eye on Leo?"

Russell nodded and grunted his assent.

Tim stood. "I really must be off. Be careful old chap, eh?"

"Please, keep me informed."

After Tim departed, Uncle Jun joined them and handed over a large bottle of brown liquid to Russell. "You drink and gargle, every morning and evening, one good mouthful. Throat feel better soon, eh."

Russell looked at the bottle and back to Uncle Jun. He nodded, "Thank you, Jun."

"What is it? Looks quite unappetising," Leonard remarked as he turned up his nose.

"Mostly Pinellia and Magnolia, some ginger," he shrugged. "Good for throat and voice." He turned to Russell. "You no listen to silly-boy Leo, you drink."

For the first time since making Leonard's acquaintance, Russell laughed.

Chapter Twenty-Four

The three most unlikely of friends sat and chatted amicably together while drinking copious amounts of tea. Eventually the topic came back to the disappearance of Harold Bedingfield.

"Do you know or have you heard of Mr Elijah Riley and his brother Joshua Riley? asked Leonard.

Uncle Jun crossed his legs and leaned back in his chair. He nodded. "Both man. I know their name. I hear of them sometime, but mostly rumour."

"What rumours?" Leonard asked.

Uncle Jun shrugged. "Needing men to help with something, but not sure what. I no pay attention."

"I think I know Joshua Riley," Russell unexpectedly said.

Leonard turned to him. "How?"

"I was told by Madam Sophronia at the Victoria Hotel to treat him nice — he came to, er, visit Miss Gringle."

Leonard felt uncomfortable. "Just the once?"

"No, more than three times, perhaps four," Russell grunted. "I did not care for him, he hurt Miss Gringle. But the madam always says that he is wealthy and important."

He'd never met Joshua Riley, but already, he detested the man. It was time to learn more about him. "I think I should visit my ex-employer, Mr Pembroke," Leonard said after a moment of silence.

"You crazy, you could be hurt if men come for you, Leo," said Uncle Jun.

"I'll go with you," Russell stated, surprising him.

Uncle Jun's head bobbed up and down. "Good boy, you go with crazy Leo, stop him from make trouble."

"I can't have you come inside Mr Pembroke's house, he won't talk to me if you are there. You'll have to remain outside and wait," Leonard advised.

Russell shrugged.

Frederick and Louise Pembroke lived in a large stately home on Wellington Terrace. Leonard knew the house well having visited them on prior occasions.. It suited him to visit Mr Pembroke at his home, where he'd be more relaxed and hopefully more forthcoming. The only reservation was how he would be received.

Leonard also knew it was time to talk to his superior about his unfair dismissal from the newspaper and clear the air for once and for all. With Russell at his side, they set off in a Hansom cab bound for the Pembroke residence.

It was already dark when Leonard and Russell alighted the cab and began walking the short distance to Mr Pembroke's house. "I'll wait here, under the tree. I can see his doorway from here," volunteered Russell. "If you need help, I will come."

Leonard was grateful and felt reassured by his presence. Feeling anxious, he turned from Russell and slowly walked across the road towards the Pembroke's grand residence.

The house had virtually no front yard and extended almost to the edge of the road. He opened the gate, entered the property and walked up three wide wooden steps onto an expansive porch. A sculptured metal head of a lion was affixed to the centre of the heavy door that was framed on either side by colourful stained-glass windows. Held in the jaws of the lion's mouth was a substantial metal ring; Leonard grabbed the ring and swung it down twice. The metallic clunks resonated inside the house and he waited.

He heard movement from inside before the door swung open to reveal Mr Pembroke. At the *Evening Standard*, Frederick Pembroke was a powerful manager who commanded his domain with unquestioned dominance. His voice alone could instil fear; his praise could warm a chilled heart, and a mere smile inspired commitment and loyalty.

At the door, Leonard saw a diminutive and frail old man. Wisps of grey hair stood at oblique angles, his tie loose and slightly askew, and pale watery eyes stared quizzically back at Leonard. He could see the unexpected death of Milton Camden had affected him severely. "Uh, good evening, sir. I apologise for my unannounced visit, but, er, I thought it best to call on you here at home ..."

Mr Pembroke's mouth tightened, and his eyes refocused. His chest expanded beneath a crumpled jacket, and he exhaled a long, slow, drawn-out breath. He nodded imperceptibly and smiled. "I expected you would eventually call," he said softly; it sounded phlegmy. He coughed and cleared his throat. "You'll want to come in." He stepped back allowing Leonard to enter.

They sat in the spacious living room with large windows that offered an impressive view over Wellington. Beneath them, Leonard could see twinkling lights and a city enjoying an early evening. He lowered his head, took a deep breath to fortify himself then looked towards Mr Pembroke, who sat quietly in the comforting embrace of a large armchair. "Er ... my dismissal from the *Evening Standard* was unjust and undeserved," he began. He expected Mr Pembroke to protest. He didn't. He continued to sit and appraise him—it was a little unsettling and only added to his anxiousness. "There was a plan, a scheme, initiated by Neil Flanagan and it was intended to discredit me, not just to you, my employer, but to Mary as well."

Mr Pembroke raised an eyebrow. "A plan? Did I not speak to you of gathering evidence, I presume you have some?"

"Yes, sir, sort of, but first I need to inform you of a ploy designed to prevent me from interfering and searching for Harold Beding-field. I'm sure you recall his wife?"

"Most clearly," replied Mr Pembroke.

"During that time, my, er, inquisitiveness led me to a young woman, Agatha Gringle. Her father was killed in Courtenay Place and was a known associate of Mr Bedingfield. Miss Gringle was, ur, she um, had somewhat questionable virtues, sir." Leonard cleared his throat. "I met with her once, at her place of employment the Victoria Hotel, where she performed her … her, uh … craft. I had to pay ten shillings to speak to her for half an hour," Leonard grizzled. "But all I did was talk to her and ask questions, nothing more."

Mr Pembroke sat motionlessly.

"She wanted to give me additional information and asked that I meet her at Ivy's on Oriental Bay, where she could speak freely. The place held familial memories for her. When we met, she gave me more information, and we decided to then go to the Hutt Race Course, where she believed Harold Bedingfield could be found. Uh, it was her who shot and killed the man just north of the race course."

Mr Pembroke's eyes widened. "What did you say?"

"I was there, sir. She shot dead a man with a revolver."

"Good heavens. I heard about the death and we even reported on it, spared only fifty words on the story …"

Leonard reached into his jacket and extracted the letter Agatha had given him. As promised, Inspector Gibbard had copied the letter and returned it to him. He handed it over.

Mr Pembroke reached for his reading spectacles and read the letter quickly.

Leonard's heart was racing.

Mr Pembroke handed the letter back. "Did you influence this missive?" he asked after removing his reading spectacles.

"No, sir, absolutely not. I wasn't aware she'd composed it. She left it at my home shortly before her death."

Mr Pembroke grunted, then nodded. "This man Leon Barrow who was killed, what have you learned?"

Leonard began to explain all that had transpired. He told Mr Pembroke everything, including the attempts on his life, the poison tonic and how he believed Milton Camden was murdered. He concluded by recounting Flanagan's despicable and violent behaviour towards him.

Mr Pembroke was disturbed. The death of Milton Camden had been difficult for him and he looked downcast.

"You wanted evidence, Mr Pembroke?"

Mr Pembroke raised an eyebrow.

Leonard handed him the page he'd taken from Wellington's library that reported on Neil Flanagan's assault charge. He sat back and waited for the senior reporter to finish.

"Shoddy writing." He took a deep breath. "Seems our Mr Flanagan is easily riled and possesses a volatile temperament. No, lad, I wasn't aware of this at all." He removed his reading spectacles again.

"As I can personally attest, it appears that he is a very dangerous man."

Mr Pembroke chewed his bottom lip as he digested all that Leonard told him. "I admit, you've been unjustly maligned, not only has your career been unfairly tarnished, your personal life has become a shambles …" The aging senior reporter shook his head. "What you've disclosed provides me with insights that I was not previously privy to. Poor Milton," he sighed. "It explains much, and certainly the professional behaviour of Neil Flanagan has been far from exemplary. His performance has been lacking and when Inspector Gibbard spoke to me about him, I first believed there was a misunderstanding. And now there is a warrant for his arrest … good heavens, what is becoming of people?"

Leonard could see he looked distracted. "Is there something wrong?" he asked.

After a brief pause, Mr Pembroke twisted in his chair to better face his guest. "I don't believe it appropriate that I share with you private conversations, however, in light of all you continue to suffer through, it would be equitable for me to inform you of some details. It may not satisfy you, but you may be somewhat appeased."

"I don't understand," Leonard replied.

"Neil Flanagan was hired because Mr Beaumont insisted I employ him as a reporter to cover Recreation and Entertainment, and I adamantly refused. That position belonged to Milton Camden, and there was no reason to replace him, he'd done no wrong. Due to his insistence and applied pressure I relented, suggesting a compromise where Mr Flanagan could report on matters of the Economy and Finance, which is where we needed help. Mr Beaumont reluctantly conceded. With Milton Camden's unfortunate passing, Mr Beaumont was all too quick to ensure that Mr Flanagan immediately assumed those vacant responsibilities around Recreation and Entertainment. I believed at the time that Milton's death seemed a little too convenient. And from what you've disclosed, my concerns were justified."

"Why is the Recreation and Entertainment portfolio so important to Flanagan?" Leonard asked.

"I wish I knew, but I do suspect there is more to this. Leonard, it was Mr Beaumont who informed me of your, uh, alleged improprieties. Again, and with some conviction and raised voices, he demanded your immediate dismissal without offering you the opportunity to explicate. I defended you Leonard, but I was overruled. I found the allegations to be whimsical at best and knew it was out of character for you to behave in such a scandalous manner. Mr Beaumont believed otherwise. I have no opinion on what is motivating the man and, I admit, find it mystifying."

"Do Neil Flanagan and Mr Beaumont have an association outside their professional lives, sir, are they acquaintances?"

"I wouldn't have thought so, but now, I'm not so sure, Leonard." He rubbed the back of his head. "What now?"

"What now!" Leonard exclaimed. "I'd like my job back, Mr Pembroke!" He didn't mean to sound so harsh and hoped Mr Pembroke didn't take offence.

Mr Pembroke placed the arm of his reading spectacles in his mouth as he considered his reply. "I understand how you feel and sympathise, however the decision to re-instate you falls entirely in the purview of Mr Beaumont, not me. And my understanding is, that isn't likely to happen."

Leonard looked crestfallen. He couldn't see himself working for another newspaper,; he grimaced in exasperation and looked again at Mr Pembroke. "There is more, I haven't told you everything."

Mr Pembroke toyed with his reading spectacles.

"It was me who reported the location of Neil Flanagan to the police."

"I commend you."

"I don't think you fully grasp the whole situation, sir. Neil Flanagan was hiding in the offices of Accountant, General Commission, Agent for the New York Contributionship Company on Cuba Street."

Mr Pembroke's mouth opened. "Flanagan was there?"

Leonard nodded.

"I'd heard about the police raid, but had no idea that you or Mr Flanagan were involved. My goodness, it does shed a different light on it, doesn't it?"

"Indeed," Leonard replied. "I'm also led to believe that you are acquainted with Elijah and Joshua Riley."

Mr Pembroke's eyes narrowed. "Who told you that?"

"I'm not at liberty to say, sir. But I understand you have socialised with them."

He nodded. "I have been to a few functions hosted by the Riley brothers, but they do not share their intimacies with me, nor would I consider myself a close acquaintance. Although …"

Leonard inclined his head as he waited for Mr Pembroke to continue.

"Yes, yes … I do recall now. I was introduced to both Riley brothers by Mr Beaumont. He invited me to a function, insisting I meet them because their sphere of influence in Wellington would be beneficial to the ongoing success of the *Evening Standard*."

"All roads lead to Elijah and Joshua Riley," said Leonard.

"And you believe they are behind this whole sordid mess?"

"Considering what I have learned, then, yes, I do believe they are, but how, or what are their intentions?"

"If Mr Beaumont was somehow influenced by the Riley brothers, then that could explain his adverse behaviour towards you … seems logical." Mr Pembroke looked thoughtful.

"How much do you know about them?"

Suddenly the door opened and Louise Pembroke entered the living room. She looked surprised when she saw Leonard . "Mr Hardy … what a pleasure, I thought I'd heard voices. At first I thought it was Freddie talking to himself again."

Mr Pembroke grunted.

Leonard stood to greet Mr Pembroke's enigmatic wife. "Mrs Pembroke, lovely to see you. I hope you are well?"

"Thank you, Leonard, yes, I am fine. Busy. I've been out at a meeting."

"Mr Hardy and I have been having a little chat, dear," offered Mr Pembroke.

"Well in that case I shan't disturb you. Cup of tea, Leonard?"

"That would be nice, Mrs Pembroke."

Mrs Pembroke walked into the kitchen leaving them alone again as Leonard sat down.

Mr Pembroke leaned forward in his chair. "Leonard, let me look into the Rileys, I have resources and means to do this without arousing suspicion. I am curious to learn more, and I'm not happy about being an unwitting pawn for the Rileys, or for Mr Beaumont for that matter. I will send you word on what I learn. In the meantime, keep safe from harm and let's hope that menace Flanagan is apprehended soon."

"And I can get my job back."

Mrs Pembroke entered the living room with a tray carrying a teapot and four cups. Mr Pembroke noticed her error at the same time Leonard did.

"Louise, it's only the three of us for tea, Leonard came alone."

She raised her head, "I've invited a pleasant young man to have tea with us. I believe he is a friend of yours, Leonard."

To Leonard's total astonishment Russell tentatively stepped into the room. He looked sheepish.

"I found him waiting outside under that tree in the cold," she added as she begun to rotate the pot to help the tea draw.

"Be seated, Russell," she said and patted the sofa beside her.

Mr Pembroke shook his head. "Bloody woman," he whispered under his breath.

"What was that?" she asked.

Leonard felt the need to explain. "I uh, felt it prudent that Russell remain outside while I visited you. Er, he was, uh, keeping watch."

Mrs Pembroke looked at her husband. "Oh?"

"I will tell you later, dear."

Chapter Twenty-Five

$\mathcal{A}$ cab had just deposited them outside Uncle Jun's shop on Frederick Street when Russell turned to Leonard, "Do you trust 'em?"

"Who, Mr and Mrs Pembroke?"

Russell nodded.

It was a good question and Leonard thought carefully. "I think so. He is principled, and upstanding … yes, I do. They are good people. Why do you ask?"

They entered the shop. "Cause I have come across most of the swanky, posh men in Wellington at some time or other. They come to Frederick or Haining Street looking to satisfy their pleasures and I've never seen him before."

Leonard grinned, "Then I believe that's a good thing."

Leonard felt it was safe enough to return to his home. Uncle Jun protested vehemently, and Russell explained that he lived in a rooming house, and it wasn't an inconvenience for him to spend a few nights at Leonard's. Uncle Jun reluctantly concurred, and within a short time, Leonard and Russell climbed Leonard's street. As he unlocked and opened his front door he saw a letter on the floor. He immediately recognised the writing — it was from Mary!

He couldn't wait to open it. As Russell lit the lamps and with the fire roaring, he sat down to read. With excitement, his heart began to beat furiously as he tore open the envelope and extracted the letter.

250 Adelaide Road,
Newtown, Wellington.

Dearest Leonard,

I know you worry and have the utmost regard for my safekeeping and wellbeing. I felt compelled to write and allay your concerns. Both Bridgette and I believed it provident that we temporarily relocate to safer lodgings, although Bridgette will return soon.

We perceived an increasing need to distance ourselves from that despicable man, Neil Flanagan. His behaviour and manner became increasingly distressing and we began to fear for our safety.

After Tim Yates informed us of the problems you were facing, and upon his urging, we quietly relocated. No one knows where we are, but I'm sure you do.

While this does not mean I forgive you for your indiscretions, I don't, but I am willing to talk with you when it is again safe to return. I am increasingly troubled for your difficulties and health. Leo, please, do not act rashly, I will remain in contact.

Affectionally yours,
Mary

Leonard grinned, he wanted to cry. Mary was safe and in no danger at her aunt's home in Upper Hutt. He savoured the feeling and, that she was willing to talk— that was progress. But what had Flanagan been doing to make them fearful? He grimaced at the thought. Neil Flanagan had a lot to answer for. However, with Mary and Bridgette secure and out of harm's way, he could again focus on righting his troubled ship. With her decks awash, the ship was foundering and threatened to drag him down to the deepest and darkest depths. He shuddered.

The following two days were spent doing chores, cleaning and gardening, with Russell insisting on helping where he could. Leonard found him to be thoughtful and quick-witted and enjoyed his company. As instructed by Uncle Jun, Russell continued to take the medicine prescribed, and he informed Leonard the pain and discomfort in his throat had begun to ease.

Wellington had turned on a spectacular sunny day. They went into town to purchase food and were returning home when Leonard saw a produce cart selling fruit positioned at the bottom of Marjoribanks Street. Leonard pointed it out to Russell. "That is Uncle Jun's doing. They're watching." He greeted the two Chinese vendors as they passed by and continued up the street towards home.

"Uncle Jun is a good bloke," Russell said. "I've seen him around Frederick Street before, and thought him only another duff vendor and paid him no mind. How wrong I was."

"I've learned not to underestimate him, or the Chinese," replied Leonard.

On arrival, Leonard found a large envelope laying on the floor that had been pushed through the mail slot. Written on the front, in the familiar scrawl of Mr Pembroke, it simply said 'LH'.

Inside the envelope were documents all pertaining to Elijah and Joshua Riley. Mr Pembroke had been busy. There were lists of company and personal affiliations; Leonard and Russell went through the documents looking for clues that could help them determine what these two men were up to.

Leonard sorted through the various lists, placing them in order of relevance onto a clipboard to keep them organised.

The Rileys were well connected. Certainly, they had close acquaintances with many people involved with politicians, the police and military — no doubt because of Joshua's past role with the armed Constabulary. There were well-known charities they supported, including in the arts, theatre and music. Nothing seemed peculiar or out of character that linked them to any shenanigans, and by all accounts, these men were bastions of the community, supporting many worthwhile causes.

Leonard paused in his perusal to study an item on the list. He re-read it. It stated that Joshua Riley was a board member of The Island Bay Park Racing and Coursing Company. "See here?" he stabbed the clipboard with a finger.

Russell looked over.

"Correct me if I am wrong, but this is the only link we have found so far that connects them to horses."

Russell nodded.

"Which also means it links the Rileys to Harold Bedingfield, Balthazar Gringle … and …"

"And?" enquired Russell.

"… Milton Camden, the reporter for the *Evening Standard.* Don't you see?"

Russell looked flummoxed.

"Part of Milton's duties involved reporting on horse racing. Joshua Riley's relationship with The Island Bay Park Racing and Coursing Company connects all the deaths together through horses."

"Even that knob-head, Flanagan," Russell added.

"Yes, and presumably, because he wanted to report on the horse races. But why?"

"It makes sense to me," Russell said.

"Oh?"

"How else do punters know what horse to have a flutter on? They read the paper and find out which nag is favoured to win," Russell suggested.

"Then, if they can influence people to wager on a horse, that can determine the odds of a winning horse," continued Leonard.

"And affect the pay-out on winnings," Russell concluded.

Leonard leaned back in his chair. "Are the Rileys somehow involved in altering the outcome of horse races?"

"It seems bloody likely to me."

"And how do they affect the outcome of a race? That, my friend, is the question."

"Perhaps Mr Bed ..."

"Bedingfield."

Russell grimaced. "I'd bet you, ten-to-one, Mr Bedingfield knows exactly, and that's why they want him so bad. They want to shut his gob." He leaned forward placing his thick muscular arms across the table and grinned. "The Island Bay Race Course is having their Spring Meeting this weekend ..."

"And we do what? Wander around like a couple of well-heeled gentlemen and hope we aren't recognized? What if Flanagan is

there?" Leonard looked exasperated. "And I've yet to meet Mr Bedingfield and have no notion of his appearance. If we go asking questions, he'll disappear." He tossed the clipboard onto the settee in
frustration.

"If he'd be there …" Russell added.

Leonard suddenly looked up. "I have it!"

Russell waited.

"Harold Bedingfield doesn't want to be found, however, all we
need to do is find his horse, Sweet Hazel. Mr Bedingfield won't be
far away." Leonard smirked.

"And how do we not look dubious by asking questions and being
nosey?"

"Well then, that becomes the challenge, does it not?"

Russell looked over at the sofa, and smiled. He rose from the
chair and picked up the clipboard and handed it to Leonard. "Here
ya go, hold this." He stepped back. "Now you look all official, all ya
need is a peaky." He folded his thick muscular arms and grinned.

Leonard rushed into his bedroom and returned moments later
wearing a tweed flat cap.

Russell grinned. "And with it pulled low, even your mum won't
recognise you."

"And I have a matching jacket," Leonard added.

"And a nag to go with it?," the big man laughed.

Chapter Twenty-Six

The Island Bay Park Racing and Coursing Company was situated about four miles from downtown Wellington in the remote southern Island Bay seaside community, and involved a rather harrowing ride in Bell's Horse Bus to reach the locale. In inclement weather passengers were often required to help push the carriage when it became bogged down. However, today race goers were spared such discomforts as it hadn't rained in a week or so and the road was passable, although jolting. Like the road to Island Bay, the race course often suffered as a result of heavy rainfall and became more reminiscent of a lake. Today, the sun shone, the ground was firm and people, in droves, flocked in for a day of excitement at The Island Bay Park Racing and Coursing Company's race course.

The buses deposited all race fans on Derwent Street, near the stands, on the western side of the 1.2-mile track, and Leonard and Russell stepped from the bus, both rubbing their backs, feeling relieved they'd survived the journey without incurring a permanent injury.

Leonard led Russell away from the throngs of people near the grandstand and headed northwards where he had seen stables and training facilities. Just like the Hutt Park Race Course, when he and Agatha had searched for Mr Bedingfield, Leonard believed the elusive man would be in a similar location and looked for an isolated, off-site stable.

Russell stopped walking and looked around. Curious, Leonard paused, waiting for him to speak.

"I don't think we should walk together. Best if I follow at some distance, otherwise we could be mistaken for bovver boys[9]."

Leonard laughed. "I don't think I've ever been mistaken for a hoodlum, but a wise decision. Follow behind, but I implore, please keep me in your sight," he advised. Russell nodded and Leonard set off alone.

Anyone who knew him would be surprised at his appearance. He carried his clip board, his tweed flat cap was pulled low, and he wore a tweed jacket and khaki coloured trousers. To any casual observer he looked like a typical race official or steward; his choice of wardrobe matched what so many other horsey people were wearing at today's event. Leonard believed he blended in rather well.

He heard the unmistakeable sound of the starting gate crash open and horses thundering out. Eager spectators cheered.

Grooms leading horses walked past him and nodded courteously — Leonard began to feel more comfortable. Just ahead, in the first stall in a long array of stables, a young groom was diligently combing the flanks of a thoroughbred with a metal spiked brush.

Feeling confident, he approached. "Mornin'."

The groom turned and greeted Leonard politely. "Yep, lovely day, sir."

Leonard looked down at the clipboard and pretended to consult some notes. "Uh, I'm looking for a horse … oh yes, here it is, uh, Sweet Hazel, I need to confirm some minor details, any idea where I could find her?"

The groom frowned, thought a moment, then shrugged. "Sorry, sir, can't help ya. Try farther up." He pointed to another group of stables and continued with his chore.

9   *Bovver boys - Hooligans*

"Thank you." Leonard walked off and then looked over his shoulder. Russell followed discretely, but close enough that he felt reassured by his presence. Leonard turned to watch as jockeys, riding crops flailing as they urged their mounts to gallop even faster, roared past—the noise was deafening.

Once the horses had raced by, a rather loud outspoken gentleman with a beautiful woman on his arm approached. The man, obvious by his flashy, gaudy appearance, exuded wealth and Leonard nodded politely in greeting. The man held Leonard's gaze briefly, didn't respond and rudely walked past. He overheard the man telling his attractive consort about the success he'd enjoyed as a successful horse breeder and how he had the necessary talents to identify a good filly. Leonard couldn't disagree on the last point.

More people passed him as they made their way towards the grandstand and nearly everyone acknowledged him with either a hello or a polite head nod. He was just beginning to feel more at ease in his pseudo role as a race official when he observed two men walking in his direction. One was small, and with a start, he recognized him immediately. It was the small American who'd fled his house when they tried to poison him. He felt the prickling of dread. In fear of discovery, he raised the clipboard to hide his face and pretended to be engrossed in some officious detail. He held his breath as they walked by.

"Morn'n," said one of them.

"How ya doin'?" The small man said, his American accent distinct and unmistakable.

Leonard exhaled and replied at the same time, it sounded like a cough. Then it dawned on him, Russell! They would recognize him immediately. Without thinking he turned to look behind and saw the two men continue. Of the big man there was no sign, he'd vanished. The small American paused and began to look curiously back behind him. Leonard looked away and quickened his stride.

He could hear his heart thumping in his chest and threatening to explode. He forced himself to walk and not run in panic. *Be calm, relax*, he told himself over and over again as he quickly tried to gain some distance at the same time appearing unconcerned. Behind him, fans yelled in delight as the leading horse crossed the finish line.

He didn't hear the sound of pursuit and with some relief turned behind a lengthy row of stables. Once out of sight, he stopped and risked a quick peek around the corner. Both men were arguing, but the small man was pointing in his direction. *He must suspect something*, he thought grimly, and of more concern, Russell wasn't anywhere to be seen.

He knew he needed to hide. If they decided to come back and search, they might give up if they didn't see him. Carefully he eased his head from behind the stable wall for another quick look. They'd begun to walk his way.

He ran. With the clipboard under his arm he rounded the far side of the stables and headed in an easterly direction on the far, north side of the race course. He knew he couldn't be seen, but not for much longer. He needed to find some shelter, anywhere, a place that offered concealment.

The gates crashed open and another race began.

In the distance he could see a small group of cottages nestled together on a low rise. They were set back from a small track, surrounded by railed fences and a few stables. In desperation, he headed towards them. Immediately ahead, the ground began to slope down; a moderate grade that ended at a stream and he knew he'd be out of sight for a brief time, but when he crossed the stream, he'd have to climb up the far side, and that was when he'd be visible and vulnerable.

Gasping for breath, he paused, bent over with hands resting on his thighs and sucked in a few needed lungfuls of air. Having regained some energy, and his breath from his quick rest, he crossed over some thick wooden planks that bridged the stream then turned and walked slowly backwards as the terrain angled upwards. He saw them then, two little figures in the distance. They'd stopped and were looking around, searching for him. Leonard watched them enter a stall, then exit and enter another.

Leonard decided he would make a break for it once they entered the adjacent stall in line and knew he'd have about twenty seconds before they remerged. He waited, then saw them enter the stall. Seizing opportunity, he turned and ran, counted twenty seconds, then fell to the ground, hoping his clothes would blend in to the tufty, longish grass and render him invisible. The two men reappeared, then methodically entered the next stable. They were searching each stall for him. Leonard rose to his feet and sprinted again for another twenty seconds before again falling prone to the ground. He lay unmoving, chest heaving from the exertion. Directly ahead, he could see more stables that would offer him more concealment – only one last sprint.

The two men reappeared and then disappeared into the next stall in line. They were determined, he thought grimly. But where was Russell?

Leonard took off running as fast as possible. He reached the stable and rounded the corner on the count of eighteen. Once out of sight, he leaned back against the wall trying to catch his breath. Thankfully, he hadn't heard a cry of alarm signalling he'd been spotted. He was relieved, but would they come this far looking for him or would they give up? In the distance he heard the roar of excited race-goers as another race began.

"Can I help you?"

The voice startled Leonard, and he jumped. "Uh, uh, I apologise, I didn't see you."

An older man sat on a chair in the shadowed gloom of the open stable, nursing a glass of amber liquid. A bottle of whiskey sat on the ground at his side. He raised the glass and took a sip before speaking again. "You appear troubled and you've come onto private property." It wasn't a question, just a simple statement.

While the man didn't appear hostile, Leonard could see he wasn't thrilled about his unexpected appearance and wanted an explanation. He thought quickly, "Forgive me, sir. I, er, I was being pursued. Two men …" He was still short of breath and he filled his lungs. "… This was the only place I could seek shelter." He stepped back and quickly looked to where he'd last seen them. They didn't appear, and feeling some relief removed his cap and wiped his brow.

The older man looked alarmed and stood. "What men? Where are they?"

Leonard pointed in the direction of the stables at the north end of the race course. "That way, but I do not see them now." His heart still raced and he knew that as concerned as the older man might appear, there was little he could do to defend himself against two thugs in prime physical condition. *Where was Russell*?

The man grimaced and cursed.

"Uh, I will leave, please give me a moment to collect myself.

Where may I find the road, sir?" Leonard asked as he leaned back against the stable wall trying to recover.

The older man remained silent and stepped into the darkness of the stable and returned moments later carrying a shotgun.

A shotgun! "I will take my leave, there is no need for that, I have no quarrel with you, sir." He raised his arms defensively to demonstrate he had no weapons and posed no threat. "Please, tell me where I may find the road and I shall quickly be on my way," he appealed. The eagerness of the old man to brandish the old gun in such a threatening manner was a little disconcerting. *Why was the shotgun so close at hand and easy to access,* Leonard wondered? "Uh, sir, please point that elsewhere."

"Harry!" yelled the man over his shoulder. With creaky legs, he stepped past Leonard and looked around the stable's corner to where he'd pointed. He squinted into the distance. "I don't see anyone."

"They were following me, and searching for me in the stables, that's when I ran here."

"Harry?" the man yelled again.

"Coming," the response was faint.

Leonard heard the reply and looked in the direction of the voice. Moments later another man appeared carrying two buckets of water. He looked up at Leonard and his expression changed. He looked apprehensive and stopped. The heavy buckets swung from beneath his hands as he stared.

"This bloke came running up here, said he was chased by two men," advised the old man.

The man carrying the water seemed to relax a little, and continued towards the stable and lowered the buckets to the ground. "Where?"

"From those stables," Leonard pointed again.

"What did they look like? How were they dressed?" he asked, as he removed his hat and scratched his balding pate.

Now that the man was closer, he could see him more clearly. Leonard estimated he was in his mid-thirties, average height and quite lean. A man used to the rigours of hard work, or just under-nourished, he thought. "They were city men, and dressed in suits, one man was smaller, and American."

Both men exchanged a look.

"Do you know them?" Leonard asked, sensing their discomfort at his description of the pursuers. He looked from the younger man back to the older man, hoping for a clue.

The younger man walked past him and carefully eased his head around the side of the stable looking back towards the path leading to the race course. "I don't see 'em," he stated, then turned back. "Unfortunately, we are *very* familiar with them."

Leonard could see both men were agitated. "Look, I apologise. Please show me where the road is and I shall make my departure."

The younger man sighed. "There is a path that will lead you down and take you onto Clyde Street, but you'll be seen by anyone down near the race course. If those men are looking for you, they'll see ya," he warned, then inclined his head. "Why is it they want you?"

Leonard thought quickly and decided the truth would be best. "Those men are part of an organisation who have murdered people. They are involved in some sort of illegal enterprise to do with hors-es. I just don't know what, and that is what I was hoping to learn by coming to the race track today." Surprisingly, both men didn't react to his allegations.

"And you came alone to the race course knowing this?" asked the younger man, shaking his head at Leonard's foolishness.

"No, no," Leonard replied quickly, "I have a friend, but we were separated. He came with me today as a form of protection." Leonard sighed, "I just don't know where he is…"

The older man returned to his forgotten whiskey glass and up-ended it in a big gulp. He pulled a face and shook his head as he felt the burn. He belched. "What are we going to do, Harry?"

Leonard's head spun to face the younger man. "Harry? Harold Bedingfield?"

The younger man's expression changed as he glowered at Leonard. "Who are you?" he asked, his anger unmistakeable.

Chapter Twenty-Seven

The old man placed the shotgun against the exterior stable wall and returned to his seat where he began refilling his glass. "This will be good," he grumbled.

Leonard wasn't sure if the old man was referring to his whiskey or the ensuing conversation. "You are Harold Bedingfield?" he asked the man again who carried the buckets.

He nodded, "I am he. Now tell me who the hell you are." His eyes darted to the shotgun.

After all this time, I finally found him. "My name is Leonard Hardy," he began, "up until recently I was employed by the *Evening Standard* newspaper, and was given a simple task to write a community notice that listed Harold Bedingfield as a missing person."

The old man laughed. "Missing alright, went into bloody hiding, more's th' truth." He began coughing.

Leonard could see that Mr Bedingfield was understandably anxious and fearful.

Harry stepped back towards the stable for another quick look towards the race course. He recoiled. "Damnation, they're coming!"

Leonard's mouth dropped open. "What should we do, run to the road?"

The old man rose from his seat and reached a bony hand for the shotgun. Harry beat him to it. "Grab the pitchfork," he instructed. "You, Mr Hardy, would be well advised to enter the stable. Derris, you go in there as well. Use that pitchfork if you have to." Harry lowered himself behind a water trough and rested the long barrel of the shotgun over the lip and aimed it where he knew the men would appear. Not requiring a reminder, Leonard hurried to the tenuous safety of the stable.

He heard the two thugs breathing hard as they scrambled up the path towards the stable. One man slipped and he heard the blaspheme clearly. Both men paused briefly and then rounded the corner and simultaneously froze. The unmistakeable sight of the shotgun barrel aimed at them wasn't a welcome they expected. Again, Leonard could hear his heart thumping in his chest and held his breath in anticipation of the shotgun discharge.

"Look, Bob, if it isn't Harry here to greet us. We've been looking everywhere for you."

"Are ya gonna use that thing or just swat flies with it?" casually questioned the American.

"You've been a naughty boy, Harry. We've been searching for you for some time, and here you are," stated the taller hoodlum with a big smile. "You've been misbehaving and we've been rather perturbed." He frowned to emphasise his point.

The old man with the pitchfork standing in front of Leonard hiccupped. Leonard winced and slowly exhaled.

The two men heard the sound. "Let me guess … Derris, ya bum, be neighbourly and come say hello," instructed the American.

Leonard knew they'd discover him soon enough, and now regretted not running when he had the chance. He couldn't help it, and held his breath again.

Derris walked from the stable with his pitchfork extended like a lance. Both thugs laughed and neither seemed perturbed by the fact a shotgun was still pointed at them.

"I'd like you to both leave, you've been warned, now go!" ordered Harry.

Derris brandished the pitchfork, thrusting it aggressively at the two men to emphasize the point.

Leonard looked for another door, an alternative exit from the stable, but he saw nothing that could aid in his escape.

"You see," said the American, "there's another fella we want to welcome. I'm quite sure he's here somewhere. Mr Hardy? Leo? Be a chum and step out so we can see ya." He quickly snatched the pitchfork from Derris and pushed him roughly to the ground. The older man didn't stand a chance against these two roughnecks.

Leonard closed his eyes and waited for Harry to discharge the shotgun. He didn't.

"Leo, come and say hello!" they taunted.

He had no option, and stepped, blinking, from the darkness of the stable into the bright sunshine.

"It's our lucky day, isn't it, Bob?" said the taller thug. "We found them both."

"Then perhaps you should use your luck at the race course and leave us in peace," Leonard suggested.

The two thugs ignored Leonard. Without warning, the tall one stepped forward, leaned down and yanked the shotgun from Harry's hand. He broke open the gun and grinned. "Look, Bob, no shells." He laughed and tossed the shotgun aside as the small American pulled a revolver from his jacket pocket and pointed it at Leonard.

Harry looked downcast. Resigned to his fate, he slowly stood. Derris awkwardly rose to stand beside his friend.

"Now this one *is* loaded, wanna take a gamble, Leo?" taunted the American called Bob. The revolver didn't waver and he held the weapon with the assuredness of a professional.

Leonard wisely kept his mouth closed and just glared at the small man, hoping Russell would appear.

In the dark recesses of the stable, a horse moved and inadvertently kicked at the side of the stall.

"Is that our Sweet Hazel?" remarked the taller man. "It's not too late Harry, we still have a gift for her, and we can all make some money, eh? What race have you entered her into, because I presume you have?"

Harry's shoulders were slumped. "Last race, the big one."

"Wonderful, then it isn't too late," he replied. He reached into his pocket and extracted a small bottle, holding it up for everyone to see. He shook it. The innocent looking pink liquid gave Leonard the chills. "But first, we need to make sure Leonard doesn't get up to any mischief." He stepped around his three captives and walked into the stable, returning with a coil of rope. "Best thing we can do, until we decide what to do, is keep you here, Leo. Can't have you getting up to any naughtiness, now can we?"

He walked up to Derris and gave the old man a push in the back. "Into the stable. You too, Leo."

Once Leonard and Derris were in the stable, he sat them down, back to back, and tied them securely together. "This will keep you two out of bother, eh?"

"What we gonna do with 'em? We can't leave 'em tied up and we can't use the cocktail," stated Bob, the American, when his associate stepped from the stable.

"When it is dark, we could take Leo to the beach and drown him. Considering all his recent misfortunes, his suicide won't be unexpected."

Bob nodded. "That's acceptable, but what about the old fella, Derris?" he asked.

"Perhaps he has a fall and breaks his neck," shrugged the taller man.

Bob gave the matter some thought. "Well, we didn't expect to find both Leo and Harry here today, so it puts us in a bind. The old man … he's a drunk, who would take his word earnestly? He's just a nuisance that we have to attend to somehow."

"You can't just go murdering anyone who interferes with your scheme," stated Harry. "Haven't you killed enough?"

"You just worry about Sweet Hazel and get her ready for the race, or you'll be floating face down in the trough," warned Bob, as he swung the revolver and struck Harry cruelly across the side of his head.

Harry cried out and stumbled. "I … I … have to take her down to the race course, the jockey will be there soon looking for her," he said rubbing his head where he was struck.

"Then get her ready!" yelled the small American. He raised the handgun as if he were going to belt him again. In fear, Harry ran inside, still rubbing his temple.

The American leaned against the side of the stable at the entrance and watched the activity inside as his associate helped Harold Bedingfield prepare Sweet Hazel for her race later that afternoon. The revolver dangled casually from his hand.

Leonard sat, immobile, bound to Derris and looked at the small American and wondered if his life would truly come to an end. His bindings were tight and struggle as he might, all it did was cause the coarse rope to cut into his skin. "So you give race horses a tonic containing a drug to enhance their performance?" he asked.

Bob laughed. "Our little cocktail assures us that a good horse will outperform and almost always guarantees us a victory. Nothing like a little stimulation, eh?"

His associate laughed. "And the punters are all too happy to lose their money."

"Is it worth murdering for?" Leonard shook his head in disgust.

The American smirked, then suddenly jerked forward, bending double as an involuntary whoosh sound escaped his mouth. The revolver fell to the dirt as he collapsed to the ground, clutching his stomach and wheezing for air. Russell quickly stepped up, discarding the pitchfork and pocketing the gun before hauling the American to his feet and delivering a powerful fist into his bruised midriff. Again, Bob fell to the ground with a grunt, frantically struggling to breathe.

Hearing the commotion, the taller thug inside the stable turned and saw his associate fall. In response, he fumbled in his pocket and withdrew his own revolver. He raised the weapon at the same time the reins from Sweet Hazel's bridle dropped over his head. Harold Bedingfield jerked the sturdy leather straps as hard and as quickly as he could. The tall man was totally unprepared as the reins snapped cruelly against his exposed throat and he was unable to prevent himself from toppling backwards. In reflex, he squeezed the handgun's trigger and a bullet disappeared harmlessly through the roof. The soft tissue and cartilage of his neck were more forgiving than the stout leather reins and like his American friend, he fell to the ground, painfully gasping due to his injured throat.

The gunshot was unbelievably loud in the confined space of the stable, and Sweet Hazel panicked. She reared and began kicking the sides of the stall. Harry dropped the bridle and turned to his horse as Russell began to untie Leonard and Derris.

"Grab the gun!" Leonard yelled to Russell in warning.

Russell looked up and saw the thug Harry had partly choked reach for the discarded revolver on the stable floor. Still in a frenzy, Sweet Hazel continued to kick the stall and was at serious risk of injuring herself, while Harry was doing his best to grab her halter and soothe her with calming words.

With remarkable agility, Russell dove for the revolver as the stricken, partly choked thug tried to raise it. He was too slow and Russell crashed into him with his shoulder, slamming the thug's head into the thick planking of the stall.

At the entrance to the stall, the small American stirred with a groan, scrambled to his hands and knees and floundered for the pitchfork laying nearby.

"Russell!" Leonard cried out in warning.

Russell rose and stared in disbelief as the small American, now on his feet, advanced with the pitchfork extended. He reached into his pocket for the revolver he'd confiscated, levelled his arm and squeezed the trigger. Nothing happened. In disgust, he tossed it aside, and without fear or regard for his safety, angrily stomped towards the American.

The small American pulled the implement back, then lunged forward as Russell came within striking range. With nary a care in the world, Russell easily swiped the dangerous tool aside and reached for the small man. In pure desperation, the American stepped back, gathered himself and by using it as a club, took a wild swing with the pitchfork, aiming for Russell's head.

Leonard could only watch helplessly as the lethal tool arced towards Russell   . He closed his eyes.

With a meaty paw, Russell caught the swinging handle, easily snatched it free, drew his arm back and swung with all his might. The metal tines of the pitchfork impacted the side of the American's head with a sickly crunch. Without a sound, he collapsed to the ground and didn't move.

No one spoke. It was deathly quiet; even Sweet Hazel had calmed down and, to Harry's immense relief, hadn't injured herself.

"I need a drink," said Derris, breaking the silence.

"I think you killed him," said Harry, standing over the lifeless body of the American. "He isn't breathing."

Leonard didn't want to look; despite his reluctance, he glanced over at the body and wished he hadn't. Blood seeped from the back of the misshapen skull. The damage the pitchfork had inflicted on the American's head was grotesque. He turned away and retched.

Russell, who hadn't said a word, looked pale.

"I think we need to report this to the police," Leonard suggested after wiping his mouth.

Russell turned to Leonard. "I, I will go to gaol, I killed him," he rasped.

Derris coughed—he was seated back in his chair refilling his glass. "I don't believe you need to worry. You defended us, and if ya hadn't done what ya did, then he would'a killed us. You saved our lives." He raised his glass in salute. "Whoever you are, bottoms up!"

"I agree, Russell. What transpired was witnessed by three people. Once the constabulary are aware of the circumstances they will understand and I can't imagine they will charge you," Leonard consoled, although he wasn't sure. When it came to the intricacies of the law, he knew nothing.

Behind them, seated and propped against the wall, the remaining thug wheezed and breathed with some difficulty. He couldn't move, having been bound by Harry with the same rope previously used on Leonard and Derris.

"I'll go down to the race course," volunteered Harry. He retrieved his jacket from a hook. "Since we won't be racing now, I need to scratch Sweet Hazel from the race and notify the jockey. I'll return with the Police soon as I can."

Leonard crouched near the injured thug and held a small bottle of tonic he'd pulled from the thug's pocket, but found no form of identification on him. "What is your name?"

The man stared resentfully back but remained silent, his breathing raspy and forced.

"Perhaps you can illuminate me as to the ingredients in the bottle?"

"I can tell ya that," exclaimed Derris from the comfort of his seat. "It's a potent cocktail of nitro-glycerine, opium, carbolic acid, and rose water."

Leonard's face crinkled at the revelation.

Russell sat on the edge of the water trough, brooding, and toyed with the revolver he took from the American.

"And they give this to racehorses?" Leonard grimaced.

"Makes 'em run fast but will kill 'em in the end. Nothin' can survive repeated doses. Is cruel and inhumane, " Derris informed him.

Leonard again looked down at the injured man. "Who is behind this?"

The man managed a sneer.

Leonard gave up and walked away to stand in front of Derris.

"Are you familiar with the Riley brothers, Joshua and Elijah?"

Derris shook his head. "I heard of the names, but no, I don't know 'em."

"Do you know or have any suspicions as to who is behind this organisation?"

"We've been trying to find out, or rather Harry has, but he ain't got nowhere."

Leonard looked thoughtful. "Do you know who killed Balthazar Gringle?"

Derris had his glass raised to his lips. He froze then slowly nodded. "T'was him," he waved his glass at the body of the American laying beneath an old blanket. "Bastard!"

"How do you know?"

"I was there at Courtenay Place." Derris took a generous sip. "Balthazar wanted no part in medicating horses, and told 'em so. He threatened to go to the authorities, and then one day, that little American chappie arrives and chokes him. I thought I'd be next and took off to warn Harry who was at the Hutt Park with Sweet Hazel."

"So, Harry is also against the, the, uh, horse medicating?"

Derris nodded. "Said t'was bloody cruel to the animals, not to mention it being unsporting."

Leonard began pacing in circles around the front of the stable. He paused and turned back to Derris. "Harry's wife, what is her involvement?"

"Oh dear, she's colder than a dead fish, that one is." He shook his head. "She's been trying to force Harry to go along with the scheme for a while. As it turned out, Sweet Hazel was a perfect candidate for that, that, stuff."

Leonard's inclined his head in puzzlement as the old man continued.

"She began threatening him. Only got worse for Harry… the bitch." Derris took another sip from his glass. "Harry wanted no part in it, or with her, and he ran away, absconded, he did."

"To Courtenay Place?"

"At first he did, was to make her think he was an inebriate. So she'd leave him and Sweet Hazel alone."

Leonard tried to make sense of the facts and resumed his nervous pacing. "Surely there were other horses they could administer the tonic to?"

Derris laughed. "You can't medicate a horse likely to win, you don't make any money that way. You gotta gives it to a horse that only has a slim chance of winning, but unlikely to. That way, once given, you wager heavily on that horse as the betting odds are much better."

Leonard paused his pacing and listened.

"By continuing to medicate, they'd already killed a couple of horses, uh, Pearly White and Jasmine, if I recall their names, and Sweet Hazel was the next in line." Derris looked into his empty glass. "Not only that, dear old Balthazar reckoned he had it all figured out and knew who was behind it, then they went and killed him. That left Harry. They wanted his horse, and to make sure he kept his mouth shut." He refilled his glass.

Leonard turned away and stared into the distance. *So, Balthazar Gringle had it all figured out. He must have told Agatha, which is how she came to know so much.* He turned back to the old man. "Did Mr Gringle inform Harry of what he learned?"

Derris belched and shook his head.

Chapter Twenty-Eight

Derris was quietly nursing his whiskey while in the distance, race fans cheered for winners or yelled in despair at losers. The quiet unexpected sound of a footstep interrupted the general race-day ambience that washed over them. Russell looked up as the tall man, free of his bonds, lunged for Derris. In his hand glinted a knife.

Russell bellowed a warning and tried to intercept the thug, but he was too far away. Surprised by the sound, Derris turned in his seat, exposing his body to the oncoming blade. The tall thug coldly thrust the lethal *stiletto* deep into his chest and in a single, fluid motion, yanked the weapon free, leapt over him, and ran around the side of the stable.

Russell charged after the fleeing man, but rounded the corner to see him disappear behind a large flax and continue running. He knew he'd never catch him. In exasperation, he turned back to aid Derris.

Leonard was already on his knees trying to stem the flow of blood. "I can't stop the bleeding!" he cried.

Together both men did their best for the elderly man, but to no avail. Blood continued to pool beneath him and in a short time he stopped breathing.

"These men are evil, Mr Hardy. Until they are apprehended, you will never be safe."

Leonard looked towards him. "We tried Russell. I tried to save him, but the wound was too severe, and the blood … the blood, it was too much."

Russell walked into the stable and retrieved the rope that had bound the tall man. He held it up. "Severed. He had a hidden knife."

"Didn't Harry do a search before tying him?"

"He wouldn't think of looking in his boot," Russell said and tossed the rope aside. "That's where these type of men hide such weapons. It isn't Harry's fault. I should have checked."

With utmost care, they moved Derris and placed him beside the body of the American, and again, re-covered both bodies with the old saddle blanket.

Leonard stood over both dead men feeling helpless. "What can I do, Russell?" His body shook.

The large man stepped over to stand beside him. "With all the information you know about these people … they will come for you."

Leonard looked up at Russell's face. "And you know about as much as I do — you are in equal danger."

"Story of my bloody life, Mr Hardy," he replied in his hoarse raspy voice.

Harry was on his knees with head bowed in silent prayer before the cold lifeless body of his friend. A few feet away, a seasoned veteran policeman, Sergeant Michael Bromley, watched dispassionately. His junior associate, Constable Martin Moreland, stood a step farther back and tried to avoid looking at the exposed faces of two dead men. Sergeant Bromley's moustache twitched, indicating his unspoken irritation. Today was to have been an easy day in the sun watching horse racing. He'd even wagered a small amount on a sure winner. But now, procedure took precedence and what was to have been a pleasant day now amounted to a long night of paperwork and unanswered questions.

Sergeant Bromley cleared his throat. A signal that for now, police business was the priority, grieving could come later. Harry eased himself upright and turned to Leonard. "I… I'm sorry, I never saw the knife, and now Derris, poor Derris, is dead."

"You weren't to know," Leonard reassured him.

"Alright then, gentlemen," said the sergeant. He held a notepad and pencil. "Let's start at the beginning shall we."

"Sir?" Leonard interrupted.

The sergeant raised his bushy eyebrows and looked at Leonard.

"Uh, I believe that what happened here today is quite relevant to an ongoing investigation, um, headed by Inspector Gibbard."

If, by all initial appearances, the sergeant's eyebrows were elevated to their maximum limit, they unbelievably moved even higher. "Is that so?" Sergeant Bromley was no fool. If Inspector Gibbard were here and brought his own staff, then his workload could be considerably reduced. Like magic, the eyebrows lowered to their normal position and the sergeant raised a hand to smooth his prodigious whiskers. "Why don't you tell me about this *investigation* of Inspector Gibbard's eh, mister?"

"Uh, Hardy, Leonard Hardy."

The sergeant diligently recorded the details.

Leonard explained, as briefly as he could, about the other deaths but deliberately omitted telling him about the Riley brothers.

Sergeant Bromley tapped his pencil repeatedly on his notepad as he considered his options. Coming to a decision, he scribbled a few lines on a blank page, tore it from the book and inhaled deeply. He turned to his junior, "Martin, make haste. Return to the depot and get word to Inspector Gibbard. Inform him that there have been two deaths that *may* be linked to his investigation, and I would enjoy the pleasure of his seniority and expertise, forthwith. I've listed the pertinent details on this." He handed the folded note to the constable. "Quickly now."

"Yes, sir." Constable Moreland picked up his bicycle and began wheeling it towards Clyde Street at the bottom of the winding path.

Sergeant Bromley turned his attention towards Russell, who was sitting quietly on the grass with his head on his knees. "You are familiar to me."

Russell raised his head.

"Haining Street?"

"Frederick Street. I used to be employed by the Victoria Hotel," Russell replied morosely.

"Ahh, yes. Been in a spot of bother yourself, haven't you?"

Russell shrugged. "Part of the job. But I don't go causing trouble, and if I did, then you'd a known where I worked."

Sergeant Bromley silently conceded Russell had a point. In the distance, race fans cheered another victory, and the sergeant wondered if he'd just won a bob or two on a race. "Now, then, let me get started and record some details, we have a long wait. Mr Hardy, your address, employer, and what did you witness?"

If Inspector Gibbard was peeved at being called out on a late Saturday morning to attend to the scene of a multiple killing, he didn't show it. His horse, lathered in sweat, was being attended to by Constable Tim Yates. Due to the familiarity of the case, Tim was called upon to accompany the inspector along with Senior Sergeant Hale and another constable. Harry provided feed and water for all the horses.

Out of earshot from Leonard and Russell, Inspector Gibbard and Senior Sergeant Hale conferred with Sergeant Bromley and were briefed on the details surrounding the deaths of both men. Leonard watched the inspector nod his head a few times, and saw him ask numerous questions.

"Leo, were you harmed?" whispered Tim.

"Not physically, but I dare say, seeing two men die doesn't sit well," he replied while keeping an eye on the inspector. He knew he'd receive a tongue-lashing from him at best.

Tim continued to rub down the inspector's horse. Both of them had ridden hard to arrive as quickly as possible. "You were indeed fortunate to have that brute accompany you today."

"He's saved my life more than once — he is a good man. I am forever grateful to him and certainly in his debt." He looked at Russell who still sat on the grass, then turned back to Tim. "Any word from Mary?"

"Mr Hardy!" exclaimed Inspector Gibbard. "A moment of your time?"

Leonard rolled his eyes, "Here we go." He walked over towards the inspector and waited for the admonishment that was sure to come. The sergeant and Senior Sergeant Hale stood at Gibbard's side with his hands clasped behind his back.

"Inspector?" Leonard asked and steeled himself for what was sure to come.

"By what flawed supposition prompted you to come to the Island Bay races when you are totally aware of the danger you are in?" His expression was cold and unfeeling.

Leonard, who could see the inspector's simmering anger, felt contrite and decided to be open and honest. He explained his reasoning and when finished, waited for the expected tirade. Inspector Gibbard didn't disappoint, chastising him thoroughly for his foolishness and interference. Leonard knew the inspector was correct so wisely remained silent. In hindsight, men had died needlessly and as the inspector pointed out, they'd still be alive if he and Russell had stayed home. After receiving his admonishments, he listened attentively as the inspector recounted the details as reported to him by Sergeant Bromley.

"Is this information correct and do you have anything further to add?" The inspector's voice was cold and unfeeling.

"Yes, sir. It is correct and no, at this time I have nothing more to add, although…"

"One thing at a time, Mr Hardy," interrupted the inspector. "Do you believe that Russell Baylor could have avoided killing the American?"

Leonard shook his head. "No, it was unavoidable."

"Very well. Thank you, I will speak with you again. Remain here until Senior Sergeant Hale has released you."

Leonard nodded.

"Mr Baylor?"

Russell looked up.

"A word?"

Inspector Gibbard spoke individually to Russell and Harry, and then spoke to the three of them as a group. "I see no reason, at this time, to charge anyone as no crime was committed by any of you. I am satisfied that the death of the unknown American was a simple matter of self-defence. The killer who fled … let's just say, that's a different story and I'd like to have a quiet chat with him." He turned to Senior Sergeant Hale. "Please continue with the investigation here, and Sergeant Bromley can resume his normal duties once the coroner's wagon has departed with the deceased. Mr Hardy, if I can impose on your time …?"

Inspector Gibbard began to walk away and Senior Sergeant Hale and Leonard followed.

"That will be all, Senior Sergeant," said the inspector.

"Very well, sir," replied Hale, looking miffed.

They walked from the stable towards one of the cottages. When satisfied they could talk privately, the inspector stopped and faced him. "Now then, I believe you have more information?"

Leonard sensed the inspector's disposition had mellowed somewhat. "We've uncovered a horse … er, and for want of a better description, a horse medicating scheme."

The inspector waved away a fly and scratched at his face.

"I know what caused the death of Milton Camden and Agatha Gringle." He reached into his pocket and pulled the bottle containing the narcotics he obtained from the tall man who escaped. He handed it to the inspector. "I believe it's another bottle of the same substance I handed to you at the Mount Cook Depot. However, I now know what it is. No doubt the coroner will confirm that this vile liquid is comprised of nitro-glycerine, opium, carbolic acid, and rose water. Those men feed this potion to race horses. It makes them perform much better and assures them of a race victory."

"And you're still convinced this same substance was administered to Miss Gringle and Mr Camden?"

Leonard nodded, "I am."

Inspector Gibbard held the bottle up into the sunlight. "Looks harmless, eh?"

"That's how they were intending to kill me at home. Give me a dose equivalent to what they administer to a horse." Leonard scowled.

"What of Elijah and Joshua Riley? Any facts or evidence to associate them with this scheme?"

Again, Leonard shook his head. "No, not yet."

Inspector Gibbard turned and stared out across the race course in the distance. "I've met with some resistance about pursuing an investigation into the activities of the Riley brothers. Until such time I have facts and irrefutable evidence linking them to any form of crime, my hands are tied, Mr Hardy, there is nothing I can do. Earnestly, I advise you on a personal level to avoid these men, and do not provoke them further or you, too, will be lying on the coroner's table. Professionally, I can't tell you to find evidence because that is the role of the police. However, if you do obtain anything that I can use, please do not hesitate to notify me immediately." He turned and glared at Leonard.

"I will, inspector. I want to see these men pay the penalty for their crimes, not to mention for what they've done to destroy my life."

"The big man, Russell Baylor, can you trust him?"

Leonard replied quickly. "With my life!"

"Good, keep him close." The inspector began to walk back to the stable. "Now I must return home, or Mrs Gibbard will have me drawn and quartered for arriving home late when we are entertaining guests this evening."

Chapter Twenty-Nine

Both Leonard and Russell tried to sleep during the journey back to Wellington. The rough road made it difficult, but after the exhausting and horrific events of the day, they each closed their eyes and managed to doze, although only for short stretches of time.

It was during the walk back up Marjoribanks Street towards Leonard's home that they again began to talk about what happened.

"We are still no closer to discovering who is behind this scheme," Leonard declared in frustration. "We know a little, but cannot confirm who the principals are."

They passed the Chinese vendors selling produce from their cart and acknowledged them with a wave and a greeting and continued up the steep street.

"Those Riley brothers seem the obvious choice," volunteered Russell.

"And yet Inspector Gibbard is prohibited from investigating them until there is conclusive evidence linking them."

Leonard stopped. "But they must be bringing that potion into the country somehow. New Zealand doesn't grow opium in sufficient quantities and it would take too long to cultivate, so it is imported … but on which ship?"

Russell shrugged.

Leonard lit the fire and paced his sitting room while Russell sat quietly watching. Something bothered him but he couldn't identify what it was. He paused at the writing bureau and stared at the clutter. He recalled the handwritten notes inside Leon Barrow's pocket-book and immediately searched for the note paper where he copied the names he found. He retrieved the note and re-read it. At the time, one name stood out, but he recalled how when he first saw it, it seemed unimportant. *Tyne, Lewis & Chatswood*, and beneath was written *Rhodes* and *Newcastle*. He stared at the names. "Of course! This is it!"

Russell raised his head.

"Tyne, Lewis and Chatswood are shipping agents."

He turned to Russell and waved the paper at him. "This is a clue. Why would Leon Barrow have a note in his pocketbook with the name of a shipping agent unless something was being shipped? And what do we know is being shipped?"

"Household chattels?" he shrugged.

"No, chemicals and potions. Ingredients to make the tonic for the horses! But what ship?"

"And how many ships arrive in Wellington?" Russell added, "More than I can count. There have to be about twenty ships in the harbour at present. And then, where do they place them?"

"Moor."

"Eh?" Russell queried.

"Moor or berth, you don't place a ship."

"Well, there are enough wharves to moor many ships in Wellington … be like looking for a needle in a haystack," Russell added.

Leonard stepped back to the lamp and again held the scrap of paper to the light. "Wharves! I think you may have solved the conundrum, Russell. Look, the paper lists the shipping agent. Then there are two other words, *Rhodes* and *Newcastle*. *Rhodes* is the name of a wharf! Therefore, I can only assume that *Newcastle* is the name of the ship because it isn't the name of a wharf…"

"And what are we gonna do with that information?" Russell asked.

"Good question, and one that is worth pondering," Leonard said as he slumped into his chair, the silence marked by the crackling fire.

"Household chattels. Furniture!" Leonard exclaimed.

Russell sat up with a start.

"I have an idea," said Leonard with a big grin. "Russell, we're going into the furniture business."

A persistent drizzle settled over Wellington and its busy residents dressed appropriately to ward off the moisture. However, it needed more than inclement weather to prevent Wellingtonians from going about their daily duties.

"You do look rather dapper, quite the gentleman," remarked Russell as they both stepped from a Hansom cab onto Lambton Quay.

Leonard wore a formfitting Chesterfield overcoat with full shoulders, a colourful English square silk tie over a tailored white shirt and matching collar and cuffs. To compliment the ensemble he wore a derby hat, and felt very conspicuous in his unusually stylish attire. "Is paramount that I am perceived to be a gentleman with means," he added as he looked at the building which housed the premises of Tyne, Lewis & Chatswood, Shipping Agents. "I suggest you watch from across the road. I shouldn't be long, however if you don't see me in thirty minutes, come for me." Leonard reached for his pocket watch, and checked the time. "Wish me luck."

Feeling less assured than he did when he conceived the brazen idea, he walked up the steps and entered the building.

A receptionist looked up. "Good morning, sir. How may I assist you?"

"Good morning, I wish to speak to one of the principals regarding shipping," Leonard replied, trying to sound confident.

"Do you have an appointment?" she asked.

"I do not." He smiled graciously. "However I do expect that a potential new customer will be seen promptly."

"May I ask your name, sir?"

Leonard smiled. "Miles Harrington."

"And the nature of your visit, Mr Harrington?"

"Shipping furniture."

"Of course, Mr Harrington. Please be seated and I shall enquire when you can be attended to."

Leonard felt a trickle of sweat around his neck. He smiled and nodded, then turned towards two comfortable-looking chairs and walked towards them. He didn't sit, but instead looked out the window. He didn't have to wait long.

"Mr Harrington?" came a voice, the American accent unmistakable.

Leonard turned and saw a diminutive man with oil-slicked hair and large spectacles balanced precariously on the end of his nose. His head was tilted slightly forward as he peered over the top of the heavy rims in curiosity. "Good morning."

"I apologise, sir, we have no record of your appointment. But I have time to speak with you."

"My visit is unannounced, and I wish only to make enquiries, Mr …?"

"Abner Tyne, at your service, Mr Harrington. Please, this way."

He extended his arm, indicating Leonard should follow.

Leonard's heart raced furiously as he followed Abner Tyne to a large, well-adorned office. Framed pictures of ships graced the dark, wood-panelled walls; two replica model ships protected in glass cases sat on a large credenza; and behind the expansive desk on a book shelf sat some framed pictures of horses. Leonard's mouth felt dry.

Separated by a low mahogany coffee table, two green leather armchairs sat in front of the desk, and Mr Tyne indicated for Leonard to sit. Rather than sit behind his desk, Mr Tyne sat in the other armchair after Leonard was seated.

Leonard crossed his legs and brushed some imaginary lint from his trousers.

"I'm familiar with many of Wellington's gentlemen, and yet I do not recognise you. How can I be of assistance to you today, Mr Harrington."

Leonard forced himself to make eye contact with the shipping agent and held his gaze. "I am a recent arrival to Wellington and have yet to socialise or experience the entertainment and recreational amenities Wellington has to offer."

"Then I shall look forward to seeing you out and about. Now, then, what can Tyne, Lewis & Chatswood do for you?"

Leonard leaned back in his chair. "I am in the business of furniture, Mr Tyne. I have one or two small factories in England producing quality fitments and furnishings and intend to have them available to purchase in New Zealand. It is my wish to ensure that a suitable shipping company represents my interests and ensures safe, landed delivery at a reasonable cost. Is Tyne, Lewis & Chatswood worthy of my trade, Mr Tyne?" Inwardly Leonard winced and hoped he wasn't laying it on a bit thick.

Abner Tyne took the bait. He leaned forward. "Is it too forward of me to ask the quantity, sir?"

"Mr Tyne, I am trying to ascertain your company's suitability. If I choose you to represent my shipping interests, then, at that time, I will provide you with the required details. But for now, let me say, uh, substantial."

"Of course, sir," smiled Mr Tyne.

"Do you represent other furniture makers?"

"No, we do not, but under contract we have shipped furniture numerous times."

Leonard uncrossed his legs. "And your business clients, are they reputable, upstanding companies?"

"Of course, Mr Harrington," replied Abner Tyne without pause.

"The value of my cargo would be significant, and it is foremost that I review your past business dealings before I make any commitment. Do you understand Mr Tyne?"

"Indeed, and by all means, this is standard practice, sir. I can provide you with suitable testimonials and a customer registry if you require."

Leonard nodded. "That would be satisfactory — I accept your offer," Leonard replied.

"Give me one moment. Please excuse me." Abner Tyne stood and left the office.

Leonard exhaled. He was tense and his heart still beat furiously.

It wasn't long before Mr Tyne returned carrying a large envelope. Leonard stood.

"Mr Harrington, all the information you require is contained here. If you have any questions, I am always available, and please, feel free to schedule an appointment anytime. I look forward with confidence that we can agree on acceptable terms." He extended his hand with the envelope.

"Thank you for seeing me unannounced, Mr Tyne. We will speak again." Leonard took the proffered documents.

"You have an interest in horses, Mr Tyne?" Leonard pointed to the pictures.

He saw a flicker of annoyance from the shipping agent.

"We, er, I enjoy the finer points of all equestrian sports, Mr Harrington." He cleared his throat. "This way."

Mr Tyne escorted Leonard out of the office, past the receptionist and to the door.

"Thank you Mr Tyne, I shall be in touch. Good day."

It was still drizzling outside when Leonard approached Russell. Without pause he walked past him and said, "Follow me." Once around the corner and out of sight from the shipping offices, he stopped and waited for him to catch up. "Someone may have been watching. I have no trust in that objectionable man at all." Leonard held up the folder. "But I do have this," he grinned.

Chapter Thirty

"You went to a lot of bloody trouble to obtain that," Russell growled, when they arrived back at Leonard's home.

Leonard sat at his writing bureau with Russell seated beside him on a kitchen chair. The envelope sat before them. "Then let's hope it was worth it."

He extracted the documents, and as expected, there were a couple of sales and advertising brochures that had no value. Leonard moved them aside and spotted the testimonials —finely crafted and obviously professionally written commendations. Again, nothing important. Finally, the last pages were a list of valued customers. Leonard grinned, this was what he wanted. He ran his finger slowly down the column of businesses that were clients of Tyne, Lewis & Chatswood, Shipping Agents. His finger stopped. There it was, the New York Contributionship Company. *They were a customer.* In and by itself, not incriminating, but, as Leonard explained, it completed another piece of the puzzle.

"What we have confirmed, is that Elijah and Joshua Riley have business interests with a shipping company," said Leonard.

"And to what means?" Russell shrugged. "Don't help us a great deal, or does it?"

"Not sure yet." Leonard again ran his finger down the list of customers. "If the Rileys are importing this tonic, they are using Tyne, Lewis & Chatswood—"

"And what do they do with it once it gets here?" Russell asked.

"They need to transport it to a safe location and store it."

"Are you intending to go to every—"

"Wait," interrupted Leonard. "We know the shipping company, the name of the ship, and we know the ship berthed at *Rhodes* wharf. So all we need to do is find out who moved the tonic and where."

"How the hell are ya gonna do that?" Russell rasped.

Leonard turned to him and smiled. "Quite simply. We go to the Harbour Master. From the ship's manifest, his office should be able to provide a date and tell us who the carrier was and to where the shipment was delivered. I can only hope they agree to provide it." Leonard looked at his watch. "We can go now, is still early and they've all had lunch — all we will have to do is wait."

"Mr Hardy, we're frightfully busy today, what is your need?" stated Andrej Janjić, one of the Harbour Master's clerks who regularly attended to Leonard. He gave Russell a long second look.

No welcoming pleasantries or, how are you today Mr Hardy? It was business as usual at the chaotic Harbour Master's office. Resigned to a long wait, Leonard placed a piece of paper on the counter that detailed all the facts the Harbour Master's office would need to find out where the shipment was sent to.

"One moment," replied Andrej, as he disappeared to solve a dispute between another clerk and a shipping agent. Some shouting ensued and finally the shipping agent stormed from the Harbour Master's office, slamming the door behind him.

"Is it always like this?" Russell asked after the shipping agent rushed from the office.

"No, most frequently it's worse. Today seems like a more quiet day."

Russell grunted.

The clerk returned and read the note. "This is a little unusual, Mr Hardy. It's going to take me a while, you will have to wait." Again, he nervously shifted his gaze to Russell.

"It *is* urgent, Mr Janjić," Leonard implored. He turned to Russell. "At this place, I've learned to be patient."

The clerk looked uncertain. "Let me see."

There was a bench seat along the far wall and they sat alongside others who were destined to spend their afternoon staring at the dreary four walls of the office.

"Uh, the convenience …?" Russell asked.

Leonard gave him directions and continued to read a newspaper while Russell excused himself and disappeared briefly.

The clerk returned about thirty minutes later . "Mr Hardy, I have the information you need." He waved a piece of paper at Leonard, placed it on the counter and went to assist another customer.

Once outside Leonard read the document.

Office of the Harbour Master
09:00 hours
Vessel—Newcastle. Berth—Rhodes, north. Agent—Tyne, Lewis & Chatswood.
August 28th, total 6 (six) crate shipment oriental spices signed for by T. Pickett, on behalf of Thorndon Haulage.

Delivery address—14 Abel Smith Street, Te Aro.

Leonard slapped the paper with his hand. "There, now we know where it is."

"Where what is, I don't see anything that says it's that tonic. It says spices," said Russell. "Could be soap for all we know."

"It can't be anything else but opium, but we do need to confirm. Then, dear boy, we can go to Inspector Gibbard and he can begin to investigate the Riley brothers."

They began to walk back towards Marjoribanks Street and Leonard's home.

"But we do need to find a link between the Rileys and that shipment," Leonard added as an afterthought. "Perhaps Uncle Jun can help, he has connections. Shall we detour to Frederick Street?"

Russell was quiet as he walked at Leonard's side. After a short while he edged a little closer. "I think someone is following us. Don't turn around or you'll alert 'em."

Leonard resisted the urge to look over his shoulder and walked on for a few steps. "Do you know who?"

"Two men I've never seen before."

"What should we do?" Leonard asked as the first pangs of anxiety stabbed at his stomach.

"We continue to Jun's in Frederick Street, where I will have a brief discussion with the gentlemen," Russell replied. "When I tell you, scarper, make your way to Jun's shop."

"For fear of being assaulted, I will not hesitate," Leonard said, feeling apprehensive.

Ahead was the intersection of Taranaki and Frederick Streets. When they turned left at the corner, they would be out of sight from the men following for a brief time.

They turned the corner and Russell told him to make haste. Needing no urging, Leonard took off as quickly as he could. He looked back over his shoulder and saw Russell waiting.

Suddenly two men appeared. Immediately, he saw Russell set upon them, catching them both unaware. Leonard slowed to watch as one man fell to the ground, then the other. The big man wasted no time in dealing with them. Thankfully no other pedestrians were nearby to witness the assault and robbery. The last thing he saw before arriving breathlessly at Uncle Jun's shop was Russell bending over each man going through their pockets.

"Leo, what you do?" stated Uncle Jun as Leonard ran into his shop. He was astute enough to recognize Leonard was running from something. "Quick, you go in back." He pointed to the curtain separating the shop from his private residence.

Leonard sat at the table in the private area at the rear of the shop and waited for Russell and Uncle Jun while he caught his breath. It didn't take long.

The curtain was yanked open, and Leonard looked up with a start as Russell, with Uncle Jun following behind, entered the kitchen.

"Leo, what happen?"

"We were being followed by two men. Thankfully, he took care of them," Leonard pointed to Russell.

Uncle Jun turned to Russell. "What you do to men?"

"Uh, we had a brief talk and I borrowed their pocketbooks." He placed them both on the table.

Leonard picked them up to look for identification.

"Where are bad men now?" asked Uncle Jun, looking concerned.

"Uh, I expect they are feeling remorseful and nursing their aching heads, possibly due to the effects of alcohol," Russell grinned.

"You frighten me, Leo," admonished the aging Chinaman. "Trouble follow you."

Leonard explained what happened and the reason for their visit, as Uncle Jun put water on the stove to make tea.

"Where is warehouse?" he asked.

"On Abel Smith Street, number fourteen. We need to look in there and see if they are storing those drugs."

"We no like other men bring drug here. Many Tong[10] bring opium to New Zealand and difficult to control. Once other men do this, price and quality change. Not good, bad for people and create many problem." He poured tea into three cups. "I must tell *Tong* of this, they will not be happy. He lifted his cap and scratched. "I come back, drink tea." With that, Uncle Jun departed through the curtain and was gone, only to return minutes later.

Leonard and Russell could only watch in puzzlement.

"Important man will come here to speak to you, Leo. You tell him about opium, and where." His head bobbed up and down. "Now, tell me what you learn about these bad men and horse, yes?"

Leonard explained what had happened at Island Bay during the races. Uncle Jun was distressed.

"This gang, not good, much crime." He shook his head again. "You in big trouble Leo," Uncle Jun waved a bony finger at him. "Gang not good, very bad."

"It wasn't my doing; they came after me," Leonard appealed. "They ruined my life."

Uncle Jun leaned forward. "When man come here, you must tell him everything. No hold back, tell him all, you un-erstan Leo?"

Leonard was frustrated. He didn't have any real facts that could incriminate anyone. While he was making progress, they were no closer to discovering who these men were and who sent them. Uncle Jun refilled their cups and they sat and talked until someone entered the shop. Uncle Jun rose from his chair and hurried to attend to the customer.

10 Tong – Secretive Chinese organization often associated with criminal activities.

271

Moments later the curtain parted and Uncle Jun returned along with an elderly Oriental. Like Uncle Jun, he was dressed similarly in loose straight-cut pants and jacket with a traditional peasant *jin* cap on his head.

They spoke in Chinese as Leonard and Russell waited. Finally, Uncle Jun turned. "Leo, Russell, this Wang Yong."

Leonard and Russell both stood as Wang Yong bowed his head respectfully.

"A pleasure to make your acquaintance, sir," Leonard said.

Wang Yong nodded and smiled.

"Good afternoon, sir," said Russell politely.

Wang Yong gave Russell a long hard look then spoke to Uncle Jun in Chinese.

"He say, you a monster," Uncle Jun laughed. "A big man, and dangerous. He know of you, and say you are not bad and are kind honourable person."

Russell looked embarrassed. "Thank you," he replied hoarsely.

Once seated, Uncle Jun respectfully turned to Wang Yong. "Please, Leo will tell you."

Wang Yong looked at Leonard. "It is indeed a pleasure to make your acquaintance, Mr Hardy. Chen Jun has told me much about you and the peril you presently find yourself in."

Leonard was surprised. Wang Yong spoke with eloquence and articulation. English educated he assumed, and with no trace of a Chinese accent.

"It is with some concern that I learn that men are possibly manip-ulating the outcome of horse racing by artificial means. The Chinese community is alarmed as this has a bearing on some of our recre-ational passions. It unfairly tips the balance. Forgive my inquisitive nature, perhaps I can impose on you to share with me what you have learned?"

Leonard couldn't help but like the enigmatic and understated elderly gentleman. He nodded, and began to recount everything that happened to him, and what he'd come to learn. Wang Yong, Uncle Jun and Russell sat attentively.

"I commend you, Mr Hardy. Both you and Mr Baylor are resourceful and have learned much, but not everything. I am aware of many of the things you have told me, but only now can I put it all into context and perspective. In the grand scheme of things, what these men are endeavouring to accomplish has a negative impact on our community and in light of political connections and influence, you are correct, the authorities are limited in their efforts to curtail the activities of these ambitious, unscrupulous men. We call it organised crime, Mr Hardy."

Please, my friends call me Leonard, or Leo," he responded. "As I suggested, I cannot connect Elijah and Joshua Riley to any impropriety. We need to confirm that the components used to create the tonic are being stored at the warehouse on Abel Smith Street. If I am correct, that could be sufficient for the police to take action." Leonard shrugged, as though he believed it was just a formality for the Police to become involved.

Wang Yong spoke briefly to Uncle Jun in Chinese before turning back to Leonard.

"Leonard…" Wang Yong inclined his head in acknowledgement at his use of the Christian name, "Chen Jun has interests in keeping you safe. I understand this and concur, especially as people have already died. We do not wish to see you come to harm, even though you have the persuasive influence of Mr Baylor at your side." Wang Yong smiled at Russell. "Allow me to arrange for that warehouse to be investigated, and if we locate the chemicals, as you believe, then you can inform the police. Is this agreeable?"

Leonard leaned back in his chair. He knew he had no option but to agree. He nodded. At least he could minimise his own risk. "I think that is acceptable, thank you."

Wang Yong smiled. "Leonard, where do you live? On Mount Victoria?"

"Yes, Marjoribanks Street."

"Is it safe for you to return home?"

"I have people watch him, from produce cart, and on street," Uncle Jun explained.

"That didn't prevent Flanagan and the American from trying to kill me," Leonard responded.

Uncle Jun looked up at Leonard. "Those men, no good, lazy. Now better men, not lazy, they watch."

"I wonder if that is adequate?" Wang Yong scratched at the sparse, wispy hairs on his chin. "I urge you to heed caution, Leonard. If this gang is aware of your relentless pursuits and private investigation, then I'd be most wary. They will, and with vigour, take steps to ensure you cannot impede or affect their interests. Mr Baylor is but one formidable man, but he cannot protect you from many. We have an old saying, Leonard, 'an overturned cart ahead warns the one behind.' These men, this gang, they have killed before and will do so again."

Leonard looked down at his feet as he considered Wang Yong's advice. He looked up and met his eyes. "You are astute and wise, thank you for your guidance. We will return home early this evening and collect some clothes and find a hotel."

Uncle Jun extended an arm and affectionately patted Leonard on his back. "You silly boy, Leo."

Wang Yong smiled. "I will send word to Chen Jun on what we learn from this warehouse. Be here tomorrow evening." He turned to Uncle Jun, and again they conversed in Chinese.

Uncle Jun and Wang Yong rose from their chairs, and, Leonard and Russell respectfully followed suit .

"I will look forward to seeing you both again," said Wang Yong after bowing his head. He followed Uncle Jun from the private area to the front of the shop. Leonard and Russell were a step behind. Outside on Frederick Street there was a bustling crowd, comprised most of distinctly Chinese. Uncle Jun watched as Wang Yong was swallowed by the throng and seemed to disappear as the horde dissipated. Suddenly it was quiet again.

"All those Chinese—" said Russell.

"They outside to protect Wang Yong," stated Uncle Jun. "He is powerful man, many would see him dead. Come, we have tea."

Chapter Thirty-One

"We will go home, have dinner, gather some clothes and then find a hotel to stay in," Leonard said as they walked towards Marjoribanks Street. "I think Wang Yong speaks with considered reason. The more desperate these men are to protect their horse medication scheme, the greater the lengths they will go to prevent anyone from interfering. As Wang Yong said, 'We know they've already killed, and they won't hesitate to do so again.'"

Russell nodded and turned up the collar of his jacket. The weather was changing and becoming colder.

Approaching the intersection of Marjoribanks Street, they were about to cross the road when a man walked towards them. As he approached, he acknowledged Leonard with a polite head nod and, in recognition, stared briefly at Russell.

"Mr Hardy?"

Leonard turned in surprise. The man had stopped.

"Mr Hardy?" repeated Andrej Janjić, the clerk from the Harbour Master's office.

"Good evening, Mr Janjić," Leonard replied curiously, "I didn't recognise you."

The clerk looked nervous as Russell loomed over him.

"Do you recall, Mr Janjić is with the Harbour Master's office," Leonard told Russell.

"I, I, uh, wonder if I could have a brief word?" asked the clerk. "Uh, privately."

"Mr Baylor is a trusted friend," Leonard replied.

The Harbour Master's clerk looked uncomfortable.

Russell coughed. "Uh, let me …"

Leonard sighed. As his home was just up the street, he saw no harm in letting Russell go ahead — he fished in his pocket for the door key. He leaned towards Russell and whispered, "Worry not, our friends are watching." Leonard indicated towards the Chinese produce cart across the road. Two of Uncle Jun's men were keenly observing them.

Russell's head swivelled in all directions looking for threat or danger. Satisfied they were safe, he nodded. "Very well, I will see you back at the house." He took the proffered key and crossed the street.

After Russell walked off, Leonard looked for a place they could talk without blocking the footpath and at the same time seek shelter from the frigid wind. A nearby doorway to a barrister's office offered some privacy. He stepped to the entrance and Mr Janjić followed.

Leonard turned back to face the Harbour Master's clerk. At his office, the clerk was always so self-assured and confident, away from his dominion and here on the street he seemed servile. "I apologise for my friend, he can appear a little intimidating." He smiled. "How can I be of assistance, Mr Janjić?"

Mr Janjić cleared his throat. "You've been coming to our office for some time, and are patient and kind. I know the wait is infuriating for you, but we are limited with staff … we do what we can."

Leonard acknowledged the apology with a nod and wondered where this conversation was leading.

"Uh, perhaps I am out of order, and this is not my affair, but I feel you should be made aware …"

Leonard's eyebrows furrowed. "Aware?"

"After you departed earlier today, two men, both unknown to me came to the bureau enquiring after you. They demanded to know what you wanted from us."

Despite his warm coat and hat, Leonard felt a chill. "Do you know who they represented, er, were they police?"

Andrej Janjić shook his head. "No, I don't believe so."

Leonard could see the poor clerk was discomfited.

"It is not our policy to divulge our customers affairs to others, but these men suggested if I didn't assist them, they would cause— uh, they threatened me, Mr Hardy," Andrej exclaimed. "When I saw you here, walking, I thought it only fair to tell you."

Leonard felt immediate concern, perhaps he'd underestimated these people. He wondered if they were the same two men who had earlier followed them towards Uncle Jun's shop. He looked around for any suspicious characters and saw only the two Chinamen across the road. Other people passing them by showed no interest.

"Mr Hardy?"

This new revelation only confirmed that he and Russell needed to find an alternative and safe place to spend the next few nights. Standing exposed here on the street certainly wasn't prudent — he needed to go home quickly. He regretted sending Russell ahead. Leonard collected himself and focused his attention back on the clerk. "Thank you very much for sharing with me, Mr Janjić. I am most grateful. Uh, had you seen these men previously?"

Andrej shook his head. "Are you in trouble? Do you require the police?" the clerk looked perturbed.

"Perhaps when this is over, I can explain to you," Leonard added. "But I must return home at once. Please forgive me for rushing off."

"Be careful Mr Hardy," said the clerk. He remained watching as Leonard crossed the road and began to walk towards home.

It wasn't a fancy house like some other grand colonial estates perched on Mount Victoria. Leonard's cottage had been built in England about forty-five years earlier, in the mid 1840s, then transported to New Zealand by ship and assembled on site. Leonard presumed the cottage had been assembled on a Saturday when workmen were thinking about Sunday rest and not on the finer points of precise craftsmanship, as evidenced by continuous water leaks and constant draughts. Despite its dubious construction, previous owners had taken good care of the cottage and kept it well-maintained.

A narrow veranda spanned the south side, facing the street, and the front door was centred perfectly in the middle, bracketed by large sash windows that Leonard always had difficulty opening. Inside, a hallway separated the living room on the right from the main bedroom on the left. The kitchen and a second bedroom were in the rear.

Leonard and Mae had purchased the cottage about two-and-a-half years earlier where they had been very happy. She had tended lovingly to the garden, and after her death he had continued to maintain her precious shrubs, herbs and vegetables to the best of his limited ability. In his opinion the house was still the finest on the steep street. It was his last link to Mae.

Leonard greeted the two Chinamen with a friendly wave as he passed by the produce cart, and began to climb Marjoribanks Street with some urgency. He'd almost reached his front gate when the gloom of early evening was disrupted by a sudden bright flash. A jet of orange flame shot skywards from his chimney. In incredulity, he watched as the windows turned instantly orange and lit up the street before the walls blew out and he was enveloped in a hail of debris, glass shards and timber. A millisecond after the flames erupted from his chimney, it exploded outwards. Bricks spun wildly through the air like errant missiles, smashing through windows and damaging roofs of neighbouring houses. Leonard never registered the full sound of the thunderous explosion and destruction as he lay bloody and unconscious on the footpath almost within reach of his gate.

In disbelief, people began to run from their homes to stand on the street. Fearful their own homes would soon catch fire, some screamed and ran in panic. Those who lived farther away and whose homes were in no immediate danger gathered to stand in the street gawking in astonishment as flames hungrily engulfed what remained of Leonard's house and began to lick above rooftops. Within moments the distant, shrill peal of police whistles repeatedly cut through the night, signalling an emergency as local residents, now galvanised, dutifully began a bucket brigade to extinguish the multiple fires that were springing up. Seeing a body lying prone on the footpath, a brave neighbour dragged Leonard to safety just as a wall came crashing down, unleashing a curtain of sparks and embers that descended over them both.

Thankfully the damage was mostly localised. While neighbouring homes suffered from mainly broken windows and a few small fires, they were quickly attended to and promptly extinguished, while Leonard's home was left to burn—its ruin complete. The fire brigade finally arrived long after the last wall collapsed, and in collaboration with the police, began an official investigation to ascertain the cause of the fire and devastation. However, the full extent of the damage and destruction wouldn't be evident until morning when they could comb through the wreckage.

Chapter Thirty-Two

"Mr Hardy! Mr Hardy, can you hear me?"

Leonard stirred and immediately felt pain. It hurt everywhere and he groaned.

"Mr Hardy, Leonard?" appealed the voice.

His head hurt. Slowly raising a hand to his face, he felt bandages and grunted in pain.

Russell? "Russell!" he croaked. His eyes opened and he tried to sit up, but a hand on his chest prevented him from moving. "Russell … Baylor, he—he was in my home. Is he hurt?" His mouth was dry.

"Drink this." A nurse held a glass to his lips and he sipped the cool liquid. Feeling immediate relief, he focused his attention on the room and his surroundings. He saw the nurse who was attending to him, and nearby stood Inspector Gibbard and Tim. Their faces both conveyed looks of concern and pity.

"Russell? Where is he?" he asked as he quickly surveyed the hospital ward he was in.

Inspector Gibbard leaned forward and spoke privately to the nurse. She nodded and moved reluctantly aside as the inspector stepped closer to the bed. "Mr Hardy, unfortunately, Russell Baylor … uh, he did not survive. I'm sorry."

Leonard felt his eyes well with tears. "I tried, I tried to hurry home …"

The nurse stepped in and handed him a handkerchief.

"What happened Inspector? I recall very little."

Inspector Gibbard sighed heavily. "A preliminary investigation leads us to believe that your house exploded. The source of the explosion originated from the fireplace. We know nothing more at this time."

Leonard closed his eyes. He heard someone step closer.

"Leo, you were indeed fortunate and are lucky to be alive," said Tim. "You were struck by debris and found on the street, not far from your gate."

"And spared serious injury, so it seems," added Inspector Gibbard.

Leonard opened his eyes. "But not Russell, he wasn't spared. He was a good man and didn't deserve this …"

"No one deserves to die in such a brutal manner. If it wasn't an accident, then those responsible will be apprehended and punished, I promise you that, Leonard," the inspector added.

Leonard shook his head in frustration and winced at his effort.

The inspector cleared his throat. "But I'd be remiss if I didn't ask you a question or two.

The nurse frowned.

"Did you store any substantial quantity of combustible products in your home?"

Leonard coughed. "Enough to destroy my house? No, I did not." His chest hurt, and he winced at the effort of talking.

"Er, do you recall seeing anyone? Do you have any information to help us identify who the culprit or the accomplices are?"

Leonard thought a moment. "From memory, I saw nothing unusual."

"Inspector, Mr Hardy requires rest. I suggest you return tomorrow." The nurse folded her arms and glared, daring the policeman to defy her.

The inspector sighed. "Very well, I shall return tomorrow. I hope you feel better, Leonard." He turned and walked through the ward and before the nurse could intercede, Tim stepped up to the bed.

"Leo, I'm doing my darndest to get word to Mary." He looked like he wanted to say more, changed his mind, and then turned to follow after the inspector.

Leonard squeezed his eyes shut in an attempt to block the emotional trauma. *Perhaps Mary shouldn't come*, he thought. *Everyone who has been assisting me has been killed.* The savage reality of recent events was too much, and all he wanted was to be alone with his grief. With the help of the nurse, he rolled carefully onto his side and was pleased to hear the swish of her starched uniform as she walked away.

Thankfully, he had no visitors the following morning and was able to dwell in his misery, which suited him just fine. His mood didn't improve when Inspector Gibbard arrived shortly after his midday meal.

The inspector stood at his bedside and remained silent as a nurse removed the crockery and utensils. "Food will restore your vitality and health," he said.

"Then you eat it," Leonard replied petulantly and looked away.

Gibbard's mouth tightened. "It was dynamite."

Leonard's eyes opened wide.

"We found physical evidence of diatomaceous earth—"

"I have no conception of what Dia– is," Leonard interrupted.

"Seashells, Mr Hardy. Miniscule portions of powdered shells in sedimentary rock, similar to chalk are used in the manufacture of dynamite. Based on the amount of residue, we believe no less than two sticks of dynamite were placed in your hearth. We surmise the dynamite was cleverly hidden and that lighting the wood in your fire caused the dynamite to detonate. The intent was to destroy your home and you in it. Providentially, you were spared … unfortunately, Mr Baylor was not."

"And did your clever analysis discover the names of the murderers? Perhaps they left a calling card attached to the dynamite."

"That's enough! Do you need reminding that people, your neighbours risked themselves to come to *your* aid while their homes were damaged? And you have the arrogance to mock the fine effort of our emergency services who do their duty, often in perilous conditions, without regard for their own wellbeing so *you* can lay in bed and feel sorry for yourself!" Inspector Gibbard's face was crimson.

Leonard's mouth opened but he couldn't find words.

"I thought you a better man than that, Mr Hardy. Good day to you, sir." He spun quickly and strode away.

Patients and staff stared at Leonard. There was nowhere for him to hide or run. He pulled the sheet over his head in shame.

Even the nurses kept their distance and left him in peace. He spent the afternoon contemplating his misfortunes in solitude, and while he felt physically better, he struggled with his emotions — feelings of despondency and wretchedness overwhelmed him. His life was in tatters, he had no employment, no home, his fiancé had forsaken him and those who had provided him with assistance had been murdered. There was little to look forward to, and no matter how he reasoned, his future looked bleak. Even his safety at the hospital was tenuous, as he knew that those men who'd destroyed his house and killed Russell would stop at nothing to see him dead.

Any sudden noises or disturbances in the ward gave him a start and he fully expected men to storm in wielding weapons. Sleep was difficult, resting was almost impossible and his injuries, although numerous, were minor amounting to nothing more than cuts, bruises and a painful lump on his head.

So when he heard a commotion and raised voices, he quickly sat up in bed and waited for the inevitable. He was rewarded with the sight of Bridgette. Her fiery red hair was pinned beneath a fashionable postilion hat, its colour complimenting the emerald green of her dress that she wore with style and pure confidence. She breezed into the ward like a princess on a regal visit, waving and greeting fellow nurses by name and with a laugh. Even some patients believed they'd been honoured by the presence of royalty and perked up as she glided gaily past them with splendour and pomp.

Despite the darkness of his present disposition, he couldn't help but smile. This was Bridgette at her finest, and her performance worthy of homage.

Having sashayed through the ward Bridgette stopped at the foot of his bed, her smile broad and joyful. A porter entered the ward carrying a small travelling valise, spotted Bridgette and walked over. "Thank you, Mr Roundtree," she said. "Right here will do," and turned the full extent of her vivacious personality onto Leonard. "Leo, darling, what are you doing in this dreary place?"

The ward matron stood frowning in the entranceway, and Bridgette turned and gave her a small finger wave and smile.

"If you were unaware, my home was destroyed and a friend killed. They say I'm fortunate to be alive, although I wonder about the truth of that statement."

"Oh come now, homes can be rebuilt, and I know you have provisions for indemnity. But it is sad your friend was killed, and I'm sorry for your loss. I never met him, but I'm told he was a remarkable man. You were privileged to have made his acquaintance, even if it was for a short time. But misery is a bad bed-fellow and suits you not, Leo."

"I have little reason to be as joyous as you, Bridgette."

"Well then, we shall change that, shan't we?"

Leonard looked a little perplexed. "How is Mary, is she here too?"

Bridgette leaned down and whispered, "No, she isn't here, but she is safe, Leo."

"I'd hoped ..."

"Come, come, get up, I purchased some clothes for you. Get dressed, time to go," she said, giving the bed a pat with her hand.

"If you brought along your wits, then you'd also be aware that I've been somewhat injured and require hospitalisation," he said while folding his arms in petulant defiance.

"Not any more, Leo, you've been discharged and are under my care. Your injuries are minor and you are capable of walking. Come, come, we haven't all afternoon to dilly dally."

He looked at her with his mouth agape.

Bridgette rested her hands on her hips.

"You're serious, aren't you?" he finally managed to say.

"Of course, hurry along Leo, I've bought clothes for you. She pointed to the valise the porter had dropped near the bed.

He looked up at her and saw her charming smile.

Constable Tim Yates was waiting near the hospital entrance talking with a porter when Leonard, walking gingerly alongside

Bridgette, exited the building. "What took you so long, Leo?" he said with a grin.

"I think he rather preferred the company of nurses who attended to him," said Bridgette.

"At least they left me in peace," Leonard replied grumpily.

Tim quickly hailed a Hansom cab and once loaded and squeezed inside, they headed off to Bridgette's home a short distance away. Bridgette explained to Leonard that Mary was concerned for her safety and had gone to her aunt's home in Upper Hutt. She told him how Neil Flanagan had threatened and even shoved her. While arguably it was only a firm push, they felt it best to quietly leave Wellington until it was safe to return and Mr Flanagan was no longer walking the streets. Leonard seethed at the revelation, and quietly vowed to ensure Neil Flanagan faced justice and paid for all his numerous crimes.

"Inspector Gibbard received permission to have a constable watch over you, Leo," Tim volunteered once they were at Bridgette's. "Just like the old days, remember that?"

"It wasn't that long ago," Leonard added, "and only one constable?" he harrumphed. "I doubt a lone constable will be a deterrence to those thugs."

"You question my ability?"

"No, I fear those men who are willing to kill people with such ease and without remorse."

"Uh, that brings me to another point, Leo," Tim shifted uncomfortably on his chair. "Your friend, Russell …"

Leonard looked at his friend.

"He was, uh, buried at the Mount Cemetery. He had no family, all we knew is that he was Catholic," Tim added.

Leonard sat quietly and nodded. "I will visit his grave as soon as I can, I owe him that much."

They sat in Bridgette's kitchen while she prepared a meal. "Oh Leo, I've been remiss, we are having guests this evening,' she stated.

Leonard felt sorrowful, he'd just come from hospital, was still mourning the death of Russell and wasn't up to socialising with Bridgette's friends.

"Uncle Jun is coming, along with someone I'm unfamiliar with, a Mr Yong."

Leonard sat up. "They're coming here?"

"I visited Uncle Jun and told him what happened to you, and our plans to bring you here. He asked if he could bring his friend Mr Yong," Tim offered.

Leonard remembered their last conversation when he and Russell were at Uncle Jun's shop. He hoped they brought good tidings, he certainly needed it. "That's the first good news I've had, and yes, Mr Yong is a well-connected friend of Uncle Jun."

Chapter Thirty-Three

Uncle Jun shook his head, "You silly boy, Leo, you could have been kill."

Leonard, morose and looking down at his feet, slowly raised his head and met the gaze of his elderly friend. "And Russell *was* killed, Uncle Jun … those men you had watching the street, did they not see anything?"

This time Uncle Jun didn't respond. Wang Yong, who sat beside Jun, coughed politely. All heads turned to him. "We are all deeply saddened by the unfortunate loss of your friend, he was an honourable and well-respected man." He shifted position slightly as he composed his thoughts. "Why our men saw nothing is a mystery to us, we have questioned them extensively and believe they were intentionally distracted. I take responsibility for their failure as I underestimated the resourcefulness of our adversaries." He took a deep breath. "However, collectively we can overcome them, which brings me to the reason for being here with Chen Jun." He dipped his head in respect to his friend.

Other than the ticking clock on the mantelpiece, the room was silent. Leonard, Bridgette and Tim sat spellbound as they listened to the eloquent friend of Uncle Jun. Wang Yong was an enigma. Chinese through and through, he outwardly propagated the appearance of a simple oriental merchant, yet he articulated English without any accent, and his words were carefully crafted. He was like a general addressing his officers—he didn't demand respect, he earned it.

"We took the liberty of entering the warehouse at 14 Abel Smith

Street and searched thoroughly," began Wang Yong.

Tim sat a little straighter —Mr Yong's admission of illegally entering the building didn't sit well with him.

Wang Yong gave a Tim a quick look and smiled. "We took nothing, and upon leaving, there was no evidence to suggest we had entered and searched the building's interior. What we discovered is of interest, and I believe the constabulary would be elated to know that sufficient quantities of unregistered opium and other chemicals are being stored at that location. For what purpose you may well ask? We can only surmise that they are being blended to create a powerful tonic to enhance the performance of race horses. Constable Yates?"

Tim swallowed. "Sir?"

"What other corroborating information do you require so that your superiors can approve and launch an official investigation to lawfully search these premises?"

"Sir, I have no authority to initiate a search and will need to speak to Inspector Gibbard first."

Wang Yong nodded. "Then with urgency, I suggest that you speak to the inspector at your earliest convenience."

"And that proves Tyne, Lewis & Chatswood are importing the opium ... but how can I link them to the Riley brothers?" Leonard questioned.

"I will take this opportunity to leave and inform the inspector," said Tim, rising from his chair. "I don't wish to know what you are going to do, Leo, but whatever it is, don't infringe on the law or put yourself in any more peril. I will return shortly."

Leonard smirked.

Bridgette returned after seeing Tim to the door and entered her sitting room. "If I may—"

Leonard was stretched out on his chair with his hands behind his head as he was wont to do when deep in thought, and Uncle Jun and Wan Yong were having an intense discussion in Chinese. They all turned to her.

"Far be it for me to offer suggestions," she said, then paused.

Leonard sat upright, interested to learn what she had to say.

"Please continue, Mrs Leyton," encouraged Wang Yong.

"Uh, I believe the Riley brothers are too well protected and directly pursuing them will prove to be, um, fruitless. A waste of time and dangerous."

Uncle Jun smiled and nodded, eager for her to continue.

"Um, I think the best course of action is to pursue and apply pressure to that woman, the one where this all began, she is the weak link."

"Mrs Bedingfield?" Leonard asked.

"Yes, she obviously has an association with the Riley brothers and I believe the solution to this entire sordid mess is through her. As a woman, I can see that she doesn't love her husband, but she *does* love someone! A member of her family?"

The thought of further encounters with *that* woman gave Leonard chills. "But how? We need some form of leverage," he stated.

"We watch her; she may visit someone." Uncle Jun suggested.

"I believe Mrs Leyton has succinctly stated the obvious. And Chen Jun is correct that the woman will meet with people and she will talk," Wang Yong said.

Bridgette stepped to Leonard's side. "And what of Leonard's safety? Tim has gone to see the inspector and Leo is again unprotected."

Wang Yong and Uncle Jun again conversed in Chinese. After a moment, Uncle Jun turned to Leonard. "We think it better you come to shop. We can protect you there Leo, here much harder."

Leonard knew Uncle Jun was correct. For now, it seemed the most sensible option.

"Your friend, Tim, he can sleep there too, more the merrier, eh?" Uncle Jun grinned.

Leonard sighed. "Very well, I will come tomorrow, I must wait for Tim to return first."

"Good boy, Leo," said Uncle Jun. "But Leo, your house, you have protection?"

"You mean do I have indemnification?"

Uncle Jun nodded.

"Thankfully I do—oh dear, I really must begin proceedings and file a claim and should visit my bookkeeper in the morning," Leonard replied. "So, uh, I will be somewhat delayed and will arrive at the shop in the afternoon, Uncle Jun."

"Do not be silly boy, come soonest, eh?"

The next morning Tim and Leonard stepped from a cab onto Manners Street where Leonard's bookkeeper was located.

"Here we go again," grizzled Constable Yates. "Nursemaid to the esteemed Leonard Hardy, esquire."

"You should be so fortunate to be attending to me and not someone like that virulent woman, Mrs Bedingfield," Leonard replied. "And, may I add, you are being paid a suitably handsome stipend for the privilege. Rather than wait in the dreary offices, I suggest you wait out here," Leonard suggested as he started to enter the building.

"Ah, good morning Mr Hardy," said Keith Morecomb as he greeted Leonard in his offices. "How can we be of service? Oh my, your face, you've been in a frightful …"

"That is what I've come to see you about, Mr Morecomb."

The bookkeeper extracted a well-used handkerchief and dabbed at his nose. "Hayfever."

Leonard grimaced in sympathy. "Mr Morecomb, my home was destroyed in an unfortunate, er, accident, and I believe I need to file the necessary paperwork to receive indemnity."

Mr Morecomb wiped his nose again. "Yes, of course. Is that how you suffered your injuries, looks, er painful?"

"Only when I laugh, Mr Morecomb, and that is less frequent these days."

The bookkeeper snickered. "Let me retrieve your documents — one moment."

Mr Morecomb departed his office and returned soon after, clutching a number of files. "Now, let me see, somewhere here …" He opened a glossy green folder, flicked through various pages and finally found what he sought. "Here we are, thank goodness for accurate filing, eh?"

Leonard waited as the bookkeeper scanned page after page. He closed the file and turned to a credenza behind his desk from where he extracted a form. "We just need to provide the required information to begin the process. I must sympathise for the inconvenience and pain you are currently enduring Mr Hardy. I hope this process alleviates some of it."

Leonard smiled. "I hope so too, Mr Morecomb."

The bookkeeper asked numerous questions and Leonard answered truthfully until he was asked about the cause of the fire. "Of course, Mr Hardy, I will need to obtain a report from the police to verify your claim."

"That shouldn't be a problem. Inspector Gibbard was attending to matters," Leonard volunteered.

"Oh? He is quite senior for such duties ..." He looked at Leonard and received no response.

"Nonetheless ... uh, yes, a good man," stated Mr Morecomb. "Very thorough. Now then, I will request the information from the police and file your claim accordingly. You do understand that these things do take time. If I have any questions, I will be in contact. Er, do I have your new address, Mr Hardy?"

Leonard thought quickly and decided it best to give Bridgette's residential address rather than Uncle Jun's. Mr Morecomb made a note and stood from behind his desk. "I think that covers all pertinent details. If I have need of more information, I will correspond accordingly. Is there anything else I can help you with?"

Leonard rose slowly from his seat. "Thank you Mr Morecomb, you've been most kind and helpful."

Tim was pleased to see Leonard when he appeared. "You could have built a new house in the time it took."

"It took an age. But now the paperwork is done, and I must wait."

They caught another cab to Bridgette's, where Leonard retrieved the valise with clothes Bridgette had purchased for him, and then early afternoon arrived at Uncle Jun's shop.

The next few days were spent writing letters and informing family and friends of the unfortunate circumstances around the destruction of his home. Bridgette offered to purchase more clothes for him, and he secretly enjoyed that. Her sense of style was un-matched, and his new clothes did not only fit perfectly, he actually felt quite dapper. His aches and pains diminished and the wounds on his face were healing nicely.

Uncle Jun informed him that people were watching the home of Mrs Bedingfield, but as yet she had received no callers, or left her house, and remained cloistered inside. "Patience, Leo," reminded Uncle Jun.

Leonard had not seen or heard from Inspector Gibbard since he angrily stormed from the hospital ward, and he wanted to apolo-gise for his churlish behaviour. Inspector Gibbard reassigned Tim, replacing him with an aging constable with a limp. It wasn't reas-suring— Leonard doubted the man could defend himself, let alone anyone else. Tim assured him that the constable's mere presence was a deterrent. Leonard wasn't so sure.

The week at Uncle Jun's passed slowly, and on the seventh day, Tim arrived. "Leo, Leo, I have news."

Leonard was reading a book in the private curtained area of Un-cle Jun's shop when Tim rushed in. The aging constable, currently on duty, politely moved towards the rear door out of earshot. "Leo, I'm pleased you are seated."

Leonard closed his book. "It would serve me well if you brought good tidings or take your leave."

Tim sat as Uncle Jun entered.

"Earlier today, Inspector Gibbard finally obtained permission to search the warehouse on Abel Smith Street. The inspector and I, with two other constables assisting, scoured through the warehouse and found no opium or any chemicals that would be deemed illegal, let alone suspicious. I'm sorry Leo, we tried."

Uncharacteristically, Uncle Jun cursed.

Leonard was crestfallen and shook his head. "Why did it take eight days? You reported the findings from Mr Yong eight days ago, Tim!"

"Leo, Inspector Gibbard immediately sought approval from Superintendent Taggett and was told an answer would be forthcoming. It wasn't the fault of the inspector, he is as frustrated as you are."

"So they were forewarned, the Riley brothers were told of the search and covertly relocated their potions ahead of time."

"That's what the inspector believes, too," replied Tim.

Leonard grunted in disgust. "Can anything else go wrong?"

Tim's expression softened. "What you don't understand is, if we received new information to the whereabouts of the opium, the inspector doubts permission will be granted to conduct another search."

"I go tell Wang Yong," Uncle Jun suddenly said and quickly exited the shop.

Leonard was furious. "I see little reason to stay in Wellington. My life is in danger, the police are inept, my house destroyed, I have no employment and my fiancé has deserted me. Tell me, Tim— what reason do I have to remain here?"

Tim met his harsh gaze. "Your friends, Leo. Those who care about you and value your companionship. As for Mary, you forget she is in peril, too, and as far as I'm aware, she hasn't deserted you. I think you've forsaken her."

"When the affairs of my home are settled, I think I shall return to England." He folded his arms and leaned back in the chair.

Chapter Thirty-Four

Bridgette found Leonard in a foul, irritable mood. Tim had warned her ahead of time, and she breezed into Uncle Jun's shop like a whirlwind. Uncle Jun laughed with her, delighting in her spirited energy.

Jun pointed to the curtain separating the shop from his private area. "He sulk, you bring smile to silly boy Leo."

Leonard was ready and prepared for Bridgette's uplifting disposition, but when she parted the curtain and entered the kitchen, his resolve collapsed – he couldn't help but grin. "I'm in a disagreeable mood, Bridgette, and you have no right to bring me joy and happiness." He tried to pout but was unsuccessful.

"I hope I do bring you some joy, Leonard Hardy, I have a missive for you and I can only hope this improves your life." She reached out and handed him a letter. "I cannot linger, I'm required to be at the hospital. Fair well and cheer up, it isn't the end of the world." With that she kissed him on the cheek and departed, leaving him alone to stare at the envelope.

The sender was the Morecomb & Associates Bookkeeping Company. Leonard tore the envelope open and extracted a very brief, concise letter. He read it quickly and was somewhat perplexed. Keith Morecomb requested that he visit his office on Victoria Street with some urgency, that was it. He scratched his head, then rose from the chair and went in search of the constable. "We're going into town, Victoria Street, bring your coat as it looks like rain."

"Mr Hardy, thank you for coming so quickly," greeted Keith Morecomb after wiping his nose.

"I came as soon as I received your letter," Leonard replied. "Is there a complication?"

"Ahh, one moment, let me retrieve your files, eh."

Leonard was left alone to ponder the reason for his summons and felt the familiar stirring of anxiety in his stomach. He tapped his fingers on the chair's armrest as he waited.

Mr Morecomb returned and fussed with files, and again referred to the glossy green folder. "Yes, yes," he muttered to himself before looking up at Leonard, wiping his nose again. "Hayfever."

Leonard leaned forward in his chair. The green folder … he'd seen one like it before ... somewhere else.

"Now then, it appears that there is a quandary over the claim submission for your home."

Leonard's eyes opened wide. "You must be mistaken, surely you've fulfilled your obligations and ensured I am protected with indemnity as I requested?"

Mr Morecomb removed his spectacles and gave them a vigorous wipe with his soiled handkerchief. He placed them back on his nose, then removed them for another buffering. "My responsibilities are not in question. Your claim was denied because—"

"Denied? Denied!" Leonard cried.

"Mr Hardy, please. Allow me to finish."

Leonard took a deep breath.

"Under the indemnity contract you signed," Mr Morecomb held up Leonard's copy of the contract, "you agreed that no recompense would be paid if the cause was due to wilful damage or neglect."

Leonard opened his mouth to speak and Mr Morecomb raised a

hand to forestall him. "According to the report issued by the police, your house was destroyed as a result of an explosion or incendiary device."

"That is correct, sir, the police believe at least two sticks of dynamite were used," Leonard affirmed.

"Ah yes, and herein lies the muddle. Er, the, uh, claims adjuster has determined that as no perpetrator has been charged with an offence, nor are there any witnesses observing a third party committing any wrongdoing, then it is deemed the explosion is a result of negligence through the hoarding and storing of volatile substances."

"Preposterous!" Leonard shouted and rose quickly from his chair. "That assumption is absurd!"

"Mr Hardy, some decorum, please."

Leonard sat and seethed.

"My role is to provide bookkeeping services for you. I completed the necessary documents with information you provided, obtained an official account of the incident from the police and submitted the claim on your behalf. I am merely an agent and not responsible for this decision."

"I apologise, Mr Morecomb. It's just, is just that this judgement is pure nonsense. Can I appeal, who is the company responsible for the indemnity?"

"Of course you can appeal the decision. It is your right."

"Please, Mr Morecomb, provide me with their name and address and I will seek an immediate meeting with a company representative and seek to overturn this."

Mr Morecomb nodded. "As would I." He flicked through a page or two and scribbled the address and company name and handed it to Leonard. "A good reputable company."

Leonard stared mutely at the paper. His mouth opened but he couldn't speak. He closed it, swallowed and tried to subdue the anger that threatened to erupt. He fought to establish self-control but the rage welling from deep within was as combustible as the dynamite used to destroy his home. He closed his eyes for a moment and felt his racing heart pounding wildly in his chest. After a deep calming breath he slowly re-opened his eyes. "Is, is there an error, is this correct?" he squeaked.

Mr Morecomb finished wiping his nose and leaned over his desk to look at the note he just wrote and was relieved to see that he'd not made an unforgiveable blunder. "Yes, the New York Contributionship Company, their offices are on Cuba Street," he confirmed with a smile.

Leonard stormed from the offices of Morecomb & Associates Bookkeeping Company in a fury. He stomped past the constable who stood waiting outside the bookkeeper's office and strode quickly up Lambton Quay onto Willis Street. The aging policeman, unable to keep up, soon lost sight of him.

By the time he walked along Manners Street and arrived at the lower end of Cuba Street, his rage had dissipated—replaced by a determined, callous resolve and purpose. He had few options but one; everything had been taken from him, he had nothing. *What do I have to lose*? he asked himself repeatedly, and continued up Cuba Street with hardened resolve. A few heads turned in curiosity as he strode briskly up the street.

He'd last seen the offices of the New York Contributionship Company at night from across the street with Yan, when Neil Flanagan had appeared outside the building. During day time, the premises didn't look any more inviting. Outside, in the deep shadowed entranceway, a man stood casually, with hat pulled low, shrouding his face. Leonard sensed he was a sentinel, a guard keeping watch. Before the man could react, he strode quickly past, yanked the door open and stepped inside.

The interior was surprisingly spacious. Ahead, at a lengthy, richly burnished wood counter, two secretaries had their heads down busy with work. On the wall behind them, a large sign proudly proclaimed in bold green letters, edged with gold, that these were the offices of the New York Contributionship Company. He turned his head to see that the man who previously stood outside had followed him in and paused against the wall. It mattered not. With a grim expression Leonard strode purposely towards the counter.

On his left were small offices. With wood panelling covering the lower half of each office wall, the top section was made with frosted glass which allowed light to pass through and still offered privacy, similar to the *Evening Standard*'s bullpen door. He heard voices, and saw indistinct shapes inside a couple of the confined rooms.

"Good morning, sir, how may I be of service?" greeted the younger, and he presumed, junior of the two women receptionists.

"I think Mr Joshua Riley is expecting me ..." It took all his self-control to offer the woman civility. "I am Leonard Hardy," he stated with economy, and then forced a smile that more closely resembled a grimace.

She looked down at her desk, presumably to consult a diary or calendar, then spoke in hushed whispers with the elder woman while he glanced around the room seeking a clue to the location of Riley's personal office. After a moment the elder woman looked up. "I don't believe Mr Riley has an appointment scheduled with you, sir." She waited for a response.

Leonard was still scanning the interior, when the door from one of the small offices on his left opened and a large, impeccably dressed man exited the room. He looked over his shoulder and spoke to a man inside the office. "See it's done immediately, Mr Hill," and walked down the hallway towards the stairs.

From the man's comportment, Leonard assumed he might be a Riley, but which one?

"Mr Hardy?" questioned the receptionist.

Leonard ignored her and walked quickly to the room the man just vacated.

"Mr Hardy?" the receptionist yelled. "These are private offices!"

Leonard stuck his head through the open doorway and in a congenial tone asked the lone inhabitant, "Was that Mr Joshua Riley himself?"

"Indeed, sir, uh, can I assist you?" the man replied quizzically.

Leonard heard the clack of hard shoes on the marble floor and guessed the guard had seen enough and was coming to escort him from the building. Without thanking the man, Leonard ran down the hall, chasing after Joshua Riley. The guard followed about six strides behind him.

"I'm Leonard Hardy!" he shouted.

Immediately the well-dressed man stopped and slowly turned. He was an imposing figure with a barrel chest and a strong jaw and stood well over six feet tall. His clothes were immaculate, and with piercing blue eyes he glared at Leonard.

"I have him, Mr Riley, sir," said the guard as he grabbed Leonard's elbow.

Leonard shook his arm free and took a step closer to Mr Riley.

"I believe we need to talk, Mr Riley. You can either speak with me now, or I'm quite willing to cause you and your company some awkwardness that may require some explaining. Not the type of attention a man like yourself seeks, is it?"

Again the guard reached for Leonard's elbow and tried to twist his arm behind his back.

"Mr Riley!" Leonard yelled loudly, feeling some discomfort from the guard's attempt to separate his arm from his shoulder.

Employees vacated their offices and everyone craned their necks to see who was causing the commotion.

"Release him," instructed Mr Riley. "This way." He spun and climbed a flight of stairs to the first floor. Leonard, massaging his arm, followed a step behind. In his shadow, the guard stalked. Mr Riley entered a plush office and stood in front of his desk with arms folded. His expression hadn't changed — he still glared malevolently as Leonard entered. The guard remained outside the door.

"If you seek an appointment, Mr Hardy, then be civil, do so through conventional means and not by causing a ruckus. This is highly irregular."

Leonard didn't immediately reply and looked around the room. He saw books on shelves, mostly volumes on legal matters. There were a few on ships and shipping, some almanacs, and in a corner behind the desk, he saw two books that wouldn't normally be found in the office such as this. He took a step closer to better see. One was titled, *A Chromolithographic Pharmacy Catalogue*. The other was a book published by the Pharmaceutical Society of Great Britain. *Most unusual*, Leonard thought. Some uninspiring paintings of horses graced the walls. One looked similar to the painting of the horse in the *Evening Standard*'s conference room, but then again, horses all looked the same. He turned his attention to the imposing man, still leaning with arms folded against his desk. "I doubt whether you would have availed yourself to me."

Joshua Riley exhaled and unfolded his arms. "What can I do for you? I'm a busy man and there are many things that are in need of my attention."

Leonard took another step closer to him. While physically commanding, he wasn't intimidated by the larger man. "My home was deliberately destroyed, Mr Riley. Evidence the police uncovered prove at least two sticks of dynamite, strategically placed and hidden in the fireplace were the cause. It wasn't an accident. Yet you denied my indemnity claim, and stated it was negligence on my part."

Joshua Riley shrugged then stepped behind his desk and eased himself down into a large leather chair.

Leonard continued. "But we both know that you were responsible."

Riley opened his mouth to protest, but Leonard gave him no opportunity to respond. "A man died in that explosion, and prior to that, others have been killed." Leonard thrust out his hand and pointed at the man, "And *you* are accountable!"

"That is enough!" bellowed Mr Riley, standing quickly to reinforce his point, his face red from outrage. "I will not sit here in this office and have slanderous, unfounded accusations made against me." He placed both hands on his desk and leaned forward. "Your home was destroyed because you foolishly stored hazardous materials." He raised a hand and pointed. "You were negligent and acted irresponsibly. The death of a lowly harlot and her ruffian minder are inconsequential, of no importance, and purely a result of excessive opium use by her. The police are most satisfied with the conclusion of the investigations and due to a lack of resources, they will not probe any further. Attempting to apportion blame on me is ludicrous, totally absurd. If you persist with this, Mr Hardy, I will have formal charges brought against you. Mr Mason!"

Leonard was stunned. Mr Riley all but confessed. Anger had loosened his tongue.

The guard entered the office.

"Mr Hardy is to leave these premises immediately. And see to it he is reminded of the error of his ways and that we do not welcome his return."

"I will see justice served!"

Riley laughed at Leonard's assertion and stepped from behind his desk. "Justice serves the privileged."

The guard walked quickly towards Leonard who was still glowering at Joshua Riley.

Leonard knew with absolute certainty that Riley was behind the deaths of his friends and others. The guard yanked his arm, and again twisted it behind his back as he was escorted painfully down the stairs, through the hallway, towards the gloomy rear exit of the building.

"Mr Riley wants me to impress upon you how much he doesn't wish to see you come back," said the guard as he roughly manhandled Leonard past the kitchen at the rear of the building.

"You might … wish … to reconsider," Leonard replied between shoves.

The guard managed to laugh as they reached the door. "Why would that be?"

"Because I will return and bring the constabulary with me. You will stand beside Mr Riley when the charges are made against you and pay for your crimes."

The guard laughed again, "Not bloody likely." He unlatched the rear door, and kicked it open as sunlight streamed in. With Leonard's arm held firmly behind his back, the guard pushed him outside into the alley, delivered a vicious punch to his kidney and followed him out. The door swung closed—the click of the lock loud and final.

Leonard grunted and fell to his knees as he received a hard slap to the side of his head. The guard wasn't finished yet and as he drew his leg back to deliver a kick a shout made him turn. What he saw caused him to pause, and he took an involuntary step backwards as half a dozen Chinese youths rushed at him. He couldn't run back inside to safety, the door had closed and locked automatically—he was trapped. They descended on him with a series of blows to his upper torso and head, and when he fell, they kicked savagely. He couldn't defend himself against so many and was overpowered with ease. Leonard could only watch in mute horror as they beat him senseless. He feared they'd kill him.

But they didn't. The guard lay moaning pitifully, curled into a protective foetal position near the locked door. Leonard eased himself unsteadily to his feet as the Chinese approached.

"Are you hurt, Mr Hardy?" one of them asked as he walked towards him. The other youths spread out and kept watch.

Leonard was surprised they knew his name. He rubbed the side of his head. "I think I will survive," he mumbled as he began brushing dirt from his clothes.

"We must take you from here before others arrive. Please come with us," the youth said.

Leonard had no choice and followed the youths down the alley where they entered the rear entrance of a nondescriptive structure, then walked through a dark hallway to exit onto Cuba Street. They quickly crossed the busy thoroughfare and walked inside yet another building. No one gave the youths a second look or questioned them.

Leonard was told they would wait here until safe to proceed. Many of the young men disappeared, leaving him alone with just two of them. "Were you sent by Wang Yong?"

"Yes, sir," answered one of them in perfect English.

Leonard was rubbing the side of his head where the guard had painfully slapped him. "Thank you for your timely help. I fear that man would have cruelly beat me. Uh, how did you know …?"

"Wang Yong asked that we watch for you if you enter these streets. You were seen walking up Cuba Street, so we wait when you enter building, some in front and others in back."

"And why are we waiting in here?" Leonard asked the young man.

"We don't want anyone to see us take you to Chen Jun Qiang. We will cause distraction when no one is watching, then quickly leave here."

Chapter Thirty-Five

"Have you lost your mind, Leo?" In anger, Tim paced back and forth in the rear of Uncle Jun's shop.

"Actually, yes. I believe I lost it somewhere in between losing my job, my fiancé and my home!"

Tim threw his hands up in frustration. "Leo, we can't help you if you continue to behave this way and take matters into your own hands. You could have been seriously injured or worse, killed. You were reckless and foolish!"

"Help me?" Leonard's voice rose an octave. "Help me? You provided me with a lovely elderly gentleman wearing the uniform of the constabulary, but who'd be better suited darning socks and protecting the infirm. You've made no headway in solving all these crimes—none, none at all, and are no closer to prosecuting the guilty than before. What am I to do, wait until Christmas, and hope between now and then a festive miracle happens and I can then make an attempt to restore my life, or what little remains of it?"

"We are doing the best we can," Tim offered. "Inspector Gibbard—"

"Ah, the esteemed and prominent inspector who watches dispassionately from the snugness of his cosy, warm office and does little else. Bah, I've had enough of him," Leonard waved his arm dismissively.

Tim silently fumed in irritation and continued to pace. Behind the curtain, Uncle Jun could be heard dispensing advice and tending to customers.

Leonard suddenly sat straighter in his chair. "Do you recall when Agatha was killed and Inspector Gibbard stated that he would not make public the actual cause of her death, that it would be documented as suicide and not a result of opium or laudanum?"

Tim stopped his pacing and looked at Leonard. "I do, and you are correct, her death was listed as a suicide, nothing more. Why do you ask?"

"Something Joshua Riley said. I clearly remember, he said she died from excessive opium use. How would he know that?"

"I know what you're thinking Leo, and perhaps Joshua Riley is responsible, but you have no evidence to prove anything! The man is untouchable, so don't go near or provoke him. If he complains you are harassing him, the police must respond and you could be charged."

Leonard folded his arms and leaned back in his chair. "Poppycock!"

For the remainder of the day, he sat alone in the rear of Uncle Jun's shop. Out front, the elderly constable sat on a chair keeping watch, ostensibly to provide protection, but that was laughable Leonard thought. His mood deteriorated as he considered how to move on with his life. He couldn't afford to build a new home, and with no employment his future seemed bleak and prospects dim.

Later in the afternoon a messenger arrived with a missive. Leonard immediately tore open the envelope to read it. It stated quite simply that he was invited to have dinner with Mr and Mrs Pembroke at their residence that evening.

His clothes had all been destroyed in the fire and he didn't have many options, but he did his best and felt he looked somewhat presentable. *Bridgette would be pleased*, he thought with a rare smile.

As instructed, he arrived promptly at 6:00 p.m., with a younger and more agile constable assigned to watch over him during the evening. The constable adamantly insisted he would remain outside when Mrs Pembroke met them at the door.

As always, he was taken back and marvelled at the décor and artwork that graced the walls of their majestic home when he was led inside. The house and its interior were so out of character with the austerity portrayed by the *Evening Standard*'s senior reporter and editor, and Leonard assumed that it was Mrs Pembroke who had the grace and propriety to tastefully decorate.

Mr Pembroke was seated in his comfortable over-stuffed armchair in their sitting room reading when Leonard entered. His spectacles were balanced precariously upon his nose and he raised his head, "You're tardy, Mr Hardy."

"He is no such thing Freddy," interjected Louise Pembroke as she pointed to a sofa for Leonard to sit. "I kept him talking at the front door with the young constable."

Mr Pembroke closed the book with a snap and removing his spectacles, placed them on a reading stand beside his book. Leonard saw the book was titled, *Capital. Volume I: The Process of Production of Capital*, by Karl Marx.

"English translation," offered Mr Pembroke when he saw Leonard's interest. "Would behove you to indulge in such insightful reading."

Leonard nodded. "Yes, I have been meaning to obtain a copy, sir."

Mr Pembroke's mouth twitched. He may have smiled, Leonard wasn't sure.

"Now then, it seems your woeful life has taken an objectionable deviation for the worse …"

"Freddy, please, be civil," chastised Mrs Pembroke.

"Leonard knows full well what I mean," sighed Mr Pembroke. He twisted in his chair to better face his guest. "What on God's green earth is happening, Leonard?"

"Leonard, dear. What Freddy means is that we are both concerned for your wellbeing. When I heard about your home … well, I was appalled, you could have been killed … poor Mr Baylor. I liked him — such a lovely man."

Leonard looked down at his feet and composed his thoughts. He looked up after a brief moment. "I admit, I am at my wits end, and have little recourse but to return to England. I have lost everything. There is nothing left for me here."

"Bollocks!" exclaimed Mr Pembroke.

"Freddy, your language!"

"You must fight for what you believe in. Walking away solves nothing and you'll be forever haunted with regret," Mr Pembroke sternly advised.

"What do I know of these men, the Riley brothers who've destroyed my life? I have no wealth or resources with which to defend myself or retaliate."

Mr Pembroke leaned forward. "Karl Marx said, 'Ignorance never yet helped anybody.'"

Mrs Pembroke smiled and nodded.

"Think, dear boy. You are astute… intelligent, and a problem solver. You may not have a treasure chest filled with gold at your disposal, but you have a treasure chest. It's the people around you, those whom you know, your resources and your wealth are in knowledge and wit."

"I have tried, Mr Pembroke, all I succeeded in accomplishing is causing aggravation to the police and creating further irreparable damage to my life and reputation."

Mrs Pembroke rose from her chair and quietly disappeared into her kitchen.

Leonard and Mr Pembroke remained silent.

"I received a letter yesterday," began Mr Pembroke. "It was addressed to the *Evening Standard*, and to your attention." He retrieved an envelope from his reading stand and waved it in the air.

Leonard looked up.

"Are you familiar with Mr Andrej Janjić?"

"Yes, he is a clerk at the office of the Harbour Master. Why would he write to me?"

"Yes, and a good question. However, he stated that on behalf of the *Evening Standard*, you'd made a previous enquiry about a, a, uh, particular shipment."

Leonard thought quickly. He had made an enquiry and had Mr Janjić believe he was still employed by the *Evening Standard*. Technically untrue, of course. He didn't want Mr Pembroke to be made aware of that slight oversight. "Ah, yes. I do recall that."

"Hmmm." Mr Pembroke gave Leonard a long hard stare before continuing. "Then again, how would he know you were no longer employed by the *Evening Standard*, eh?" He raised a single bushy eyebrow.

Leonard felt the relief. "I concur."

"According to Andrej Janjić's letter," continued Mr Pembroke, "another similar shipment is expected to arrive next week, except the transportation details have suddenly and inexplicably changed.

Would you know anything about this?"

Leonard thought carefully. It could only be another shipment of opium. But because the police were aware of the warehouse where the previous shipment had been stored, the Riley brothers must have chosen another, new location for storage. "Perhaps."

Mr Pembroke's eyebrows raised in unspoken question.

Leonard took a deep breath. "I can only believe it is another shipment of opium that is to be delivered to the Riley brothers. I can't think of what else it could be."

"And please tell me, Mr Hardy, why would a clerk of the Harbour Master be so forthcoming and willing to share these details with you? No doubt this information is presumably confidential and in violation of his employer's precepts."

"Because he likes and feels a modicum of sympathy for me."

Mr Pembroke coughed.

Leonard looked sheepish and turned away.

"Very well." Mr Pembroke rose to his feet and walked to one of the large windows that overlooked Wellington. "Presumably another shipment of opium arrives, how can you prove that it belongs to either or both of the Riley brothers?"

"That is a question we have been pondering over for some time. Frankly, I'm out of ideas."

"Think, Leonard."

Leonard stood and moved to stand beside his former employer, looking out the window over a darkened city. A few lights flickered below. "Wouldn't that depend on where the shipment is stored, and, even better, if the Riley brothers personally check the shipment and ensure it contains what they paid for, then that would be proof, would it not?" Leonard answered.

"Only if the police catch them."

"The police are limited in what they can do. Inspector Gibbard has been told not to pursue the Riley brothers unless he has conclusive indisputable evidence."

"Then, Leonard, I suggest you inform the esteemed inspector of this new development, and perhaps he can gather that evidence." Mr Pembroke turned from the window and handed Leonard the letter written by the clerk. "The shipping information is accurately detailed."

Leonard unfolded the letter and read its contents quickly as Mr Pembroke returned to the comfort of his armchair.

"I think you are very fortunate, Leonard. Use this opportunity to put this mess behind you. More importantly, use your treasure chest to ensure a victory—think!" Mr Pembroke advised.

Mrs Pembroke entered the sitting room. "Dinner is served gentlemen."

"And the constable?" Mr Pembroke asked.

"He is seated on the veranda with a plate, dear."

Leonard accepted an invite from Mr Pembroke to return for dinner in a week's time. After thanking both of them for their lovely meal and saying farewell, he asked the young constable if he minded walking back to Uncle Jun's shop. It wasn't that he didn't want to use a Hansom cab, although he absolutely detested them, he wanted to take the opportunity to walk and think. Mr Pembroke had given him plenty to mull over, and the more he thought about it, the more convinced he was that Mr Pembroke was absolutely correct. If he planned and thought through each step carefully, he knew he could catch the Riley brothers inspecting their cargo of opium and provide the police with enough evidence to begin legal proceedings against them. But how?

Chapter Thirty-Six

It was not yet dark, and a light persistent drizzle made it uncomfortable waiting. Leonard adjusted the collar of his coat again. Feeling better, he tightened his scarf and buried his hands deep in his pockets to ward off the wet and chill. The young constable stood bundled in his overcoat, standing in the shelter of a nearby warehouse as Leonard waited impatiently for Andrej Janjić to walk past on his way home. He'd been here for almost an hour, and there was still no sign of the clerk. He was beginning to believe he'd missed the man when he saw a lone figure walking along the wharf towards him.

"Mr Janjić?" he questioned with uncertainty as the man approached. Like himself, the man had his head and hands buried deep in his coat.

On hearing his name, the man immediately raised his head and Leonard, with some relief, recognised him immediately.

"Mr Hardy, a bit miserable to be out."

Leonard fell into step beside him and began walking. The clerk saw the constable emerge from shelter and follow.

"He's with me," stated Leonard. "And yes, not a pleasant evening. I, uh, I was waiting for you."

Mr Janjić stopped.

"I received the letter you sent, please accept my gratitude."

The clerk nodded and looked a bit uncomfortable.

"Uh, why did you send it? You had no obligation, and presumably your employer may not take kindly to sharing confidential information? Surely, you put your employment at risk?"

Mr Janjić turned his head and looked around. There was an entranceway to a building with a substantial eave that offered some privacy and escape from the drizzle. "May we converse over there?" he pointed.

They walked in silence then stood beneath the eave as the gentle rain continued to fall. The clerk appeared ill at ease and Leonard reminded him of the question.

"I find it extremely difficult to discuss my motives with you Mr Hardy. However, regardless of how I feel, I know my diffidence is nothing compared to what you have so recently suffered through."

Leonard took a step closer. "Thank you for your, er, considerations, Mr Janjić, but—"

"My resolve is weak, and is best that I continue before I change my mind." He smiled.

Even in the darkness, Leonard thought it was forced and unnatural.

"I am a man of moderate means and live a miserable existence. I do what I can to provide adequately for my family, but I receive nothing in return, or nothing that a normal husband receives from his spouse. Sadly, I am married in name only." He took a deep breath and continued. "A short time ago I sought the pleasures of female company outside the bonds of marriage, and had the gladness to meet Trixie."

Leonard's eyebrows furrowed. *Trixie? Agatha Gringle!* "Yes, Miss Gringle." He quickly calculated the effect it would have on the man, which could prove to be somewhat shameful and embarrassing if his association with her were made public. "When you saw both Russell and I on the street that evening, is that why Russell was in such a hurry to leave? Because he was being circumspect, and wanted to respect your privacy?" Leonard asked.

"Yes, I expect so. He was a good-hearted man."

"I understand." Leonard said. He had to commend both Russell and Agatha; their ability to be discrete was impressive.

Andrej must have known what Leonard was thinking. "I knew why you sought that shipping information Mr Hardy, er, Russell told me."

"He did what?" Leonard exclaimed rather loudly. The constable standing some distance away and out of ear-shot turned at the outburst.

"He told me when you last came to the office and asked me to provide you with information about that shipment. And especially in light of Miss Gringle's unfortunate death, I was only too willing to offer assistance." He sighed. "Dear Trixie."

Leonard recalled how Russell had excused himself when they were at the Harbour Master's office. That's when he must have spoken to him. He looked at Mr Janjić closely. "Agatha must have shared a lot with Russell, certainly more than I realised. Thank you for all you've done. I hope I can avenge Miss Gringle and Russell and see those deplorable men responsible for their deaths face justice."

Leonard could see Andrej Janjić was struggling to remain composed and his eyes were glistening.

The clerk bit his lip and shook his head. "I loved her, Mr Hardy. I would see her smile, and her laugh gladdened my heart. Our liaison wasn't just carnal, no, we would often converse and she gave me what my wife couldn't—the privilege and joy of intimacy. Frankly, I'm devastated … heartbroken … I tried to get her to stop taking laudanum, I tried my best …"

Leonard nodded. For some strange reason, he understood completely—Agatha Gringle had that way about her.

"She may have had a questionable virtue, Mr Hardy, but her probity was indisputable." Andrej wiped his eyes with the sleeve of his coat. "How can I help you? What can I do to avenge her death?"

"Uncle Jun, do you think your friend, Mr Yong would agree to meet with me?"

The elderly Chinaman sat opposite Leonard, noisily slurping tea from a cup. He leaned back in his chair and crossed his spindly legs before answering. "Why you do this, Leo?"

"When I had dinner with Mr and Mrs Pembroke, they gave me some encouragement to continue with my quest to see the Riley brothers prosecuted." Leonard saw Uncle Jun about to interject and he held up his hand. "Before you jump to conclusions, I have no intention to seek revenge on my own." He shook his head. "No, I want to help the police gather enough evidence so they can begin a legitimate investigation of the Riley brothers and their illicit, well-organised enterprise. However, I need to know if Mr Yong is willing to continue to assist me. After all, he is well connected, and has considerable resources at his disposal."

Uncle Jun smiled, uncrossed his legs and leaned forward. "Very good, Leo, you use head."

Leonard smiled and remained silent.

Uncle Jun studied him for a moment and saw the wounds on his face, the contusions and remnants of a blackened eye. The elderly Chinaman knew there were many wounds he couldn't see—emotional scars, some fresh and inflamed — others, thinly disguised and still raw. He knew Leonard needed support, not just for vindication, but to free himself of the binds that still held him to Mae Ling.

This young man was like a son-in-law, part of the family, and in a way, he was a living thread to his dear Mae Ling. Like Leonard, he was still tied to Mae. He fought back his emotions. "I speak to him, and tell you, Leo." He up-ended the cup and drained its contents before placing it on the table, then rose from his chair, paused a moment, then patted Leonard on the shoulder before leaving through the shop's rear entrance.

Leonard had some thinking to do to find a way to outsmart the resourceful Riley brothers without incurring the displeasure of the police and putting his life in jeopardy. Since his dinner with the Pembrokes he'd thought of nothing else and wondered how he could achieve his goal. He'd begun to formulate some ideas, but needed the cooperation of many people, including Inspector Gibbard.

Although there was a reprieve from rain, a light but very chilly, southerly breeze rustled leaves on gently swaying branches, which ensured that anyone outside walking the streets was bundled up and suitably attired. Standing behind the trunk of a sturdy tree in the suburb of Mount Cook, Leonard was again waiting. Not far away, the young constable assigned to watch over him paced to-and-fro in a valiant effort to keep warm. They hadn't been here long, and Leonard fervently hoped Inspector Gibbard would not be delayed, and would soon pass by on his way home.

He didn't disappoint. Already, he saw the distinctive form of the inspector walking briskly in his direction. Thankfully the information Tim provided him about his schedule was accurate.

Before Leonard could speak, the inspector paused. "Mr Hardy, I find your unorthodox methods of communicating with me rather perplexing." He glared at the young constable who was standing rigidly at attention. "Why is it that you feel the need to waylay me on my way home?"

Leonard always felt compelled to be guarded when talking with the senior policeman. "Uh, I was hoping we could have a frank and private discussion."

The inspector scratched the sparse whiskers that invaded the pockmarked skin of his face and grunted.

Leonard took that as a cue to continue. "Can you confirm with me that you are unable to investigate the Riley brothers unless you have evidence that will bear legal scrutiny in the court?"

"Are you asking for personal reasons or for the benefit of the *Evening Standard*?" Inspector Gibbard asked.

"Personal, of course."

"Your question is more reminiscent of a reporter looking for a story."

"If you recall, my employment with the *Evening Standard* was terminated."

"Hmmm. Mr Hardy, as I previously explained, both Mr Elijah and Joshua Riley are extremely well connected with influential friends. Until such time as there is tangible evidence, I'm not permitted to probe into their activities without suitable cause." He began walking and Leonard remained at his side.

"What if the opportunity to obtain solid evidence presented itself to you?"

The inspector stopped. "Are you telling me you have or can get that evidence?"

Leonard grimaced. "Perhaps. Inspector, I have come across some information that could assist you, if, and I repeat, if, you want to see the Riley brothers prosecuted for their crimes."

"As long as no applicable laws are broken, and all evidence is obtained legally, then yes, most certainly. But what do you have? If you have details of a crime and do not share them with me, then that is an offence and you will face consequences," warned the inspector with a hard edge to his voice.

"No, no, far from it. I want to aid you and I am formulating a plan where you can obtain solid and reliable evidence so that the Riley brothers are held accountable."

"And what do you have?"

"I have knowledge of when the next shipment of opium will arrive in Wellington and, with thought and planning, we can link that delivery with irrefutable proof to the Riley brothers so they can be arrested."

"Last time you presented me with similar information it turned out to be of no value whatsoever."

"True, but only because the Rileys were forewarned."

Inspector Gibbard inclined his head. The hard edges of his face softened and he sighed heavily. "Yes, agreed. I believe that, too."

"And I do not wish for that to happen again. In this instance, no one must know, and those in the constabulary must not be told, because someone could intentionally warn them."

"I cannot perform my duties without the support of my colleagues and resources in the constabulary—"

"What if other people provided you with support, and uh, legally of course," Leonard added with his best, most charming smile.

The inspector continued walking. "That depends … I need more information."

"Very well, if I arranged a meeting at a secure location where we could discuss those details, would you attend?"

Inspector Gibbard pursed his almost non-existent lips. "I'm presuming that others who would assist would also be in attendance?"

Leonard nodded.

"And you have formulated a plan?"

Inwardly, Leonard cringed. The best he had was some ideas, but a plan ...? He swallowed. "Yes, and it will put an end to the Riley brothers' shenanigans once and for all."

"Let me think on it, Mr Hardy. This is most irregular and inappropriate. Let me know when and where this meeting will be and I will give it due consideration."

Leonard thought this was a positive indication. "Very well, Inspector, I will send word to you within the next few days."

"Good evening, Mr Hardy."

Leonard watched Inspector Gibbard stride away. *A most peculiar man*, he thought. *But without question, upstanding and beyond reproach. "*Time to return home, constable!"

"Do you actually have a plan?" Tim asked with incredulity.

"Well, not exactly — it's a work in progress," Leonard meekly responded. They were in the private area of Uncle Jun's shop where Leonard was still staying.

Exasperated, Tim rubbed his face. "Leo, here you go again, you're calling a meeting to thrash out and implement a plan that doesn't exist. What will you discuss... recipes?"

"I have some ideas," Leonard volunteered.

"Ideas! Good heavens!" Tim cried. "I think you've received one too many knocks to the head."

Leonard picked up a small plate that held a scone topped with jam and cream. He stared at it, trying to decide the best way to devour it without creating a mess.

Tim knew Leonard well enough to know what he was thinking. "A civilised person would put less cream on top and cut the scone into manageable pieces," he offered.

"Yes, but that would limit each mouthful to a small portion, when the satisfaction lies in consuming as much of it as possible on the first bite." He rotated the plate and assessed the scone from a different angle. "I admit, Bridgette was thoughtful and managed to heap an extraordinary amount of cream on top. It presents a minor hurdle, but not insurmountable."

"Just like your non-existent plan?" Tim added.

"Herein lies the challenge, Tim. This scone represents the opium the Riley brothers are expecting. Just like me, they want to look at and assess it. Ensure that they have received exactly what they paid for."

"You didn't pay for the scone, it was a gift from Bridgette."

Leonard grinned. "At least have the courtesy to play along."

Tim sat down on a chair opposite Leonard and leaned forward. "I'm listening."

"The scone came directly to me, but the opium can't be delivered directly to the Riley brothers on Cuba Street or they risk discovery. No, they must keep the opium at a secure location and then go to where it is stored. There are two very relevant facts …" Resisting the urge to eat the scone, he placed the plate back onto the centre of the table, licking his fingers which had inadvertently touched the cream. "Point one. The opium is transported from the ship to a safe place to store." He pointed to the scone on the table. "That is the storage facility. We need to know where this warehouse or location will be."

Tim nodded.

"Point two. The Riley brothers will, in all probability, check their shipment to ensure they received what they paid for."

"You hope," Tim suggested.

"They will. However, we do not know when this will happen... but sometime very soon after it arrives at their storage location. So the challenge is, we need to shadow the shipment to where it will be stored, and then follow the Riley brothers to the location and catch them inspecting their opium." Leonard leaned back in his chair and folded his arms.

"Unless someone steals it," replied Tim. He reached forward, and before Leonard could react, picked up the scone and took an enormous bite."

Leonard shot to his feet. "That's unfair!"

A substantial glob of cream fell from Tim's nose and ran onto his uniform. Despite the mess, he couldn't contain himself and began to laugh.

Leonard doing his best to look stern, failed, and joined in.

Chapter Thirty-Seven

With a grunt, Chen Jun Qiang swung both heavy doors of his shop, and closed them with a clatter. Leonard watched as the elderly Chinaman dropped a wooden beam into sturdy metal supports, then threaded a large padlock through a hole and snapped it into place. His shop was now locked. Leonard couldn't recall the last time he'd seen the place closed this early. Normally he was open for business from sunrise until well into the evening, often past 10:00 p.m.

Uncle Jun looked up at Leonard, wiped his hands on his linen breeches, and smiled. "We go, eh?"

Leonard returned the smile, "After you."

The young constable discretely followed a few steps behind affording Leonard and Uncle Jun some privacy so they could talk without being overheard. People acknowledged and greeted Uncle Jun as they walked towards Taranaki Street, and he in turn bowed his head in respect and always said a few kind words in reply.

Leonard looked casually around and noticed a few Chinese youths loosely positioned around them. At first glance, they appeared to be nothing more than pedestrians, but he quickly noticed how they randomly changed from one side of the street to the other, behind or in front, and were never farther than twenty yards or so away as they kept the pair constantly surrounded. To any casual observer, there was nothing untoward, they were just two men walking together with a a lone constable trailing. It felt reassuring.

They crossed Taranaki Street and turned into Vivian Street. Here, there were fewer people and Leonard noticed how the youths spread out even more. After a short distance they turned into an alley that ran parallel to Cuba Street, and Leonard knew exactly where they were headed. He'd been there before, with the young woman, Yan.

They entered the building where they were greeted by swelter from fires heating large kettles of water for washing clothes and the prattle of workers as they conversed in Chinese. As previously instructed, Leonard reminded the constable to remain outside and to wait for his return, then they walked up a stairway to the first floor where Wang Yong waited.

Immediately, Mr Yong and Uncle Jun began a conversation that Leonard couldn't follow, which ended with a hearty laugh from both men.

"Good evening, Mr Hardy, is a pleasure to see you yet again," smiled Wang Yong. "Please be seated and make yourself comfortable ."

Leonard was again struck by Mr Yong's command of the English language and how he spoke flawlessly.

Uncle Jun took a seat beside Wang Yong, while Leonard sat down opposite. On a low table between them, a pot of tea steamed alongside three cups. Leonard felt movement behind him and turned to see a familiar face. The beautiful young woman Yan appeared, greeting him with a warm smile. She dipped her head in respect to Wang Yong and Uncle Jun and began pouring tea. When her task was completed, she picked up a cup and reverently offered it to Wang Yong, the eldest. After he accepted the cup, he began tapping the cup with his middle finger, which Leonard knew was a Chinese custom that acknowledged gratitude. She repeated the process for Uncle Jun, and finally Leonard. Having completed her duty, she quietly left the large room leaving the three men alone.

Leonard politely waited for his host to invite him to speak. As he waited, he turned slightly to his right and, glancing out the window, saw the office of the New York Contributionship Company. He felt his stomach tighten and wished he hadn't looked. He sensed the inquisitive gaze of both elderly men on him and turned back to them.

"I am distressed to learn of your ongoing misfortune, Leonard. Your indemnity, and the loss of your friend, Mr Baylor, still upsets me."

"Thank you."

"I find it inexcusable that the New York Contributionship Company has failed in its obligation to honour its commitment and recompense you for the loss of your home," began Wang Yong. "What will you do?"

Leonard shook his head then shrugged. "I find it difficult to reconcile the loss and know not how to persuade them to reconsider. Thank you for asking, but I have no capital to begin rebuilding."

"You are looking at a loss of approximately one-hundred and seventy-five pounds, er, perhaps two-hundred pounds?"

Leonard nodded. "At the most."

"After your forced removal from their premises a few days ago, I doubt whether they would reassess their decision." He watched Leonard intensely.

Leonard felt contrite and looked down at his feet.

"Now then …" Wang Yong shifted position slightly.

With resolve, Leonard looked up and held his intense gaze. It felt like he was being judged.

"You have asked to meet with me, and after consulting with Chen Jun, I have agreed to your request. Please, feel free to speak candidly, you have my full attention."

"Thank you, Mr Yong." Leonard took a deep breath. He felt apprehensive, nervous, knowing his plan hinged on Mr Yong's acceptance and willingness to help.

He'd prepared diligently for this meeting. He reached inside his coat, extracting his notebook, where he'd jotted relevant talking points and cleared his throat. "I have made some detailed notes, and um, I understand that opium brought into Wellington is controlled …" He looked up into the blank expressions of Wang Yong, and then to Uncle Jun. He sighed. *This isn't going well*, he thought. He closed his notebook with a snap.

"I want to see the Riley brothers face justice for all they have done. Not only have they destroyed my life, they have killed people, and will stop at nothing to ensure their illegal enterprise continues unabated." This time, both men responded with a slight head nod.

"In two days' time a ship will arrive in Wellington bringing another shipment of opium for the Riley brothers—and I have a plan."

At this revelation, Wang Yong did react more favourably and turned to Uncle Jun — the look of concern obvious. "Can you be sure?" he asked.

"Absolutely. I have received this information from an irrefutable source — the details are correct," Leonard quickly added.

Wang Yong and Uncle Jun chatted in Chinese to each other. When they finished, Wang Yong turned back to Leonard. "What is this plan?"

Leonard swallowed. "The uh, problem is we don't know where the opium will be stored once it has been unloaded from the ship.

The original destination was the same warehouse where the other previous shipment was stored, but since the police discovered that location, no one knows where this new consignment will be delivered."

"And this is where you believe I can be of assistance?" Wang Yong asked.

"Well, yes, but …" Leonard slid to the edge of his seat and leaned forward. "Really, it's a bit more than that. What I want to happen is quite simple. I know exactly the time the ship will berth at the wharf and I want to have the particular shipment followed to the new undisclosed warehouse."

"The Riley brothers will be extra cautious, is this not so?"

Leonard nodded. "That is what I believe, and to create some confusion and make them less cautious, I will have the ship's mooring-time delayed. This means the ship has less time to unload and they will need to expedite the process and unload more quickly than usual. There will be more disorder on the wharf, more people waiting for goods and the Riley brothers will have their hands full, with less time to be vigilant. When the opium is finally loaded onto a wagon we need a mechanism in place to follow the shipment to its new storage location and remain undetected."

"You have the ability to delay the mooring time?"

"I do," Leonard grinned.

Duly impressed, Wang Yong raised his eyebrows. "Last time we did this the constabulary were slow to respond and they found nothing in the warehouse. Why not have the constabulary confiscate the shipment as soon as it is unloaded from the ship?"

"Because there isn't anything that links the Rileys to the shipment. Yes, the unlicenced opium can be impounded, but the brothers would remain unconnected."

"I suspect there is more to this …" said Wang Yong. He held his tea cup to his lips and took a sip.

"Yes, Mr Yong, following the shipment to the warehouse is only the simple part."

Wang Yong raised his voice and spoke in Chinese. Within moments Yan reappeared and took away the teapot as the three men waited in silence for her to leave.

Leonard was hungry and wished Yan had bought biscuits or cake. He thought back to when Tim took a huge bite from his cream and strawberry jam topped scone.

Wang Yong nodded, encouraging him to continue.

"I would like your men to take the opium from the warehouse."

Uncle Jun was taking a sip of tea. "Leo!" he spluttered, and shook his head.

"Steal it?" confirmed Wang Yong. If he was surprised, he gave no reaction.

"Let me explain," Leonard offered. "The challenge is to link the opium to the Riley brothers. If you *take* the opium, we can hold it and demand the Riley brothers pay money to you so that you will return it to them. We arrange a place for the money to change hands and the exchange to be made and then the police can be waiting."

"And what will prevent the constabulary from arresting me?" Wang Yong asked.

Uncle Jun was still shaking his head in disapproval.

Leonard smiled. "I will arrange with the police ahead of time, so that it is understood and agreed upon that you are helping them in a covert operation to apprehend the Riley brothers, and therefore are not breaking any law."

Uncle Jun shook his head. "Police agree to this, Leo?"

"In a manner, but I cannot finalise details until you've agreed," Leonard replied.

Wang Yong scratched his chin as he gave the matter thought.

"The important thing to remember is that the Riley brothers would remain totally unaware who is holding their opium for ransom. This way you avoid reprisals and retaliation." Leonard leaned back in his chair.

"If I understand you correctly, Mr Hardy, you want me to steal the Riley brothers opium shipment. Then send a demand missive to the brothers for a fixed amount of money, then exchange the opium for their money at a prearranged location that the police will know about in advance so they can arrest the Riley brothers when the transfer is made?" Wang Yong clarified.

Leonard nodded in agreement.

Immediately, Uncle Jun began chattering to Wang Yong. Leonard waited as they debated back and forth.

They stopped talking as Yan re-entered with a fresh pot of tea. Mr Yong said a few words to her, and once the teapot was on the table, she again silently left the room.

"You are asking a lot from me, Mr Hardy," said Wang Yong as his clear eyes bored into Leonard's.

Leonard nodded. "I know this. However, from my limited understanding of your business and the Chinese community, the removal of the Riley brothers business interests in this area serves you well. Am I wrong?" he forced himself to maintain eye contact with the elder Chinese gentleman. The room was quiet, and Leonard thought he may have overstepped.

"Following the opium shipment from the wharf presents no challenges for me," Wang Yong finally responded after breaking eye contact. "However, finding a suitable storage place where I cannot be implicated is another matter, but not insurmountable. I seriously doubt the constabulary will ignore my involvement in your scheme. One enthusiastic constable seeking to impress his superiors could easily have an adverse effect on your, uh, scheme, if he decided to arrest my men."

Leonard thought quickly. "Perhaps, Mr Yong, if I were the person that would meet the Riley brothers for the exchange."

Uncle Jun laughed. "Leo, you silly boy."

Again, Wang Yong spoke to Uncle Jun as Leonard watched.

"Mr Hardy, if the constabulary consented to do this, then it would be best if you were the person to facilitate the exchange, but you would need to wear a mask or disguise so you were not recognised. If they saw you, before the exchange was made, they would flee. Can you really convince the constabulary to agree to this?"

"I will need to discuss it with Inspector Gibbard. At this point, police participation will be minimal and probably only the inspector and one other constable would be there to witness the transaction. It may be required for your men to lend support to the apprehension and arrest."

"Why only two police? Surely such an event would require more active police involvement?"

Leonard nodded. "Inspector Gibbard has been forbidden from investigating the Riley brothers unless suitable evidence that will withstand legal scrutiny in court is presented. I also believe someone in the constabulary is passing information to the Riley brothers, so the fewer people who know of our plan, the better."

"Regardless of what you say, Mr Hardy, laws are being broken."

Wang Yong scratched his thin whiskers. "If you are offered an assurance that my people will not be implicated in any crime, then I agree. I will grant you this request, but with some modifications."

"Leo," Uncle Jun shook his head again, "you be careful."

Leonard sat back in his chair and smiled. His heart still beat furiously.

Chapter Thirty-Eight

Inspector Gibbard looked distinctly out of place as he sat on a chair in the private area of Uncle Jun's shop drinking tea from an ornately decorated Chinese cup. To Leonard's way of thinking, the inspector was an anomaly, an oxymoron. He had the appearance, propagated by a pock-marked face, oversized sideburns and a lipless mouth, that promoted the incorrect belief he was a malefactor, a villain. Yet, he espoused fairness, decency, and interpreted the law with total unbiased impartiality. His cold, unfeeling persona gave little away of his personal thoughts and opinions. If he had any, they were assiduously shrouded and kept appropriately private. Without question, he exemplified the honest and entirely trustworthy notion of a competent law enforcement official of significant rank. This made dealing with the man so frustrating because it was near impossible to predict his reactions.

Inspector Thomas Gibbard looked over the rim of his teacup that he held to the gash of his mouth. "I believe you've received a serious blow to the head that's removed any trace of sensibility." He took a sip from the cup and placed it with care back on the table.

"I'm offering you an opportunity to arrest criminals, Inspector, and perhaps solve multiple crimes and dismantle an organisation steeped in vice. You can't deny that, can you?" Leonard countered.

"I don't deny that at all. The point of the matter is simple — what you propose is illegal. And I won't be party to it."

In frustration, Leonard placed his cup quite firmly on the table and stood. The inspector watched impassively.

"If the constabulary wished to proceed with an operation of similar precepts to ensnare a criminal, then, that is legal?" Leonard asked.

"The constabulary are sworn officers of the Crown. If the process to gather evidence bears legal examination where the — alleged — perpetrators are believed to have committed a crime, without entrapment, then under special and approved circumstances, it is permissible." Inspector Gibbard leaned back in his chair and folded his arms.

"Then why can't that process be applied to what I propose?"

"Because, Mr Hardy, you are not a sworn officer of the Crown," snapped the inspector.

"Then make me one! What do you have to lose?" he appealed.

The inspector remained silent as he considered his response.

"We are not discussing the theft of a bicycle, or the unlawful activities of a pickpocket. We are talking about multiple homicides, influencing the outcome of horse racing, unlicenced opium, arson and assault. I can think of more, if you need reminding," Leonard argued.

Inspector Gibbard unfolded his arms and leaned forward. "Firstly and foremost, the sale of opium is not an offence if a vendor is registered. In this case the Riley brothers are not registered as vendors because their purpose is somewhat nefarious and that bears investigation. Do you understand?"

Leonard nodded. "I do, which is why they cannot report the disappearance of their opium shipment."

"Correct. To authorise such an undertaking as you suggest, requires me to formally solicit permission from my superior. That same superior has a relationship with both Joshua and Elijah Riley, which could compromise the successful conclusion of the operation and potentially jeopardise your safety, and perhaps even others. In all probability, he may even deny my request."

Leonard understood what the inspector was alluding to, it made sense. "Then how can we move forward? What I propose is the only option you currently have. I know you wish to arrest these men if they have broken the law, so, what can you do? To whom can you speak and receive counsel?"

"And that is my quandary," said Inspector Gibbard in a softer voice.

For the first time Leonard saw a chink in his impenetrable armour. He was making progress. "So what do you suggest doing?"

The inspector stared at a dirty fleck on the curtain that separated the private area from the shop and didn't immediately reply.

Leonard waited.

After a while, the policeman exhaled and shifted his gaze back to him. "I do not know why I trust you, Mr Hardy. You always find yourself in a tenuous predicament that barely falls within the bounds of legality, and yet I know you mean well and your intentions are honourable. I place my career at risk, but I shall consult with a legal expert, a solicitor, whom I believe can advise me."

Leonard grinned. *Progress.*

"But before you say something foolish, let me add, I know that time is crucial, and I will send word to you in the morning."

"Thank you, Inspector Gibbard."

The inspector eased himself to his feet. "And thank you for the tea." He parted the curtain and stepped into the shop.

Immediately Leonard heard Uncle Jun's sing-song voice as he

spoke to the inspector. It sounded like the he was trying to sell some tinctures to improve the inspector's unsightly skin condition.

He had a fitful, restless sleep that night. Leonard's vivid imagination conjured scenarios where the plan he envisioned fell apart and he was maimed, left wounded and bleeding. At one point he rehearsed explaining to a judge how his role in the plan was minimal and pleaded for clemency. The prospects of a life of incarceration gave him chills. Eventually his thoughts turned to Mary … he missed her, and hoped he could restore and improve on their relationship when she felt it safe to return to Wellington. He rose from his bed when the sound of Uncle Jun pottering around his shop made any hope of sleep impossible.

Leonard was helping Uncle Jun move some sacks of roots when Tim ran breathlessly into the shop. His large smile spread from ear to ear. "Leo! Leo, we must talk!"

True to his word Inspector Gibbard had made a decision and on the advice of a solicitor, a trusted colleague, he decided to support Leonard's plan, informed Tim. "But you need to dress suitably because you must attend a magistrate this morning."

"A magistrate?"

Tim grinned, "You, dear boy, are to be sworn in as a special constable. But we must not be tardy."

As directed by Tim, Leonard entered the Magistrates Court through the rear private entrance where he was led to a room. A brass plate attached to the heavy door indicated this was the office of the Hon, Resident Magistrate, Phineas Shaw. Tim knocked and waited.

The door was opened by a dour young man who stared at them both quizzically.

"Good morning, I have Mr Leonard Hardy here with me as instructed by Inspector Gibbard," said Tim.

The young man's gaze shifted to Leonard. "Enter."

Tim remained outside while Leonard stepped into the magistrate's office. The heavy door closed behind him with a loud mechanical clunk. At an ornate oak desk sat a reed-thin man with thick eyebrows and hooded, squinty eyes whom he presumed was the magistrate. Behind him a shelf laden with thickly bound legal books dominated the wall. In front of the desk stood Inspector Gibbard and another well-dressed gentleman whom he didn't recognise.

The lingering odour of pipe tobacco smoke did little to ease the tenseness he felt as he walked in.

The young man walked around him, "Mr Leonard Hardy, Your Honour."

Magistrate Shaw slowly looked up from a document he was reading and appraised Leonard carefully. "Are you here on your own volition?" he asked without pleasantries.

"Yes, sir, I mean, Your Honour."

"And you are cognisant of why you are here?"

Leonard turned to look at Inspector Gibbard, who nodded imperceptibly.

"I am, Your Honour."

The magistrate paused and gave him a long hard stare. "You are here before me, Mr Hardy, due to the rather unusual circumstances of a current investigation by Inspector Gibbard. Because of limited staffing resources, your service may be required in the capacity of a special constable to aid his lawful investigation. However, the decision to use you as a special constable is at the sole discretion of Inspector Gibbard, no one else. Do you accept these conditions?"

Leonard nodded.

"I can't hear you, Mr Hardy."

"Yes, Your Honour."

"Very well," replied Magistrate Phineas Shaw as the young man, presumably a clerk, handed the magistrate a document.

After a moment the magistrate raised his head and looked at Leonard. "You are here as a citizen to be sworn in as a special constable in consequence of the distinctive investigation by Inspector Gibbard. As a special constable you have the same status and power and are liable to the same punishments as an ordinary constable. Do you understand, Mr Hardy?"

Leonard swallowed thickly. "I do understand, Your Honour."

The magistrate nodded. "You will now undertake your oath of office."

The young clerk stepped around the magistrate's desk and handed a document to Leonard. He pointed to it. "Add your full name here."

Leonard cleared his throat and held the document nearer to his face. "Do you wish me to recite this aloud?"

"If you please," stated the magistrate.

"I do swear that I, uh, Leonard Hardy, will well and truly serve our Sovereign Lady the Queen, in the office of special constable at Wellington and the neighbourhood thereof, without favour or affection, malice or ill will, and that I will to the best of my power cause the peace to be kept and preserved and prevent all offences against the persons and properties of Her Majesty's subjects; and that while

I continue to hold the said office, I will, to the best of my skill and knowledge discharge all the duties thereof faithfully, according to law. So help me God."

The clerk took the oath document from him as the unknown man standing beside the inspector handed yet another document to him along with two more copies. Leonard believed he must be the solicitor friend the inspector spoke of. From behind the authority of his desk, the magistrate watched every movement like a hawk.

"Now then, Mr Hardy, please sign your name on all three documents, here." Again he pointed to the appropriate place then moved to the magistrate's desk where an ink pen and well were conveniently placed.

Leonard scrawled his name three times, as required, before stepping back. The clerk indicated for the inspector to sign next.

Once the inspector had signed all the documents, the clerk handed them to the magistrate. He looked sternly at Inspector Gibbard. "I was hesitant to allow this, but I feel given the uniqueness of your predicament I had little choice in the matter. The law must be upheld and lawbreakers held to account, regardless of social position, privilege or favour." He swivelled his thin, long neck and turned to look at Leonard. "There are people within this community who hold you in the highest regard. Without their endorsements and advocacy, I would not have acceded to Inspector Gibbard's request. I wish you both good luck and good health. Gentlemen."

Leonard nodded in acknowledgement as the magistrate added his signature. The clerk produced a stamp and with a dramatic gesture, imprinted each document. A copy was given to the solicitor, one to Leonard, and the other retained for the court. The clerk moved to the door and opened it. The swearing-in procedure was over, and now, he was a special constable.

Tim was waiting outside, grinning like Lewis Carrol's Cheshire cat in *Alice's Adventures in Wonderland,* and gave Leonard a congratulatory thump on his arm. He was rubbing his shoulder when Inspector Gibbard exited the room moments later.

"Before we progress further, Mr Hardy, I will need to meet with Mr Yong and yourself to establish protocols and boundaries, I will not have you or the Chinese running around Wellington creating havoc."

Leonard nodded mutely.

"As time is of the essence, then I suggest early this evening. Constable Yates can apprise me of where and when," he continued. "I think it also prudent to ensure there are no flaws and that we have scope to refine and improve your scheme."

"I will arrange it with Uncle Jun as soon as I return to his shop. "Leonard replied compliantly.

"Sir."

"I beg your pardon?" Leonard asked.

"You are now a special constable, and as I am of superior grade, you will address my rank with due respect."

Leonard couldn't tell if this was Inspector Gibbard's attempt at humour, although he did see his eyes crinkle slightly. "Er, yes, sir," he replied.

Leonard never saw the inspector smile as he turned away to speak with the solicitor.

Chapter Thirty-Nine

If Wang Yong was uncomfortable in the presence of Inspector Gibbard, he didn't show it. He was a gracious host and as eloquent and polite as ever. Uncle Jun sat beside Mr Yong and Leonard and the inspector sat opposite. Again they met above the laundry on Cuba Street. Tea had been served and each of them held a steaming cup in both hands, warming them from the cold weather they had experienced while outside.

Inspector Gibbard placed his cup on the low table, crossed his legs and studied his host carefully. "Thank you for meeting me this evening, Mr Yong."

Wang Yong silently dipped his head in acknowledgement and allowed his guest to speak.

"It is paramount that we understand our roles and recognise what is expected from each of us," the inspector continued.

Wang Yong smiled, then placed his teacup back onto the table and steepled his hands, placing them beneath his chin. "It is my pleasure to assist the constabulary in this matter, after all, Mr Hardy is one of many aggrieved parties," he stated. "And if Mr Hardy is vindicated and able to receive restitution for his substantial losses, then our minimal contribution is a small price to pay."

Uncle Jun's head bobbed up in down in agreement.

Wang Yong's face hardened slightly. "However, and additionally, the illicit business enterprises of the Riley brothers are of extreme concern to the Chinese community. We would like to have opium eradicated from our neighbourhood and see justice served,

Inspector Gibbard."

"Restitution is a matter for the courts to decide, Mr Yong, but I do agree with you," the inspector quickly responded. "If we are able to provide clear and indisputable proof that the Rileys are breaking the law, then with the authority of my warrant and the unequivocal support of my superiors, we will initiate judicial proceedings at once."

Wang Yong didn't reply immediately and held the inspector's gaze. After a few moments he smiled and then nodded. "Indeed."

"Now, as I understand it, once the opium shipment has been identified by your people, they will covertly follow the shipment to where it will be stored, is that correct?" asked the inspector.

"Mr Hardy will be foretold when the opium will be offloaded from the ship, and for us, it is a simple matter of keeping the wagon visible at all times while it's delivered to its eventual storage location," Wang Yong explained.

Inspector Gibbard scratched his chin. "But once it has been stored, how confident are you that you can remove the shipment without alerting anyone and keep it safe until the exchange is made so we can make an arrest?"

"Mr Gibbard, far be it for me to boast, for I am a simple, humble man, surrounded by people with remarkable talents." Wang Yong sighed heavily. "Take yourself for example. You are an upstanding and successful man with many notable career achievements, and undoubtedly excel at your profession. I have unquestioned faith in your superior abilities, Inspector. I am fortunate to have equally skillful people willing to aid us for a most worthy cause." He maintained eye contact with the policeman and smiled.

"Your point is understood, Mr Yong." The inspector paused

briefly and Leonard could see how both men were gauging each other and taking measure of their respective capabilities, strengths and weaknesses. "Once the opium has been successfully removed, how long before contact is made with the Riley brothers for the ransom?"

Wang Yong deferred to Leonard with a wave of his hand.

"I think that three days is sufficient, by then the Rileys should be fraught with worry and more willing to agree to my demands," Leonard said with confidence. "And then a time and suitable venue is arranged for the interchange, which will be coordinated by Mr Yong. It is crucial that you arrive precisely on time, immediately after the Riley brothers arrive to witness the exchange and make the arrests."

"The success of this operation does hinge on timing," confirmed the inspector. "Are there any concerns about this?" He looked from person to person.

Wang Yong sat comfortably on his chair and reached for his teacup before replying. He took a sip. "I believe everything is well in hand."

Inspector Gibbard turned to Leonard. "How much money will you demand from the Rileys?"

"Based on the size of the previous shipment, Mr Yong believes one-hundred pounds is a fair figure."

"That isn't a substantial amount, and I assume you feel they will readily pay you?" Gibbard asked.

Wang Yong nodded. "They have a sizeable investment in this shipment, one-hundred pounds is more than equitable — I agree, and perhaps even a little low."

The inspector pondered the matter and nodded in agreement.

"I am extremely confident that all contingencies have been considered," Leonard added. He knew that he still needed to coordinate with Wang Yong and select the location for the exchange, but as the Chinaman explained, it all depended on where the opium was stored. "This plan only works as long as the Rileys remain unaware of where their opium has been hidden."

For the next hour, they discussed details and timing. Inspector Gibbard was relentless in asking questions and confirming everyone knew what was expected from them. It was growing late and with nothing more to ask, he rose from his seat, politely offered his thanks and made his departure. He stepped outside into the southerly wind and walked home believing there was little chance of success.

The following afternoon, Inspector Gibbard, Constable Tim Yates and Leonard stood inside the premises of the Pier Hotel at the corner of Customhouse Quay and Grey Street, and from their elevated vantage point on the hotel's first floor balcony, they watched the activities on Queens Wharf without fear of being seen and recognized.

Out in Lambton Harbour, a scattering of small coastal ships bobbed at anchor. Some had already been unloaded and others impatiently tugged at their chains, waiting for their turn to moor and have men swarm over their decks to hoist precious cargo from spacious holds.

Inspector Gibbard looked at the piece of paper Leonard had previously given to him and read it again. He didn't need to as he'd memorized all the details earlier, but he couldn't resist and re-read the document in case he'd inadvertently missed something. The ship they were interested in was the China Steam Navigation Company's, *S.S Taiyuau.* At 1459 tons, the *Taiyuau* was delivering tea and other delicacies to satisfy the exotic appetites of Wellington's fine residents. With growing anxiety they watched the ship slowly manoeuvre in Lambton Harbour. As Andrej Janjić earlier explained to Leonard, ships arriving from international ports were given berthing priority over domestic coastal vessels.

"You said the *Taiyuau* would be delayed," snapped the inspector, still believing this operation had little chance of success.

"It will," said Leonard with more confidence than he felt.

Inspector Gibbard harrumphed.

They turned back to observing Queens Wharf and the coastal trader that was currently unloading the last of its substantial cargo of logs. As soon as it was unloaded, it was scheduled to slip its moorings and depart Queens Wharf to make way for the *Taiyuau.*

Even from the balcony of the Pier Hotel, they heard the faint and panicked warning cry from aboard the coastal trader. Suddenly men began running as one of the thick ropes, binding heavy logs suspended only three feet above the deck, parted from the jib gantry. The unbalanced load slowly slid back from its cradle onto the deck with a loud crash. Now completely untethered, a couple of the logs rolled from the ship and splashed into the water. It was pandemonium as men quickly scrambled to prevent other logs from causing further damage and rolling into the sea.

"My God!" exclaimed the inspector, "I hope no one is hurt."

Leonard watched in open mouthed amazement.

"Was that planned?" asked Tim.

Leonard closed his mouth and shrugged. "I hope so."

Inspector Gibbard shook his head as he watched the trader's

crew begin securing the remaining logs. From the Pier Hotel, they couldn't see the far side of the scow where the logs bobbed in the water but the activity on the deck of the coastal trader was frantic. He turned away from the hand-rail where he stood to face Leonard. "I presume this is the delay you spoke of?"

Leonard nodded. "I was not informed what would cause the delay, but … uh, I suppose it will take some time to recover those logs." He looked out across the harbour. "Look, the *Taiyuau* is turning!"

The inspector followed Leonard's gaze to see the China Steam Navigation Company's steam ship *Taiyuau*, was already veering away from Queens Wharf. "This mishap will cause a hindrance, and if what you say is correct, when the *Taiyuau* eventually does berth, they will be behind schedule which will undoubtedly complicate unloading." He pointed towards Customhouse Quay where empty wagons were already assembling.

"I think the disruption was more dramatic than dangerous," volunteered Tim.

"I agree," Inspector Gibbard replied. "I think it's time we took our leave. We can do nothing here and the next step falls squarely onto the shoulders of Mr Yong. Let's hope the delay causes Rileys' people to be less vigilant, as we hope, and there are no complications at Mr Yong's end, eh?"

The three men quietly exited the hotel and walked up Grey Street away from the wharves and caught a Hansom cab back to Uncle Jun's shop where they would wait for word from Wang Yong on where the opium had been delivered.

Afternoon turned into evening and still no word had come from Wang Yong. Even Uncle Jun appeared jittery. The inspector went home leaving instructions for Tim to inform him of details when they arrived. Leonard's stomach felt queasy, every passing hour making him feel more anxious, and he hoped nothing had gone amiss.

It was past 10:00 p.m. when a knock at the rear door of the shop alerted them to a visitor. Uncle Jun quickly unlatched and swung open the door as Leonard and Tim nervously waited. The young Chinese girl Yan entered and first greeted Uncle Jun, then Leonard and Tim.

Tea was offered, but she politely refused. "I come with news," she began, her voice soft and silky smooth.

"Do they know where the opium is?" Leonard spurted out, unable to hold back his curiosity.

Yan nodded. "The opium was delivered to a shipwright's warehouse on Evans Bay Parade."

"Evans Bay Parade!" Leonard exclaimed. "Why store it in Evans Bay, it's such a long way away?"

"And who'd think about searching there for opium?" Tim asked rhetorically.

"I have more information for you," Yan continued. "Wang Tong offers his sincere apologies for the delay in bringing you these particulars, however, it is important that you understand there were, uh, complications."

Leonard quickly turned to Tim with a look of concern.

"The opium shipment was not loaded onto a wagon as we expected —"

"What!" Leonard cried.

"The Rileys were clever. The opium was immediately loaded onto two watermen's boats and then they made their way back to

Evans Bay by sea."

By sea? Leonard shook his head... *of course.* An unforeseen convolution, and he knew that Mr Yong's people could not follow the watermen's boats. That option had never been discussed or even considered.

"We had to, uh, improvise and follow by land," she added.

"Two boats? Why two?" Leonard asked.

Yan nodded, "The shipment was much larger than the previous one."

Leonard whistled. "But, nevertheless, you know the location of where the opium was delivered?" Leonard confirmed.

Yan nodded. "Wang Yong thought it in the best interests that he, uh, take possession of the opium as quickly as possible. Soon after the opium was delivered to the shipwright warehouse, he sent men inside and we now have all the opium, Mr Hardy." She smiled at Leonard.

The relief was immense, and Leonard grinned. "Where is it now?" he asked.

Yan's smile vanished. "Uh, Wang Yong asks for your forbearance in this matter. He says that no one must know where the opium is and he will decide where the best place is to do exchange tomorrow."

Leonard made eye contact with Tim. *This wasn't what we had planned.*

Tim must have been thinking similar thoughts. "I know this wasn't what we had arranged, but in light of the Rileys unorthodox mode of delivery, then it is logical for Mr Yong to take the opium to a secure place. Why is he not willing to tell us where?"

Yan looked nervous. "Mr Yong believes that the Rileys should not be underestimated. He says they are clever, and if the location of the opium is known by others, then the Rileys will learn where it is. He wishes to minimise that risk."

"I see his point," Leonard answered after a heartbeat or two.

Tim didn't look happy. "I will go to the inspector's home and inform him of the developments."

Chapter Forty

Inspector Gibbard wasn't thrilled about Wang Yong's reticence in revealing where he had hidden the opium shipment; that was never part of their arrangement. All requests to meet with him had been refused, although through messengers he confirmed that the opium was secure and the operation could continue as planned.

Mr Yong also gave precise instructions to Leonard and the inspector on the location of where the exchange would take place. This came as a surprise, as the address was in central Wellington at a commercial building construction site. Immediately, the inspector, Leonard and Tim set out to reconnoitre the location and determine its suitability. Mr Yong stated the exchange should take place in one week, at exactly 9:00 p.m., on the 3rd floor of the building.

Inspector Gibbard scratched his whiskers as he stared up at the unfinished structure.

The commercial building was quite large. They could see that it would be four stories tall, and the lower floors were near completion while the fourth floor just had scaffolding and some elementary framework erected. The third floor, where they focused their attention, was still an open space where the interior had yet to be built. A main single staircase that ascended from the ground floor provided access to all the floors. Another stairwell was situated at the rear of the building but had not been fitted with stairs. The three men inspected the building site from a safe distance, far enough away that their observations would not be met with suspicion.

"Why would he choose this location? Surely there are better options?" Leonard asked as he watched labourers toiling away on the site.

"I agree with your point, however, the more I see of this place, then I see the advantages of making the exchange here," the inspector replied.

Leonard looked puzzled.

The inspector pointed. "See, access to the building and upper floors can only be from that fenced-off area by the gate and then up the stairs — the only way in and out. The Rileys are being funnelled to a very specific location and they have no options to deviate." He nodded in reflective approval. "It all hinges on the capabilities of Mr Yong's men. But we shouldn't dally, time to put the next element of your plan into action, eh, Mr Hardy?"

Back at Uncle Jun's shop, the three of them formulated the wording on their ransom demand message. As agreed, the location and time where the exchange would be made would be omitted from the first note and not revealed until the last possible moment.

After vigorously debating the note's wording — as Leonard's writing style, according to the inspector and Tim — was too articulate and verbose, they finally agreed on something elementary and crude that offered no clues as to who the sender was.

Leonard held the completed note and read it for what seemed the hundredth time, and shook his head in disapproval. "Mr Pembroke would be traumatized if he read this."

To Joshua and Elijah Riley,
I have your merchandise. I want £100 to be brought to me, in

*person, in exchange for the complete shipment. I will notify you
in four days' time where and when we will make the exchange. I
need not explain what will happen if you do not comply.*

He grinned, the last sentence was his idea and added a sense of
melodrama.

Inspector Gibbard sat back in his chair, rubbing his scarred face.
"I suppose this will have to suffice. The demand is concise and provides no clues as to the identity of the author. If anything, it is so
poorly written it deflects any attention away from you, Mr Hardy."

"Should we add a name to the closing? Perhaps, uh, Spring
Heeled Jack, or The Hag —"

"That will be enough Mr Yates, I see no need to offer a closing,
and certainly not one depicting a mythical creature."

Leonard laughed. "I wonder what would happen if I signed my
name?"

"I believe you'd be killed," added the inspector wryly.

Constable Yates departed Uncle Jun's shop and walked towards
the docks where he would hire a cab to deliver the ransom note in
a sealed envelope to the New York Contributionship Company on
Cuba Street. As per instructions from the inspector he did not wear
a uniform and wore a hat pulled low over his eyes and to further
confuse a vigilant cab driver, he affected his voice to appear Scot-
tish. Leonard said the accent sounded ridiculous, to which the inspector replied, "It matters not how convincing he sounds, but how
effective the disguise. What is important is that he not be recognised
as a constable in the service of the Crown."

Leonard didn't argue.

"If the cab driver is questioned by the Rileys and asked to provide a detailed description of who delivered the message, he could only offer a vague inaccurate depiction, or not at all," the inspector added.

Carrying the burden of responsibility Tim found a cab, handed over the letter and paid the driver before returning to Uncle Jun's shop where Leonard and the inspector waited.

"Now I must make a report to my superior," informed the inspector as he stood to leave. "He requires an update on our progress, and I must oblige."

"What will you tell him when he asks you if you know the location of where Mr Yong has stored the opium?"

Inspector Gibbard's face soured. "That, Mr Hardy, is not your concern."

Leonard was pacing back and forth in Uncle Jun's shop while reviewing the details for the ransom exchange. Inspector Gibbard had previously insisted that Constable Yates would be the person assigned to receive the ransom payment from the Rileys.

"Even if you wear a disguise to hide your features, you may still be recognized while Constable Yates is unknown to the Rileys," the inspector had said. "If you are identified then this entire operation could fail."

Leonard reluctantly agreed, although he did want to participate and be present to witness the arrest.

He hadn't seen either the inspector or Tim since yesterday and was anxious about the exchange, which would take place the following evening.

Sensing Leonard's anxiety, Uncle Jun assigned him some menial tasks to do in the shop and the remainder of the day passed quickly. Physically exhausted, he went to bed early. He didn't sleep, instead spending the night tossing and turning as bells and whistles pierced the night. Somewhere, Wellington's fire brigade had been called out. Sleep finally came to him fleetingly in the early hours, but he was unceremoniously woken with Uncle Jun shaking him as the grey of dawn seeped over the eastern hills.

"Leo, Leo! Wake up!"

It was chilly outside and he didn't want to arise.

"Leo, get up!" cried Uncle Jun with some urgency.

He remembered now, today was the day the ransom exchange would finally be made. He sat upright with a groan and rubbed sleep from his eyes. "Uncle Jun, what is happening?" he asked.

Uncle Jun released his shoulder and stooped down close to his face. "Leo, there has been fire, bad fire."

Leonard's eyes opened in alarm. "Are we in danger?"

"No, no, silly boy. Fire in downtown."

He shrugged and swung his legs out of bed. It was cold and he shivered.

"Leo, building burned!"

"What building?"

"Building for ransom exchange," explained Uncle Jun.

Leonard's mouth opened "Wh – What?"

Uncle Jun nodded. "Late last night, big fire in building. Is out now, but building no good for ransom."

"How do you know this, it isn't even daylight yet?"

"Leo, Wang Yong send messenger, he need to speak to you."

An hour later Leonard sat above the laundry on Cuba Street and sipped from a cup of steaming tea. Opposite, Wang Yong also held a delicate cup to his lips. He watched his guest intently before placing the cup on the low table between them.

"Mr Hardy, I presume you have heard the news?"

"About the fire?" Leonard asked.

Wang Yong nodded. "Very unfortunate. The building is now unusable for our purposes."

"Is a bit of rotten luck ..."

Wang Young shook his head and then leaned forward. "No, not bad luck. The fire was deliberately lit – it was arson."

Leonard's eyebrows scrunched together as he considered the implications. "Are you suggesting the Rileys knew, that they found out about the location and set fire to the building to thwart us? Surely not, that would mean someone told them ..."

"No doubt you are aware that I refused to meet with Inspector Gibbard," Mr Yong continued. His voice measured and calm.

Leonard nodded. "I am, and it displeased him. He feels you are not adhering to the arrangement."

"Mr Hardy, I have valid reasons to withhold information from the inspector — the police are complicit. Someone is passing information to the Rileys and common sense tells me, it can only be someone within the constabulary." Mr Yong leaned back in his seat and crossed his legs. "Who in the employ of the police is aware of our operation? The Inspector, Constable Yates and who else?"

"Tim Yates is a dear friend, a personal acquaintance, I trust him with my life," Leonard shook his head in denial. "As for the inspector, I only have a, uh, professional association with him, but I have no reason to suspect him. The man has proven to be an upstanding policeman with unquestioned integrity."

"Is that so," remarked Wang Yong. "And what of his seniors?"

Leonard shrugged, "I don't know. What I do know is that he consulted with his superior, Superintendent Taggett."

Wang Yong sat in reflective silence as he stroked the fine whiskers on his chin. After a short time he looked up at Leonard. "How can we discover who is passing confidential information to and forewarning the Rileys?"

Leonard rubbed both hands over his face. In frustration, he shook his head slowly from side to side then focused on the elderly Chinaman. "I have no notion or any insights. Should we just approach the inspector and ask him outright?"

"Perhaps ... as you are more familiar with him, then you can confide in him our concerns."

"But, Mr Yong, if the Rileys were told of the location where we would make the exchange, then they will also be aware of our plan. There is no possibility of catching the Rileys and linking them to the opium and killings, is there?"

Wang Yong held Leonard's gaze. "Exactly."

Leonard shot to his feet. "Then this has all been for nought, a complete waste of time!"

Wang Yong stared at Leonard and remained silent as he gauged the young man. After a few moments he sighed and leaned forward. "I strongly urge you, at your earliest convenience, please speak to Inspector Gibbard. Please inform me of his reaction and subsequent decision. Will you do this for me, Leonard?"

Leonard felt deflated and angry. In total disbelief, he slowly rose from his chair. "I will Mr Yong, trust me, I will do exactly that."

Chapter Forty-One

"What is so important Mr Hardy? I've had a rather trying morning ..."

To be assured no one could overhear their conversation, Leonard requested they talk outside. They exited the main building of the Mount Cook Depot and stood in privacy near an outbuilding. "Inspector, firstly, are you aware of the big fire last evening?"

"Yes, although I have been preoccupied with other matters. There's been a recent spate of burglary's so I've not had opportunity to glean any specifics."

"You don't know the address of the fire?"

Inspector Gibbard shook his head.

"The fire burned down our ransom exchange building —"

Gibbard's eyes opened wide. "Are you sure? Have you confirmed this?"

"I passed by the building on the way here to see you. Further, were you aware the Fire Brigade believes the building was purposely set alight? An accelerant was used."

Adding to his wide open eyes, the inspector's mouth fell open. As he became cognisant of the impact the fire had on their operation, another realisation dawned on him. His eyes turned to slits. "Someone talked—who?"

Leonard maintained eye contact, "I was hoping you could shed some light on that, Inspector Gibbard. Mr Yong and Uncle Jun wouldn't talk. Neither would Tim Yates ..."

The inspector turned away and stared at the distant, bush-clad upper slopes of Mount Victoria.

"… Unless, you've told others …" Leonard added.

The inspector's head whipped around, "What are you insinuating, Mr Hardy? That I'm responsible for sharing information with the Riley brothers?" In outrage, he shuffled a half step closer and glared at him angrily.

Leonard held his ground and didn't move. He could see a vein on the inspector's neck rapidly pulsing. "Well, have you?" he asked.

Both men glared silently at each other. "Don't be foolish, of course not … but someone has!" exclaimed the inspector. He composed himself and took a step away to again face the distant hills.

Leonard silently exhaled. "Need I remind you inspector, that our lives are in danger and someone is talking when they shouldn't!"

"I don't require reminding, thank you, Mr Hardy." The previous outrage had disappeared, and the inspector spoke softly.

"I must speak to Mr Yong and determine how we can move forward without compromising our plans to the police."

"Yes, yes, of course." Inspector Gibbard was distracted and hardly paying attention —Leonard could see his mind working furiously. "I, uh, I will be here for the remainder of the day. Good morning, Mr Hardy." With that, he strode back to the building lost in thought.

Uncle Jun was at the counter in his shop grinding some mysterious substances with his mortar and pestle as Leonard watched. "I no like police, big mouth, they talk too much." Uncle Jun dropped the pestle and pointed a bony finger at Leonard. "Inspector Gibbard, I no trust. He talk, he the one, Leo." He picked up the pestle and began grinding with some vigour. After a short while he again paused and looked up at Leonard. "Wang Yong, not happy when I tell him what inspector say. He agree and say perhaps Inspector Gibbard not good man and he is man talking to Riley."

"We don't know that for sure, Uncle Jun."

"Well, you know for certain inspector not talk?"

Leonard smirked. "Of course I don't. It's just that …" Leonard sighed. "I really don't know what to think anymore …"

"You must wait for Wang Yong to make decision. Remember, he still have the opium and Rileys want it, yes?"

Leonard relaxed. Uncle Jun had a valid point and Wang Yong had proven to be resourceful and perceptive. Now it made sense. Mr Yong deliberately withheld information from the police about where he had stored the opium because he didn't trust them. As it turned out, a clever decision. He turned and leaned back against the counter. "And what happens now, Uncle Jun, will the Riley brothers avoid prosecution?"

The grinding continued a moment longer then stopped. "Leo," began Uncle Jun, "*Chī yī qiàn, zhǎng yī zhì!*"

Leonard turned around.

"Gain wisdom from mistakes. Learn, eh Leo?"

"Yes, there is much to learn," Leonard replied.

The grinding continued, its rhythmic tempo unfaltering. *Mistakes, mistakes*, Leonard thought. *I made inaccurate presumptions and arrived at unproven conclusions.* He frowned and chewed on his bottom lip as he recalled the day when Mrs Bedingfield entered the bullpen at the *Evening Standard*. From that day, his life had changed, and he'd made assumptions that were incorrect, which only led to further setbacks. He'd assumed Mrs Bedingfield was motivated by concern for the whereabouts of her husband. How wrong he'd been. She'd deceived him and everyone else. What else had she done? Mrs Bedingfield … Mrs Beddington … he laughed out loud at Mr Pembroke's difficulty in remembering her name. Her name? His eyes opened wide. *Inaccurate presumptions.*

He thought back to the day he went to her house and witnessed her kissing a man in uniform. He only caught a glimpse of the clothes the man wore and while he definitely wore a uniform, it may not have been military as he guessed. Could it have been a police uniform? He never noticed the grinding had stopped.

"Uncle Jun, I'm going to the Mount Cook Depot!"

Inspector Gibbard wasn't thrilled to have his work interrupted yet again. Regardless, he exercised restraint and with his earlier frostiness forgotten, waited for Leonard to speak. He'd learned not to underestimate him, and more frequently respected his sense of logic and reasoning. Again they spoke outside so they could converse in privacy.

"Inspector, did you ever make any inquiries into Mrs Bedingfield's family?" Leonard could see the inspector was puzzled. "Let me clarify, does she have brothers, sisters … what is her maiden name?"

Inspector Gibbard was taken back. "Maiden name? This is absurd. I have had no cause … why on earth would you ask me?"

Leonard shook his head. "I'm not sure really, but I was thinking about how that woman deceived everyone. If she did so intentionally, then surely she must have deceived us previously. But I question the belief that I saw a military man at her home, perhaps it was a policeman!"

"How can you possibly relate her maiden name to inaccurately seeing a uniform? I apologise Mr Hardy, but this time you have me flummoxed."

Leonard smirked. "I'm looking for a link ... something that would make her go against the wishes of her husband. It must be quite a powerful incentive to make a woman turn against her spouse." He recalled Bridgette's advice when she spoke at her home. It was something about familial loyalty superseding marriage vows. He remembered now, Bridgette said, "...she doesn't love her husband, but she does love someone!"

The inspector didn't look convinced. "I see your point, but this is a very tenuous thread to go on."

"Inspector Gibbard, please, find out if she has brothers or sisters and what her maiden name is without drawing attention to it. It can't be difficult to obtain," Leonard pleaded.

"Leave it with me, if I discover something of importance I will notify you immediately."

Leonard was pleased.

"Actually I'm pleased you returned, saved me the inconvenience of sending you a message."

"Oh?"

"I'm no longer permitted the expense of having a constable assigned to you." The inspector shrugged. "I'm sorry."

Leonard turned to look at the young constable who stood some distance away. "It doesn't surprise me, and I doubt he would have been effective in preventing anyone from attacking me."

"More of a deterrent, really," replied the inspector. "Exercise caution, eh?" He patted Leonard's shoulder and walked towards the young constable.

Leonard was waiting anxiously in Uncle Jun's shop for word from Wang Yong on how he wanted to proceed. He was unsure if Mr Yong wanted to continue with the plan in some modified form, or not at all. Uncle Jun had previously passed on all relevant information to Mr Yong, and in reply, he had asked that Leonard remain available and he would send word.

Leonard and Uncle Jun were again in the private curtained area of the shop when they heard a customer enter. Uncle Jun hurriedly placed his tea cup on the table, parted the curtain and entered the shop, only to return seconds later followed by Inspector Gibbard.

Immediately Leonard stood when he saw the expression on the inspector's face, and steeled himself for what was to come.

Inspector Gibbard scanned the room. "Are we alone?" were his first words that precluded any greeting.

"Only the three of us," answered Leonard.

The inspector appeared to relax. He made eye contact with Leonard and shook his head slowly from side to side. "How did you know? How could you have made that kind of deduction? I thought it absurd at the time."

Leonard had no idea what he was referring to and stared blankly at the policeman.

"Taggett," said Inspector Gibbard.

Leonard's eyebrows furrowed. "Taggett?"

"Mrs Bedingfield's maiden name is Taggett."

"You sit, Inspector," instructed Uncle Jun.

The inspector sat down wearily with a grunt. "I report directly to Superintendent …"

Leonard remembered the name, *of course, Superintendent…*

"Superintendent Taggett," stated the inspector.

Leonard slumped into his chair. "Goodness gracious. I dare say, that complicates things a bit."

The inspector wasn't happy.

"Who is this man, Taggett?" Uncle Jun asked.

Leonard looked over at Uncle Jun. "Superintendent Taggett is the … brother?" He turned back to the inspector for confirmation.

He nodded. "Yes, the brother."

"… of Mrs Bedingfield."

"Ahhh, now you know who have big mouth and talk too much," exclaimed Uncle Jun.

"We need to discuss this with Wang Yong," Leonard suggested.

"Indeed," replied the inspector.

That evening Leonard was expected at the Pembroke home for dinner. Without the assurance of having a constable at his side, he selected a Hansom cab and made his way across town and up Wellington Terrace to the Pembroke's large house. As per usual, Mrs Pembroke greeted him and ushered him into their living room where Mr Pembroke sat in the comfort of his large armchair, reading.

Mrs Pembroke returned to the kitchen while her husband politely enquired about his wellbeing before asking about an update on the opium shipment.

"You've been sworn in as a special constable?" Mr Pembroke reacted after Leonard finished explaining.

"Yes, but it is not public knowledge. Best if you were circumspect, sir."

"Well, I never …" remarked the *Evening Standard*'s senior reporter. "And of course, I shan't say a word."

"Dinner is served, gentlemen," announced Mrs Pembroke from

the doorway. "And shan't say a word about what?"

"Don't be meddlesome, dear," retorted Mr Pembroke.

"Oh, like that is it." She gave Leonard a wink.

Mrs Pembroke cooked a superb dinner, and Leonard ate with gusto. Conversation soon returned to the Rileys.

"I do have an interesting development," Leonard began. He was interested in any ideas Mr Pembroke may have and his counsel was invaluable.

Mr Pembroke raised his eyebrows.

"How familiar are you with Superintendent Amos Taggett?"

"I'm familiar with his wife, Edith, she sits on the committee with me at Wellington Ladies' Benevolent Society," stated Mrs Pembroke with a smile before her husband could reply.

Mr Pembroke looked to her in puzzlement. "You never mentioned that before?"

"I don't recall you asking, dear, but I don't find her particularly agreeable," she added.

Leonard listened to the exchange.

"Why is that?" her husband asked between spoonfuls of bread pudding.

"Because many of us feel that by volunteering, we can genuinely assist those who are in need. Mrs Edith Taggett's motive is only about status and the public perception that she is involved in community activities because she is the wife of a very senior policeman. It's about her standing in the community."

Satisfied with her explanation, Mr Pembroke swung his head around to Leonard. "Why did you ask about Taggett?"

Leonard grinned. "Are you aware of who his sister is?"

"Out with it, don't keep me in suspense," snapped Mr Pembroke.

"Freddie, be nice," admonished Louise Pembroke.

Leonard took a deep breath. "Amos Taggett's sister is none other than Mrs Bedingfield."

Mr Pembroke's head whipped around. "Did I hear you correctly?"

"A surprising turn, eh?"

"Dear God!"

"Freddie, your language!"

Mr Pembroke raised his eyes and stared up at the ceiling as he digested the information. Suddenly his face transformed as the implications registered. "Are you suggesting that Superintendent Taggett is corrupt? That he is, uh, in bed with the Rileys?"

Mrs Pembroke stopped eating and listened attentively.

"Exactly — I believe he is part of the Riley brothers' criminal enterprise."

Mr Pembroke pushed his plate away. "Louise, don't breathe a word of this to anyone."

"I don't prattle, Freddie, you know that."

Mr Pembroke harrumphed and his face hardened. "It all makes perfect sense to me now…"

Leonard and Mrs Pembroke shared a look and waited for him to continue.

Chapter Forty-Two

Mr Pembroke dabbed at his mouth with a napkin, then scooted his chair back from the table. "We've been hoodwinked!" he finally said. "I saw it coming, and felt it odd at the time, but against my better judgement and pressure from Mr Beaumont …"

"I don't understand, Freddie, what do you mean?" Mrs Pembroke asked.

Mr Pembroke's face hardened. "We were short-staffed at the paper and I had sought permission from Mr Beaumont to promote Leonard and advance his career to a reporter."

What? Leonard leaned forward and listened keenly. Usually Mr Pembroke was reticent to discuss his privileged position at the paper, and certainly never spoke about his private conversations with the newspaper's publisher, Mr Beaumont, to employees or ex-employees.

As if reading his thoughts, Mr Pembroke turned and raised an eyebrow. "I'm sure you'll honour my privacy?"

Leonard cleared his throat. "Of course, sir."

"We shall see," he muttered before continuing. "My requests to Mr Beaumont essentially fell on deaf ears and were repeatedly denied. He claimed he needed to cut back on expenses. Then to my astonishment he suggested that I employ a fellow who'd only just arrived in Wellington from England. 'Has a splendid reputation,' he informed me. He couldn't speak more highly of the man." Mr Pembroke grimaced.

"Neil Flanagan?" Leonard asked. "And what of his cost saving measures?"

Mr Pembroke nodded. "I had strong, professional reservations about hiring Mr Flanagan, but Mr Beaumont informed me that he came highly recommended by Joshua Riley, and either the *Evening Standard* employ him or the Rileys would pull their advertising, which by the way, so I'm told, is considerable. I was determined that Leonard assume that role, it is rightfully his, and I informed Mr Beaumont of my reasons. I was steadfast and outright refused to hire Flanagan."

"I do recall that time," Mrs Pembroke added. "You were very upset."

Mr Pembroke looked pensive, then nodded in agreement. "Mr Beaumont wouldn't accept my *rationale* or persuasion and was determined that the *Evening Standard* should employ Flanagan. A day or so later, he informed me that the police were investigating some illicit gambling activities in Wellington and Neil Flanagan was perfectly suited to work with the *Evening Standard* in a dual role." Mr Pembroke raised a finger. "One, he would report on entertainment and recreation, and two..." he raised two fingers, "he would report his relevant findings to the police to aid with their ongoing investigation."

"That's absurd," Leonard stated. "There was no ongoing investigation. And isn't it peculiar that Mr Riley would be advocating Flanagan on behalf of the police?"

Mr Pembroke smirked. "I agree. At first Mr Beaumont claimed he only received pressure from Joshua Riley, and Superintendent Taggett eventually appealed directly to him when I continued to hold fast and refused to employ Flanagan. Mr Beaumont felt he had little option but to overrule me and hired the man—and I had to acquiesce, but, mind you, I did so only on the condition that Mr Camden retain his position as Entertainment and Recreation reporter. Neil Flanagan would be assigned to report on the economy and finance. A compromise he wasn't thrilled about."

"Excuse me, sir, but why didn't Mr Beaumont just overrule you, after all he is the publisher?"

"I can answer that, Leonard," said Mrs Pembroke. "Freddie has turned a struggling newspaper into a viable profitable business. Without his fine efforts and dedication," Mrs Pembroke smiled proudly at her husband, "the *Evening Standard* would be floundering."

Leonard nodded, she spoke the truth. It was common knowledge that Mr Pembroke had turned the paper around.

"How did Leonard's dismissal factor into this," Mrs Pembroke asked.

"Apparently, Joshua Riley contacted Mr Beaumont directly and complained about Leonard's carousing with that woman, the strumpet, and again they threatened to pull their advertising. Additionally, he stated he would influence other advertisers to do the same unless Leonard's employment was immediately terminated." Mr Pembroke rubbed his face with his hands. "Now I understand why." He sighed heavily. "You see, Leonard was making significant progress on discovering all about the Rileys' illicit operation, and he stood in the way of Flanagan at the paper. What I fail to understand is why, uh, Mr Bedington is so important to the Rileys?"

"I know." Leonard slowly exhaled to ease his pent up frustrations and anger. "Mr Bedingfield's horse, Sweet Hazel, is a good race horse but not top in the field. She has low odds of winning a race. By administering that evil performance-enhancing concoction to her, she could theoretically win. The winning payouts would have been considerable."

"Money … it's all about money and greed," mumbled Mr Pembroke, "and him … Flanagan."

"From my understanding," said Leonard, "Neil Flanagan was to report on horse racing and influence gamblers on horses he thought were most likely to win. This would alter the betting odds of other horses. By medicating very select race horses and improving their performance, the Rileys could, with near certainty, pick winners who previously had little to no chance of winning. They could make a fortune and begin doing this on other race courses around the country. Mrs Bedingfield wasn't interested in locating her husband, she wanted to find his horse."

Mrs Pembroke was shaking her head. "The poor horses, I think its cruel what these men are doing to them."

"I've heard it considerably shortens their lives," Leonard volunteered.

"Freddie, what did you believe about the accusations made against Leonard?" Mrs Pembroke asked, changing the topic.

Mr Pembroke sighed loudly. "As I told you at the time, I had no evidence to dispute the accusations made against him. I did insist to Mr Beaumont that we should afford Leonard the opportunity to defend himself, as the accusations were so out of character. He told me that his decision was not negotiable."

"Is Mr Beaumont aware of *all* that's been happening?" Leonard asked.

Mr Pembroke's voice rose in anger. "I believe he is, but has yet to see the entire strategic picture! Repeatedly when I have tried to speak with him, he has refused to discuss it."

"I suggest you stop procrastinating Freddie. Mr Hardy is without employment and was unfairly dismissed, Mr Beaumont has a moral duty to make amends and put things right," insisted Mrs Pembroke. She turned to Leonard and gave him another wink.

Mr Pembroke looked down at the floor. His chest rose and fell and Leonard knew him well enough to see his rancour festering. The room was silent.

He looked up, glanced quickly at his wife, then turned to Leonard. "And it *is* going to stop!" He thumped his fist on the table, rattling cutlery and dishes. Both Leonard and Mrs Pembroke jumped. "I've sat back long enough and done absolutely nothing." He turned to Leonard. "I apologise sincerely to you, I'm truly sorry for the role I played in all this. I was naïve and manipulated!"

Leonard tensed as he expected him to thump the table top again. "Thank you, sir."

"I have principles," Mr Pembroke continued, "and I will not stand by when people are being threatened, killed … when homes are destroyed, and the public is being fleeced at the race track by criminals. Enough!" The aging reporter's voice cracked, and his lip trembled as he struggled to keep his fury in check.

Mrs Pembroke leaned forward and gently placed her hand over his.

Leonard looked at his ex-employer. "What can you do, sir?"

Mrs Pembroke removed her hand and began removing dishes as Leonard and Mr Pembroke sat in reflective silence. After a while he adjusted his position on his chair. "At present, very little, but I do believe Mr Beaumont and I should have a little chat to set things in order."

Leonard could see that Wang Yong looked fatigued and anxious, and seemed to have aged since he last saw him, just days ago. Uncle Jun sat beside Mr Yong and sipped tea. As customary, they sat upstairs, above the Chinese laundry on Cuba Street.

"I chose not to invite Inspector Gibbard as I have little faith in where his loyalties lie," Mr Yong advised.

This suited Leonard and offered him the opportunity to share with him and Uncle Jun the information he had regarding Superintendent Taggett. "Mr Yong, if I may, uh, I have occasion to share with you some information of concern. I believe it will clarify matters."

Wang Yong's eyes narrowed. He dipped his head. "Of course."

"I am not surprised, but in reflection, I should have known," stated Mr Yong after Leonard had shared what he knew about Superintendent Taggett and his relationship to the Rileys through his sister. "And the inspector, is he also implicit in this and working in collaboration with his superior and the Rileys?"

"I don't know … I find it difficult to believe he is corrupt. I doubt he is," Leonard replied.

"Nevertheless, you are uncertain," Wang Yong added.

Leonard shrugged.

Wang Yong leaned forward. "Leonard, what you are unaware of is that in the last seventy-two hours, many Chinese business premises in Wellington have been illegally entered and thoroughly searched by men employed by the Rileys."

Leonard was perplexed, and the revelation came as a surprise. Again, the Rileys were unfairly asserting themselves.

"It has come to my attention that the Rileys have begun a process of elimination and are searching for their opium in businesses belonging to Chinese. They have systematically ransacked over a dozen establishments and continue unimpeded. It is apparent they will not cease until they locate their opium."

Leonard was shocked. "Have they hurt anyone or stolen anything?"

"They revel in intimidation and in some cases they have pilfered — nothing of value — but I feel this will escalate unless an, uh, arrangement is entered into with the Rileys."

"At least no one has been seriously injured, that is some consolation." Leonard leaned back in his chair and scratched his head. He recalled the conversation with the inspector when he said there was a recent spate of burglaries. Must be what the inspector was referring to, he thought.

Uncle Jun and Wang Yong sat quietly and waited.

"Er, I have some thoughts," Leonard finally spoke. "The fact that the Rileys have resorted to desperate measures to find their opium shipment tells me they want it badly. I suggest we initiate another ransom—"

"The police!" reminded Uncle Jun.

"If it suits you, we will not officially inform them, not Inspector Gibbard — no one. For the time being, we keep this to ourselves."

A smile played across Mr Yong's face. "Please continue, Leonard."

"You will need to be involved, Mr Yong. I see no other alternative."

Wang Yong's smile vanished and Uncle Jun was about to interject.

"Please, listen first," Leonard appealed. "We send word to the

Rileys that you wish to negotiate a truce, that the intimidation and burglaries must cease. In response, and for a ransom fee, you will return to them the opium. However, you must stipulate that you will only negotiate, in person, with the Rileys, no one else."

"But Leonard," Wang Yong shook his head," this will not prevent the illegal enterprise of the Rileys. With their opium returned, they will continue unabated."

"We cannot inform the police out of fear that word will reach the superintendent of our intentions, who in turn will give fair warning to the Rileys." Before anyone could interrupt, Leonard raised a hand. "We need to entice Inspector Gibbard, and as many constables as possible, to assemble at the location of where the truce will be negotiated and the ransom exchange made — without telling them the real reason. Once they arrive, they can be told."

"Silly boy, Leo. How you do this?"

Wang Yong toyed with his sparse whiskers. His aged arthritic hand repeatedly stroked his face as he gave the matter thought. "Chen Jun has a valid point, Leonard," he began. "How do you intend to lure enough police to the location without alerting them beforehand, then, once there, have assurance that they will make arrests?"

"We do not know with absolute certainty that Inspector Gibbard is corrupt, although my intuition tells me he isn't, but I do know that my friend, Constable Tim Yates is an honest policeman. Perhaps I can enlist his help."

Immediately, Uncle Jun and Wang Yong began conversing in Chinese. From the tone, it didn't sound like they were supportive of his idea. He turned to look out the window and stared at the main entrance of the New York Contributionship Company, and felt a chill. How ironic he would be making plans to put an end to their criminal enterprise from a location so close to them, if only they knew … he smiled.

"Leonard?"

He turned from the window and looked at Wang Yong.

"Would you like me to have faith in your intuition and make plans based purely on your presentiment that Inspector Gibbard can be relied on?"

Leonard swallowed. "My association with the inspector is based only on his role with the constabulary, we are not friends. There have been instances when he could have chosen to circumvent the law to make his job easier, but in every case I can recall, he chose the path of jurisprudence to the point of being extremely particular. Can I vouch for his virtue?" Leonard looked down at his feet and thought back to previous meetings he had with Gibbard. He looked up and held the gaze of Mr Yong. "I can."

"Leonard, my people do not have time to consider options, our businesses are being compromised. Next, people will be hurt and lives will be lost, and we do not have the luxury of time to investigate all our options and arrive at a consensus. I want to resolve this issue with the opium as quickly as possible. Do you understand?"

Leonard nodded.

"We have an old saying, 'Do not trust a person who claims to be honest, and never trust exaggerated friendliness.' I believe Inspector Gibbard's personality supports that proverb." Wang Yong smiled. "Chen Jun urges me to believe in you, he thinks your rationale is often flawed, but in the end, your conclusions are nearly always correct. We agree; to attain a successful conclusion to this sordid situation, we have little choice than to place our trust in the inspector. I will think of how to effect your plan, Leonard. If you can, please return here this evening."

Chapter Forty-Three

"Have you lost your mind?" exclaimed Constable Tim Yates as he glared at Leonard. They stood near the entrance to the Mount Cook Depot.

"Shush!" Leonard glanced around to ensure no one was within earshot to hear Tim's outcry. "Not so loud."

Exasperated, Tim turned away and with hands on his hips paced anxiously as Leonard watched. After a minute, he stopped in front of his friend and leaned forward. "You've put my career in jeopardy, and if your hair-brained scheme fails, then, as sure as I stand before you, my superiors will discharge me forthwith," he hissed.

Again, Leonard checked for privacy. "Tim, do you believe that Inspector Gibbard is corrupt?"

"That's a preposterous notion, of course he isn't. Why would you even ask?"

Leonard smiled, "Then there is nothing to fear."

In irritation Tim threw his hands in the air. "If I understand you correctly, you want me to inform the inspector that the Chinese have intentions to retaliate against all the recent burglaries and they will brawl with the culprits?"

"Yes, that is a brief summary. But do feel free to embellish the story."

"But that isn't really what's happening, is it?"

Leonard took half a step closer to his friend and lowered his voice to a whisper. "No, Inspector Gibbard needs to arrive at the real location with enough support to witness the exchange of opium for the ransom money and detain the Riley brothers just as we previously planned."

"Am I allowed to inform him of that?" Tim asked.

"Only after he has departed the depot and there is no opportunity for him, or anyone accompanying him, to send word back to the depot and the superintendent to advise them of our plans," Leonard replied. "Tim, a brawl is not a major incident, and it is unlikely that it will garner much attention from the superintendent. It's fairly routine, yes?"

"In a manner. But why is it so important to not inform the superintendent?"

Leonard looked at his friend. "Because someone has been informing the Rileys of our plans."

Tim looked puzzled.

"You recall that detestable woman, Mrs Bedingfield?"

Tim nodded.

"She happens to be the sister of Superintendent Taggett, and there is a distinct possibility that other members of the constabulary are also involved. I believe Superintendent Taggett is sharing information, through his sister, to the Rileys. Mr Yong suspects Inspector Gibbard may also be associated —"

"But …"

"Personally I don't, and neither do you. However, the inspector's response will be telling."

Tim shook his head in disbelief. "The superintendent, eh? If what you say is true, that explains much. Does the inspector know of this?"

Leonard nodded. "He does. I told him."

Tim took a step back. "Leo, what have you stepped into? And, may I add, you've gone way too far — stop this foolishness before you are killed."

Leonard ignored Tim's warning and continued undeterred. "Once Inspector Gibbard is underway with sufficient men to quell the *non-existent* brawl, you may tell him of the real location and about the ransom exchange."

"He will undoubtedly question the deception and not be thrilled," Tim suggested.

"He has every reason to thank us after the arrests have been made. But his prompt arrival is pivotal, and that is your responsibility, Tim. Make certain he comes precisely on time to the correct location."

Tim felt an oncoming headache and rubbed the bridge of his nose.

Leonard fished in his pocket and extracted a slip of paper given to him by Wang Yong the previous evening and handed it over.

With a loud exhale, Tim unfolded the note and read it carefully. "This is the address and time?"

"Yes, tomorrow night." Leonard shivered, another spell of cold weather was settling in.

The sky was clear and stars twinkled in unobscured brilliance. It was chilly, and if the breeze abated, it would surely be a frost, thought Leonard as he buried his hands deep into the pockets of his borrowed overcoat. In the distance a dog barked, its incessant yapping a minor annoyance, no doubt prompted by a sheet of corrugated iron that clanged haphazardly against a wall or roof. Behind him, less than fifteen yards away, waves crashed relentlessly against rocks, the spray sheeting upwards, and then gently drifting away.

Leonard had only just arrived with Yan on a wagon accompanied by a dozen men. They hid around the corner from the the warehouse until it was safe to proceed.

The Riley brothers' had strategically positioned two of their hired thugs at the bottom of the thoroughfare that led to the warehouse on Evans Bay Parade that Mr Yong had chosen for the exchange. They were overconfident and chatted casually, completely unaware of what was about to happen. Leonard observed, unseen, from a safe distance as a few Chinese stealthily crept towards the unsuspecting watchmen. With nary a sound and brisk efficiency, they were quickly subdued and securely tied before being moved away so they wouldn't be bothersome.

"Come, Mr Hardy, it is time," said Yan.

Leonard stood facing a narrow access path approximately thirty yards in length and just wide enough for a horse-drawn wagon, which ended at a turning area directly in front of a small commercial building used as a warehouse. The rear wall of the secluded building butted against a sheer rock face, limiting access to large sliding double doors at the building's frontage. On either side of the warehouse and thoroughfare, shipwright yards with half completed boats, derricks, and stacks of rough-hewn timber stood behind tall rickety fences. In this stretch of Evans Bay Parade there were no homes, only commercial businesses and over-used boat ramps. It was private and perfectly suited Wang Yong's need to ensure that the Rileys and their men could only leave by using the same path as they arrived, and that exit route was now blocked.

The moon was full, providing enough light for him to see the indistinct shapes of a covered wagon and a group of horses standing in the turning area immediately in front of the nondescript warehouse. Inside, although he hadn't seen them himself, he was told the Riley brothers had only just arrived and were impatiently waiting to begin the ransom exchange once everyone had turned up. Too old to attend himself, Wang Yong sent a trusted emissary to speak on his behalf.

Around Leonard, the men who came with him stirred and began advancing and spreading out to prevent the Rileys' thugs from leaving the premises. Yan had told him that there were eight more Chinese inside the warehouse. The Rileys had brought a total of thirteen men, and were comfortable enjoying the misguided belief they had superior numbers.

Leonard looked around with some concern. "It is too early, the inspector will not arrive for a short while yet." He scratched his face. The *faux* beard glued to his cheeks and chin itched and was uncomfortable.

"We must go inside now, they are waiting for us," she insisted.

The moon shone on Yan's jet black hair and Leonard felt the pang of loss tug at his heart. This beautiful young Chinese woman was so much like his Mae. He tried to focus on the task ahead and swallowed. "But we are to wait for the inspector," he appealed. "That was the plan." He felt his heart begin to race as tendrils of fear spread throughout his body.

Yan gently grabbed his arm. "Come, we cannot delay."

He reluctantly allowed her to lead him up the long access thoroughfare towards the warehouse. Ahead, he saw another of the Rileys' guards standing outside the entrance being quietly restrained. Just like before, the guard was unsuspecting and had been easily overcome.

"Keep your hat pulled down, do not look at the Rileys or their men, you mustn't be recognized," Yan sternly instructed.

"The inspector …" Leonard said. He felt numb from dread.

Yan leaned forward. "Leonard? Your hat."

Earlier, he'd been told to wear a flat cap and an old coat so that he would not be recognised. It was Yan's idea to attach the beard to complete the disguise. At the time he had agreed but did not understand the reason. Now with his heart pounding and fighting the overwhelming urge to flee, he began to comprehend. Mr Yong wanted him inside the warehouse. But why? *It was too soon. The inspector and his men had not yet arrived.*

Yan reached up and pulled his hat lower and then turned up the collar of his old coat. A faint yellow light spilled from the open doorway and Leonard stood frozen.

She tugged his arm and he hesitantly stepped around the corner and into the warehouse.

He kept his head down and only raised his eyes. In the middle of the floor lay about a dozen large crates. A table had been placed nearby and two lanterns provided light. It wasn't much, but enough for the Rileys and Wang Yong's representative to see each other and conduct business.

The Rileys and their men stood fidgeting on one side of the crates, while the Chinese stood at the other end and each party eyed the other nervously. When Leonard entered the warehouse, a few heads turned in mild curiosity to look, then quickly forgot about him as all attention was focused on the crates containing the opium. As far as the Rileys were concerned, they still believed they had superior numbers of men. What they didn't know was that all their guards outside were now captives and they were surrounded — no one could escape.

Despite the chilly temperature, Leonard felt a trickle of sweat run down his back. His hands were clammy, the face itched, and his pounding heart threatened to explode. He undid a few buttons on his coat; the fresh air helped. Yan appeared calm as she stood quietly beside him.

Sensing his unease and discomfort, she leaned in close and whispered, "Relax, Leonard, everything is well in hand."

She reminded him of Mae. Her mannerisms, looks, even her fragrance, and despite his growing anxiety, he found it strangely comforting. It was as if Mae stood with him.

One of the Chinese in the group near the crates stepped into the circle of light. "Have you brought the money as we agreed?" His voice, loud and clear.

Leonard kept his head dipped and his eyes raised so he could see clearly. He recognised Joshua Riley the moment he took a step nearer the light and crates.

"I am not impressed that you choose to steal from me!" he declared in anger. Behind him, his men murmured in assent.

The Chinaman shrugged and didn't reply to the statement. "You have the money as agreed?"

Joshua Riley didn't immediately respond and Leonard thought the man was probably fighting to control his fury.

Another man stepped forward into the yellow circle. Leonard didn't recognise him and because of his size and likeness to Joshua, he thought it must be Elijah Riley. He held three brown paper-wrapped packages bound in twine. "We have the money!" he shouted, his voice unnecessarily loud.

Wang Yong's representative turned his head and spoke in Chinese to a man behind. Immediately the man stepped forward, and with an iron bar began to pry open the crates. The Rileys sent a man to inspect and verify the shipment had not been tampered with.

Leonard risked a glance towards the open door. *The inspector should be here any time now.*

As if reading his thoughts, Yan leaned in and whispered. "Patience, Leonard."

Something wasn't right. Leonard felt it. He and Wang Yong had gone over the details carefully. According to Mr Yong, the inspector should arrive in time to witness the entire proceedings. But the exchange was about to take place without him. The ransom exchange was taking place ahead of the planned schedule. Why?

Leonard forced his attention back towards the activity in the centre of the warehouse.

Systematically, each crate was opened and carefully inspected. It took an age — the Rileys seemed determined to ensure they were not victims of foul play or that their precious opium had been stolen or diluted. The brothers stood together and watched dispassionately as the content of each crate was confirmed and each bottle tested. It was tense, and his anxiety and concern simmered. For the first time, he diverted his gaze to the men loitering in the shadows.

Even in the gloom, one man stood considerably taller than the others. Leonard felt the chill as he recognised Neil Flanagan. *What is he doing here?* This changed everything and now put the entire exchange at risk. *If I can distinguish him, then surely he can identify me.* No longer feeling as confident with his disguise, he shuffled back a half step and stood behind Yan next to the wall. While considerably taller than her, he hoped it was dark enough that Flanagan couldn't recognise him.

Leonard knew that something had gone horribly wrong. Tim and Inspector Gibbard should have been here already. *They were late.*

Wang Yong's representative stepped towards Elijah Riley and held out both hands. "As you can see, your shipment is untouched, the money please!"

Elijah Riley looked towards his brother for instructions.

Joshua Riley moved to stand boldly in front of the Chinaman and raised his hand to point at him. "You and your people will suffer dearly for this robbery." He jabbed his finger repeatedly at the Oriental. "You leave me with no choice but to acquiesce to your unreasonable demands," he expanded his chest and glared. "But you tell Wang Yong, from me, I will not forget this treachery!"

The threat was succinct and in response, the Rileys' men began posturing aggressively. All Wang Yong's men seemed unconcerned and stood casually at ease. Leonard saw Neil Flanagan swivelling his head and begin looking around. He appeared agitated. Slowly Flanagan eased back, deeper into the shadows, away from the crates and the activity.

Where is the inspector? He should be here. Again he looked with anticipation towards the open doorway.

"Give him the confounded money," instructed Joshua Riley to his brother. "All the opium is here."

Elijah handed the three wrapped bundles to the Chinaman who in turn handed them to another man.

Why aren't the police here, where are they? Leonard wondered for the umpteenth time. He risked a quick look to where Flanagan should have been standing. He couldn't see him. Leonard swallowed thickly and turned back towards the Rileys.

"Bring the wagon!" shouted Joshua. Immediately his men approached the opium crates, ready to hoist them onto the wagon when it was brought in from outside.

Leonard diverted his eyes and again searched for Flanagan. Other than the yellow circle of light near the crates that the two lanterns provided, the warehouse interior was completely dark. He shifted his gaze, searching the shadowed perimeter, and spotted movement. He squinted into the darkness and recognised the figure — Flanagan was making his way towards him!

Leonard leaned forward, his lips brushing Yan's hair. "I, uh, I think we should leave," he whispered, barely controlling his panic.

Before Yan could answer, they all heard the noise. Immediately, both Joshua and Elijah raised their heads and looked towards the doorway in disbelief. Their men also turned, and for a brief moment froze in indecision. The distant sound of a shrill police whistle was unmistakeable.

Someone yelled in alarm, "The police!" Rileys thugs reacted quickly.

Chapter Forty-Four

Something was amiss, Inspector Gibbard would never signal that they were coming. Why did he order the whistle blown?

Yan saw Flanagan creeping towards them, and to Leonard's astonishment, extended her arm to move him to the side, placing herself between him and the approaching threat. At the same time Rileys' men, now wielding cudgels, charged the Chinese, hoping to clear a path for the two brothers to exit the warehouse and escape to safety.

Leonard had no weapons; he had nothing with which to defend himself. As he'd previously witnessed, Flanagan was extremely volatile and prone to violence. He didn't need a weapon and could inflict serious and painful damage with fists alone. There was no mistaking his intentions as he stalked towards them, and Leonard knew he and Yan were in a serious predicament. He reached out and grabbed Yan's shoulder to pull her away. "Let's go."

She shrugged him off and audaciously faced Flanagan who was only yards away. Around them, men fought. Leonard was shocked to see Rileys' thugs savagely striking the Chinese with their cudgels. A couple of men dropped to the floor, while others fell back to relative safety and to regroup.

In response, the Chinese produced hidden weapons of their own. Even in the darkness he could see the glint of steel. These were small modified hatchets with shortened handles. A leather thong threaded through a hole in the handle kept them securely held. Now, suitably armed, three Chinese stepped forward and clashed with the enraged thugs. The Chinese were still outnumbered and as yet, their support outside had yet to arrive. It had only been seconds since the whistle blast, but to Leonard it was long enough.

Flanagan casually reached out an arm to shove Yan aside. Instead of allowing him to manhandle her, she deftly avoided his hand, twisted, grabbed his arm and kicked his knee. It was the last thing Flanagan expected and he cried out in pain and stumbled. Yan released his arm and stepped back out of his reach before he could backhand her. There was nowhere for Leonard or Yan to run or hide. A melee in the warehouse prevented them from leaving through the exit, and Leonard looked back at Neil Flanagan as he bellowed in rage.

Flanagan regained his balance and warily faced the young Chinese woman who still stood between him and Leonard. This time, and more cautiously, he raised his fists and lashed out in a series of quick jabs, forcing Yan and Leonard to back away.

Leonard wanted to help Yan, but fighting was not something he was familiar with. Flanagan was larger, skilled and angry. He'd witnessed his abilities against Russell, and accounted for himself quite well in that brief contest in his living room. Here, Flanagan faced only a young Chinese woman and it wouldn't take long for her to be overwhelmed by his size and sheer strength.

The feeling of helplessness was excruciating. Other than the opium crates and table, the warehouse was entirely empty of implements — there was nothing available that he could use to protect Yan or himself. Around them the mayhem continued — Leonard could hear cries of pain, anger and challenge, but his immediate concern was for Yan. He couldn't understand why the police and Chinese outside hadn't appeared. He heard Yan cry out and he stepped to the side to avoid her from careening into him as she staggered away, out of Flanagan's reach. She flexed an arm to ease the soreness from where she'd been struck.

Neil Flanagan was wily and certainly adept. Yan had unique skills. He'd never imagined a woman could fight, let alone do so with such lithe ability, but she was no match for Flanagan's brute force and he was taking full advantage of the mismatch.

Flanagan landed another blow, unintentionally striking Yan on her shoulder. He grunted as his fist connected with bone and he stepped back to rub his aching hand. Yan also cried out, and Leonard knew she was almost finished. She couldn't sustain this kind of punishment or she'd be very seriously hurt. This unfair contest had to stop. Flanagan shook his arm to relieve the pain, concentrated on his opponent, and again stepped in. Bravely, Yan held her ground. Leonard stood to the side, so close to them both but totally helpless. She was remarkable, and immediately visions of Mary filled his head. Dear Mary, he missed her so terribly much and he recalled with renewed resentment what this man had done to her and him.

One of Rileys' men looked up and saw Flanagan fighting. Leonard hoped he wouldn't come over to lend a hand.

Flanagan protected his face and body with arms and clenched fists, and stood side on, facing away from him. Leonard's own anger superseded logic and common sense and he desperately sought a way to gain advantage to help Yan. He had an idea.

Flanagan was breathing hard and jabbed, and jabbed again, while Yan continued to nimbly dodge out of the way. Flanagan shuffled another half step closer and Leonard held his ground. He was so close. Fearing the ex-reporter-cum-brawler would soon land a devastating blow in a flurry of vicious combinations, Leonard drew his arm back and swung with all his might. His new belt, with a substantial weighty buckle, whipped through the darkness.

He didn't know if it was just superb timing or good fortune, but with considerable force, the buckle at the end of his belt struck Neil Flanagan hard on his temple. With only a harsh croak he instantly crumpled to the ground. Yan turned to him in total surprise. With his belt dangling from a trembling hand, he stared open-mouthed at the inanimate form on the ground and wondered what he'd done.

Before he could gloat, Chinese ran into the warehouse, followed closely by uniformed members of the constabulary frantically blowing their whistles. He recognised Tim and Inspector Gibbard who immediately strode towards the Riley brothers who were cowering in relative safety behind crates of opium.

Outnumbered and beaten, the Riley thugs had no option; they surrendered with vociferous pleas of foul play. The Chinese, along with half a dozen constables, rounded up the ruffians who were still capable of walking, and those too injured to walk were carried and deposited in the middle of the warehouse for subsequent questioning.

Two constables approached Leonard and Yan, gave Leonard a strange look, and roughly carried the unmoving Flanagan away.

Leonard turned back to Yan. "Are, are you hurt?" he asked in a raspy voice.

She was breathing hard and shook her head. "Thank you, I am unharmed. Although I suggest Mr Hardy, that in the interests of decency and modesty, you raise your trousers."

Leonard looked down. In the heat of the moment, he never realised his untethered trousers had slid down his legs. He was thankful for the darkness as he felt his face flush.

As order was restored and his pants securely hoisted, Yan wandered off to assess the injuries of her relatives and friends as Leonard gratefully peeled the beard from his face. Feeling presentable, he cautiously approached Inspector Gibbard.

"The quandary I find myself in, Mr Hardy ..." he sighed loudly, "I'm unsure if I should congratulate or detain you."

From his harsh expression, Leonard thought the latter option was more likely. "Inspector, I admit that our plans were not adhered to, and I was merely a spectator here this evening. This, uh, this incident was beyond my control."

The inspector glared at him. "From what I heard, you were more than a spectator and gallantly sacrificed your modesty to confront Neil Flanagan." He smirked and before Leonard could reply, he continued. "We shall discuss details tomorrow, however, I have enough paperwork and examinations ahead to keep me gainfully occupied for some time. I need your statement. See you avail yourself to me at the Mount Cook Depot late morning."

Leonard turned away from the inspector and faced Joshua Riley, who was being restrained by a constable. He held brief eye contact with him and thought of those who had been murdered — people who had been slain because this man had ordered their deaths. Leonard didn't smile or feel satisfaction, instead he felt an overwhelming sadness and a feeling of loss.

Joshua Riley interrupted his introspection. "I *will* retain my liberty, Mr Hardy, and I promise you, when I do, you will suffer grave consequences."

Leonard didn't react to the threat, took a deep breath and walked away to the sound of laughter at his back. Inspector Gibbard looked up at the outburst and shook his head.

Sleep didn't come easily as Leonard spent most of the night tossing, turning and reliving the violence of the evening. When the sky lightened he eased himself from bed and considered his uncertain future as he dressed. Uncle Jun was chipper and congratulated Leonard on a job well done. "Wang Yong, very happy," he said.

Fortunately, no Chinese were seriously injured, and the Rileys' hired help suffered mostly bruises and mild contusions, although one thug had an arm broken. Uncle Jun reminded him that the Chinese were carefully instructed to not be overly aggressive and apply only as much force as necessary. Leonard wasn't so sure. From what he witnessed, the Chinese fought with ferocity and intensity. He was grateful none of Wang Yong's men were hurt, although he expected Yan to have some bruising on her body.

As instructed, Leonard eventually walked to the Mount Cook Depot where he was required to wait until the inspector was able to speak with him. He sat morosely against the far wall of the public waiting area and watched people as they filed grievances, complained or simply sought police action for a perceived wrongdoing. After an hour's wait, a constable came for him and led him into an interview room where the inspector sat at a table with a mountain of files at his elbow. It was obvious that Inspector Gibbard and staff had worked all throughout the night and not slept. Leonard steeled himself for what was to come.

"Sit, Mr Hardy," instructed Inspector Gibbard coldly as he waded through his files seeking one in particular. He didn't look up. A fatigued constable sat on a chair beside him completing paperwork.

Leonard silently obeyed and observed.

"Now then." Inspector Gibbard looked up and Leonard saw the sunken, tired eyes. "I've had a rather trying few hours, and now I am required to ask you a few pertinent questions and obtain your statement."

Leonard smiled obligingly.

"Before you open your mouth and say something asinine, I should inform you that Superintendent Amos Taggett has been temporarily relieved of duty until a thorough investigation has been completed. Preliminary findings indicate his involvement with Joshua and Elijah Riley is more complicated and extensive than we first believed. It appears you were correct, Mr Hardy. The superintendent was indeed passing on confidential and privileged information to aid the nefarious activities of criminals." The inspector sighed and placed both arms on the table. "You will not be charged with any crime."

"And Mrs Bedingfield?"

"We are investigating her involvement and will likely press charges against her."

Relieved, Leonard relaxed and his shoulders slumped. Strangely he felt no satisfaction, only sadness.

"Bring tea."

"Yes, sir." The constable scraped his chair back and quickly exited the room leaving the two men alone.

"However, of concern to the constabulary is the fact that both Mr Elijah Riley and Joshua Riley cannot be detained unless a warrant is issued for their arrest. As yet, no charges have been filed and they will be released at midday unless —"

Leonard sat up. "But, you can't —" he interrupted.

Gibbard raised a hand. "I have some questions to ask you. You will answer them honestly and truthfully. Do you understand, Mr

Hardy?"

The expression on the inspector's face was as cold and hard as Leonard had ever seen. He nodded meekly.

The inspector cleared his throat and picked up a file, opened it and glanced at it quickly. "What time during the proceedings of the previous evening in Evans Bay Parade did you first step foot inside the warehouse?"

"It was exactly 8:30 p.m. I know this because I was brought into the warehouse half an hour earlier than originally planned. You were supposed to have arrived at 9:00 p.m. and never did. You were late!"

"Just answer the question!" snapped the inspector. Then he diligently detailed Leonard's response.

"Please identify the names of the men you recognised who were inside the warehouse when you entered?"

Leonard scratched his chin. "Not many. I, I, uh, recognised Neil Flanagan, Joshua Riley and assumed the large man who had a similar likeness to Joshua was his brother Elijah."

"No others?"

Leonard shook his head.

"Very good. Now, from the beginning, please tell me what you witnessed from the moment you entered the warehouse until I arrived."

The constable brought tea for them both and Leonard described all he'd seen. Inspector Gibbard wrote furiously, recording Leonard's statement. When he was finished, he handed the documents to Leonard to review. "Please check to ensure there are no errors."

Leonard nodded and read the inspector's notes. "They are accurate, but your writing style needs some impr- uh, modification," he grinned.

Inspector Gibbard placed his tea cup on the table and looked at him with red-rimmed eyes.

"All the men who were at the warehouse that are, um, loosely associated with the Riley brothers have sworn that Joshua and Elijah Riley were at that location to purchase spices —"

"Spices!"

"Wait. The Rileys claim they were purchasing spices and the men with them are supporting that declaration. They say they were deceived by the Chinese who switched spices for opium. This is why we have been unable to arraign them. They also claim there are no credible witnesses to prove otherwise. You recounted that you witnessed and overheard Joshua Riley say..." The inspector ran a finger down a page of Leonard's recorded statement. "Yes, here it is, you said that Joshua Riley instructed Elijah to hand over the money because 'all the opium is here.' Is this correct?"

"Yes, indeed. I heard it quite clearly, and I saw bottles containing liquid being raised from the crates. I hope that liquid was opium?"

Inspector Gibbard sat back in his chair and for the first time Leonard saw him relax.

"Yes, your statement corroborates other witness accounts, and yes, it was opium. Mr Hardy, we have been most fortunate."

Leonard couldn't help but grin.

"Both Joshua and Elijah Riley are unaware that you were a sworn special constable. In effect, as a constable, you witnessed, first-hand, criminal activities and I believe we now have enough evidence to begin formal proceedings against Joshua and Elijah Riley. Legally, your testimony as a constable is no different than anyone else's, however a jury will likely feel your presence as a special constable adds credibility. The one-hundred pound ransom money was handed in to us, as agreed by Mr Yong's people and we have impounded the opium. Although, strangely, the Riley brothers claim that money does not belong to them."

Leonard felt the relief. "I saw Elijah Riley hand over the money. But If I understand you correctly, inspector, the Riley brothers will be charged?"

"After your statement, we will continue to detain them and will formally charge them this afternoon," smiled Inspector Gibbard. "However, I believe there is still someone else, a principal, who is involved and we have yet to identify him."

"Another person? How do you know?" Leonard was puzzled.

Inspector Gibbard rubbed his eyes. "As always, people talk when interrogated, especially when their liberty is threatened. Two of Rileys' men spoke of someone, a man working in partnership with the Riley brothers." He shook his head and shrugged. "I know nothing more."

Leonard wondered, who?

"I'm sure we'll get to the bottom of it, but thank you, I appreciate your fine efforts. I'm sorry you have had to endure so much."

Leonard leaned back in his chair. "Now, I have to rebuild my life." Then he remembered what bothered him and sat forward. "Why was it that you were delayed in arriving at the warehouse?"

Inspector Gibbard nodded. "The Rileys had thought to be clever. They had another group of men arrive after they came to the warehouse and they positioned themselves just down the road on Evans Bay Parade to prevent anyone from approaching. They surprised us, and only with the aid of the Chinese who were outside waiting for us, were we able to surround and overwhelm them."

"That's when you blew the whistle we all heard?'

"Uh, yes, not a smart decision was it?" He turned to the constable beside him who looked decidedly uncomfortable.

"But how did I not see them when we arrived?" Leonard asked, ignoring the red-faced constable.

"You were just ahead of them and slipped in just before they came. A good thing you were early, eh?"

Leonard sat back into his chair and recalled how Yan had insisted they remain quiet when they first arrived. She must have known. *Why did Wang Yong want me there early?* He scratched his head as he pondered Mr Yong's deliberate ploy to have the ransom exchange begin before the planned time.

"Good day, Mr Hardy, we will be in touch when we have more questions." Gibbard yawned.

Leonard stood and made his way to the door. He turned back to the inspector. "Oh yes, what of Neil Flanagan?"

Inspector Gibbard stretched his arms. "He received some minor medical attention and is no worse for wear." The inspector slowly eased himself from his chair. "He is being detained on a number of charges and unlikely to be released. You are quite safe. You can see yourself out."

For the first time in weeks Leonard walked without dread or the compulsive need to glance over his shoulder in fear. The Riley brothers, Flanagan, and all the others who'd relentlessly hounded him were now remanded into custody and awaiting trial. Lost in thought, he began walking towards Marjoribanks Street until he remembered his home was destroyed and in ruins. Feeling deflated, he turned back towards Frederick Street and Uncle Jun's shop.

Chapter Forty-Five

The following day Leonard was filled with unease. He hadn't slept much after the excitement of the previous night, instead spending hours fitfully contemplating the details around the Rileys and the horse medicating scheme. What Inspector Gibbard told him about how there was another person, a principal as yet unknown, bothered him and he couldn't let it go. *Who was this man?*

He fretfully paced around Uncle Jun's shop and reviewed all the facts. Everything linked to horses. *Horses.* From that morning when Mrs Bedingfield first came to the bullpen. When he interviewed her and she stared at the painting on the conference room wall — horses. *Confounded horses.* He knew he had to approach the problem differently. *Forget horses. Forget them.* He continued his relentless traipsing — there was another link, there had to be.

After a while he stopped his pacing, sat down and picked up a recent copy of the *Evening Standard.* Distractedly he scanned through its pages until he saw an advertisement for the New York Contributionship Company. He'd seen this same advertisement more times than he could remember … but it was something Mr Pembroke had said. He stared blankly at the page as an abstract idea entered his consciousness. *Could it be?* He considered countless options, contemplated viable arguments to dispute his developing theory and always arrived at the same conclusion. *It had to be*, he thought. To either disprove or confirm his fanciful theory, he needed some crucial pieces of information. He looked at the time on his watch. Mr Pembroke would be returning to the *Evening Standard* in half an hour from the weekly city council meeting he reported on. If he hurried, he could catch him. With haste he grabbed his coat and hat and ran from the shop.

The cab deposited him on Willis Street near the *Evening Standard* offices, where he waited in a shadowed doorway across the street for Mr Pembroke. It wasn't a long wait. He saw the distinctive elderly reporter walking up Willis Street, and without delay he rushed across the street to intercept him.

"Mr Hardy," exclaimed Mr Pembroke in bewilderment. "A pleasant surprise."

"I'm pleased I caught you, sir," Leonard replied. "I wanted to speak with you privately —it is of some concern."

Mr Pembroke's expression hardened. "I see … um." He looked around for a quiet place where they could talk. "This way, lad." A dozen yards away was a narrow thoroughfare that intersected Willis Street from another, conveniently it was hidden from view from the newspaper offices above them. Leonard followed.

Once in the alley, Mr Pembroke stopped and turned. "Now, what's this all about, eh?"

Leonard took a deep breath. "I need the kindness of a good turn, sir. But you'd put yourself in an awkward situation."

The elderly reporter was astute and knew if Leonard came to him with such an unusual request, then his reasons were probably justifiable.

Leonard explained in detail what he needed and asked Mr Pembroke if he could send a messenger to him at Uncle Jun's shop with the information he sought. "I will explain everything to you afterwards, I just hope I am wrong."

Mr Pembroke chewed his bottom lip as he considered Leonard's unusual request in light of everything that had recently happened. "It won't be easy …" He sighed loudly. "Very well, Leonard. I will do as you ask and will send you a message soonest."

Leonard returned to Uncle Jun's shop and spent the afternoon contemplating his as yet unfounded assumptions. He hoped he was wrong, but the sickness he felt in his stomach only worsened. The more he pieced together the circumstances and facts as he knew them, the more convinced he was that he was right. He waited restlessly for Mr Pembroke's message.

It was exactly 3:30 p.m. when a Hansom cab arrived outside Uncle Jun's shop. Leonard ran outside, paid the driver and received a sealed envelope. His heart rate accelerated as he returned to the private area behind the curtain, tore open the envelope, extracted the message and read.

It was concise and contained the details he sought, confirming his worst fear. "Oh dear," he said softly. The message slipped from his fingers and fell to the floor. The last line of Mr Pembroke's message read, *I am extremely perturbed, please explain.*

Leonard looked up into the face of Uncle Jun when he heard the curtain part. The old man studied Leonard's face. "Leo?" he asked.

Again, Leonard found himself in a swiftly moving Hansom cab as it navigated Wellington's streets towards the Mount Cook Depot. He stepped down from the cab and hurried towards the main building.

He didn't sit but remained standing as he waited impatiently for

Inspector Gibbard. It wasn't long before he was escorted to an interview room and the inspector stood to greet him. "Mr Hardy? What on earth is going on? I confess you have me quite alarmed."

"Inspector, I suggest you sharpen your pencil and take notes. I have your man."

"Pardon me?"

"The missing man, the elusive principal you've been looking for."

Inspector Gibbard leaned back in his chair and whistled after hearing Leonard's reasoning. How he managed with such thin lips astounded Leonard. "Your logic makes sense, but we have no definitive evidence," he stated. "This is all circumstantial and does not prove guilt."

"If I may make a suggestion, sir."

Inspector Gibbard inclined his head and raised an eyebrow.

"We need to talk to Mr Pembroke, at his home, and as soon as possible."

The inspector was stretched out in his chair with hands behind his head and he nodded slowly. "I concur."

Mrs Pembroke greeted both men cordially at the door before inviting them both inside. Mr Pembroke wasn't in his chair. Instead, he was standing looking out the window over Wellington with hands clasped behind his back when Leonard and the inspector entered.

"Freddie, you have guests," she said. Her voice was soft and to Leonard she appeared melancholy.

Leonard could feel the tension in the air and guessed they'd been talking.

Mr Pembroke turned. "Inspector Gibbard, Leonard … I fully expected and hoped you would come."

"Please, be seated gentlemen," Mrs Pembroke pointed to the sofa as her husband sought solace in his oversized chair, and she sat on a similar chair beside him.

Leonard felt pity for the man, he looked devastated.

"Thank you both for seeing us, and I apologise for not sending advance notice of our visit," began Inspector Gibbard. "Mr Hardy came to me today with what appeared to be nothing more than an unsubstantiated presumption, based purely on snippets of infor-mation and observations. By themselves, they amount to nothing and have no real apparent value. Collectively, however, they appear damaging."

Frederick and Louise Pembroke nodded, but remained quiet as they listened.

"As you are no doubt aware, the police have been investigating a series of crimes that include murder, assault …" The inspector shook his head. "The list is quite long. We arrested a number of individuals who have been formally charged. One of the ringleaders in this criminal enterprise remains at large and we have been unable to identify him. That is, until Mr Hardy came to me."

Everyone turned to look at Leonard. He felt ill.

"I cannot act on speculations, I need facts and evidence. I'm unwilling to proceed further unless I believe with absolute certainty he is correct. Mr Pembroke, I would like to hear your arguments to either dispute or confirm Mr Hardy's assertions."

"Of course, Inspector." Mr Pembroke replied.

"Mr Hardy, if you would kindly recount your assumptions."

Leonard cleared his throat and turned to Mr Pembroke. "In the beginning, I pieced this entire scheme together by linking horses," he stated. "What I failed to do was look for the men who tie this enterprise together. When I began a different approach, one name leapt out at me, that was Theodore Beaumont, the *Evening Standard*'s publisher."

Mr Pembroke listened keenly.

"You told me that Mr Beaumont said to you that he was under pressure from Joshua Riley to hire Neil Flanagan or he would no longer advertise with the *Evening Standard* and that his advertising represented significant income for the paper."

"Yes, he said he could ill afford to lose such a major advertiser," Mr Pembroke confirmed.

"But, as it turns out, he isn't really, is he?"

Mr Pembroke nodded. "After your prompting earlier today, I discovered the New York Contributionship Company spent no more or less than other advertisers."

"Then he lied to you?"

"Wouldn't you have known that, Mr Pembroke?" asked the inspector.

"No." He shook his head. "Advertising and the income it generates is handled by Mr Beaumont. I play no role in that. So, in fact, it was a falsehood."

Inspector Gibbard scribbled some notes.

Leonard leaned forward on his chair. "Were you aware that Mr Beaumont and Joshua Riley were part owners in a race horse?"

Mr Pembroke's eyebrows furrowed. "I knew he owned a race horse, reasonably successful too, but did not know he was part owner. But the horse died. How did you learn this?"

"There is a picture on the wall of the conference room. Mr Riley has the same picture in his office. I checked. They were both equal partners and owners of the horse. After a few surprising victories, it died suddenly, and I presume it was administered repeated doses of that tonic which eventually led to its death."

Mrs Pembroke tut-tutted.

Leonard took a deep breath. "Today I asked you to check on the financials of the *Evening Standard.* You checked with Mr Simms, the accountant, and learned that the paper is almost insolvent; it is struggling to re-pay its debts."

Mr Pembroke rubbed his face with his hands. It was obvious to everyone he was struggling to remain composed. He swallowed. "Mr Simms confirmed to me in the strictest of confidence that the *Evening Standard* is in a precarious financial position." He took another deep breath. "I had no idea. Mr Beaumont did not inform me and I believed we were prospering. As revealed by Mr Simms, the paper was generating more than sufficient income. Mr Beaumont, however, was draining its coffers."

Leonard could see how hard Mr Pembroke was taking this.

"Mr Pembroke, I know this all comes as a surprise to you, and I'm sorry," consoled the inspector. "Mr Hardy believes that Mr Beaumont and Joshua Riley are quite well acquainted, that they are in fact partners in an elaborate criminal scheme. By blending unlicensed opium with additives, they create a potent tonic, and administer it to a select horse to enhance its performance which artificially influences the outcome of a race. In effect, wagering significant amounts of money on that drugged horse and pocketing the proceeds." The inspector checked his notes and continued. "Mr Hardy asserts that Mr Beaumont wanted Mr Camden to retire and to assign Neil Flanagan as his replacement. We believe that Mr

Camden may have learned more about Mr Beaumont's motives and activities, which ultimately led to his death."

Mr Pembroke looked up, his eyes blazed in anger. "Are you suggesting that Mr Beaumont had Milton Camden killed?"

"I can't prove it, not yet, anyway," Leonard added. "Please confirm, sir. As you told me, Milton Camden discussed this with you shortly before his death?"

"Yes, Milton was rather perplexed and came to me asking why Mr Beaumont wanted him to retire. I knew nothing about this and told him so. It was preposterous."

Leonard sat back against the sofa as Inspector Gibbard continued to take notes.

"What will you do now, Inspector?" asked Mrs Pembroke.

They waited as Inspector Gibbard gave the question some thought. After a moment he looked up. "The information I have learned is not evidence, it is circumstantial at best…"

Leonard opened his mouth to protest but the inspector turned to him, his expression cold. He shut it quickly.

"Unless someone within the organisation comes forward to corroborate this theory with hard evidence or credible testimony, there is little I can do at this time. Of course I would like to interrogate Mr Beaumont … "

In exasperation, Leonard sat back on the sofa with his fists clenched tightly.

"Frankly, before I can act, I need more, I need evidence, irrefutable evidence," he concluded.

Chapter Forty-Six

Leonard arrived back at Uncle Jun's shop fuming. He felt the inspector was playing it too cautiously and he needed to frighten Mr Beaumont with some aggressive probing questions, hoping he'd say something incriminating that could lead to an arrest. But to do nothing … it was maddening.

He spent another sleepless night recounting the facts, replaying events in his mind, and imagining scenarios where Mr Beaumont was arrested and held to account. In the morning, feeling less than refreshed, he arose from his bed and decided to visit Mr Pembroke to seek clarification on a few details that still remained murky. He'd risk a visit to the *Evening Standard* and hope he didn't run into the publisher.

"Mr Hardy," simply responded the secretary when Leonard arrived at the top of the stairs. She looked uncomfortable and while she had always been friendly to him, he knew it was awkward for her because he wasn't permitted to be here.

"I, uh, I just need to speak with Mr Pembroke. Its personal and I shouldn't be long," he offered with a charming smile as he spared a quick glance at the bullpen's closed door.

She frowned, then leaned forward and lowered her voice. "Mr Pembroke isn't here at the moment. Perhaps it would be best if you left." She looked over her shoulder towards Mr Beaumont's office. A subtle hint that he was there and that to avoid any unpleasantness, Leonard should leave.

Leonard felt the renewed anger rise from deep within, and looked back at the secretary. *Inspector Gibbard may be too cowardly to ask Mr Beaumont some questions, but I am not.* "Thank you." He couldn't help himself, and instead of departing, he turned from her desk and strode with grim determination towards the publisher's open door.

Mr Beaumont shot to his feet when he saw Leonard entire his office. "What are you doing here?"

"There are few questions that need answering, sir." Leonard's heart was racing and he used all his self-control to remain civil, but he wasn't going to back down now. He was fully committed.

"Be gone with you this instant!" Mr Beaumont raised his arm and pointed to the doorway.

"I am not here as a disgruntled ex-employee, Mr Beaumont, I'm here in my official capacity as a special constable. I have one or two questions you can answer for me, and I shall be on my way." Leonard didn't know if his status afforded him any legal right to barge into Mr Beaumont's office and guessed the irate publisher probably didn't know either.

Mr Beaumont fought to control his anger. "I, I have a meeting to attend," he sputtered.

Leonard didn't give him time to think.

"I understand you are the owner of a race horse?"

Mr Beaumont looked at him like he was a cretin. He laughed. "What type of question is that and what business is this of yours?"

"Police business." He recalled the magistrate's warning about how he was subject to the same rights and punishments as a constable. "As I stated, I am a sworn special constable with the same powers as a regular constable. Answer the questions, sir, and I shall be on my way." He pulled the official document given to him by the magistrate and held it towards the publisher. The official seal was unmistakeable.

Mr Beaumont looked uneasy. "No. It died," he snapped.

"Oh, how did it die?"

"I believe it was a birth defect, a faulty heart. But why is this relevant, Mr Hardy? I am required to be elsewhere for an important engagement."

"It's relevant because you were also partners with Joshua Riley," Leonard stated.

Mr Beaumont's expression changed and he looked even more distressed. "I must protest, your visit here is most unorthodox and absurd, even for a special constable." He regained some of his earlier composure and confidence. "Perhaps the police are unaware of your visit here ..."

"I require clarification on a few more details, Mr Beaumont, then I shall take my leave."

"Absolutely not! I insist, you must depart immediately! I will report your behaviour — special constable or not," he barked.

Leonard understood that he'd overstepped and knew he was in serious trouble. It was obvious that Mr Beaumont wasn't going to answer any more questions and he'd learned absolutely nothing. He could already hear Inspector Gibbard's voice as he gave him a verbal thrashing about overstepping the bounds of his authority. He may even have broken the law.

"I have no time for this nonsense and I have a scheduled meeting that requires my presence." Mr Beaumont reached down and picked up his document case from the floor, placing it with a thump on his desk. Leonard knew it was time to go and was about turn away when Mr Beaumont opened the case to place some documents inside.

Leonard saw and recognised it immediately. Inside the publisher's case lay a glossy green folder. He'd seen a similar folder at his bookkeeper's and at Mrs Bedingfield's home — it was the distinctive green folder used by the New York Contributionship Company. Why would Mrs Bedingfield have such a file? Why would Mr Beaumont have one? It was obvious it had nothing to do with any indemnity policies as they were generally retained by a bookkeeper or were filed away and seldom did a policy holder actually read the policy documents. Why would Mr Beaumont have such a folder so close at hand? Without thought of consequence, he leaned over, reached across the desk and snatched the green file from within the case.

"Mr Hardy!" cried Mr Beaumont. He dropped the documents he held and tried to grab the file from Leonard's swiftly retreating hand.

Leonard twisted out of the way and opened the file. He quickly scanned the top page, then the next and froze. The sound of his thumping heart drowned out Mr Beaumont's admonishment.

In clearly written script he saw dates, times and addresses. It was a virtual chronological timetable detailing past and future events. He saw familiar names boldly crossed off a list. Balthazar Gringle, Agatha Gringle, Milton Camden, Russell Baylor — all meticulously handwritten by Mr Beaumont. He saw his own name, Leonard Hardy, not crossed off but underlined, not once, but twice. In amazement he saw opium shipment delivery dates and other names — names of people he was unfamiliar with. Of more concern, there were notations and comments that outlined the scope

417

and plans of Joshua Riley and Theodore Beaumont's illegal enterprise. In absolute astonishment, he shook his head, then raised it and slowly turned to face the publisher. His mouth opened but he could find no words.

Mr Beaumont stood rooted behind his desk, unmoving and paralysed in uncertainty. Then, as the damning realisation of discovery settled over him, he slowly slumped onto his chair and placed his hands over his face with a groan.

"Mr Beaumont, your appointment!" reminded his secretary from the open doorway.

The publisher remained unresponsive.

"Mr Beaumont, sir?" she repeated, then turned to Leonard.

Leonard refocused. "Mr Beaumont sends his apologies, he is unable to attend," he said softly.

The secretary backed away from the door in confusion.

"I expect you'll arrest me," said the *Evening Standard*'s publisher.

Leonard swallowed. "I, uh, don't know how."

Inspector Gibbard spent considerable time delivering a scathing rebuke of Leonard's actions and conduct at Mr Beaumont's office. It ended with the red-faced inspector looking exhausted and spent, and Leonard presumed only because the inspector ran out of profane adjectives. Mr Beaumont denied the allegations, and like Joshua Riley, claimed he would be released soon, the inspector added. There were some legal implications that lawyers would hash out, but for the most part, all principals had been arrested and were now awaiting a trial date.

The *Evening Standard* went into voluntary receivership and Mr Pembroke was asked to temporarily assume the role of publisher. Leonard had yet to be updated on what the future held for the newspaper, but for the present, the *Evening Standard* continued to remain in business.

The following days were filled with boredom and inactivity. He hadn't heard from Mary and he was becoming increasingly anxious. While he'd sent letters, he had yet to receive any replies and all he could do was wait. He was checking the newspaper searching for a room-to-let in a respectable boarding house when Uncle Jun stepped from behind the curtain.

"Leo, Wang Yong wish to see you tonight 6:00 p.m. at Mandarin Cuisine Restaurant, on Haining Street. You know place?"

Leonard's eyebrows furrowed. "Yes, I know of it. But why does he wish to see me?"

Uncle Jun shrugged his bony shoulders. "You come. Six o'clock, not be late, yes?"

For the remainder of the day the elderly Chinaman hummed a tuneless song and went about his business, leaving Leonard alone until he locked his shop early and departed. Leonard's eyes settled on an advertisement for a passage to England and thought about his future.

He casually strolled down the busy thoroughfare of Haining Street. It was a hive of activity. Hawkers, pedlars, and undesirables flocked to this area for opportunity and need. Tea rooms, opium dens, and gambling halls were in abundance, and all were well frequented. His destination was the Chinese eating house called Mandarin Cuisine Restaurant, which was situated near the end of the notorious street. Leonard grinned — a Chinese restaurant with the French word, *cuisine*, as part of its name. It was just ahead and again he wondered why he had been summoned.

Outside, two hefty Oriental men stood guard and neither looked friendly or welcoming. He pulled out his watch to check the time; it was exactly 6:00 o'clock. He approached the entrance warily. The curtains were drawn so he couldn't see inside, although from the noise, the restaurant appeared to be quite crowded. A sign near the door boldly stated that the Mandarin Cuisine Restaurant was closed for a private function.

Leonard looked at one guard, then the other. "Good evening, uh, my name is Leonard Hardy, I'm expected by Mr Yong."

Without acknowledgement or a word, a guard opened the door, inviting him to enter and Leonard cautiously stepped over the threshold. Immediately all conversation inside the restaurant ceased and Leonard paused in uncertainty, then froze in incredulity. His eyes didn't look around the crowded room and he didn't greet its occupants, instead, he stared fixedly at the person who stood alone at the room's centre. Time seemed to stop and nothing else mattered but her. Only her. His eyes misted over as she took a step towards him. "M-Mary …" he croaked.

She rushed into his outstretched arms and the room erupted.

It took a while for Leonard to make sense of what was happening. When he pried himself from Mary, wiped his eyes and could again see clearly, he glanced around the restaurant's interior and saw them all. Bridgette , smiling broadly and looking radiant. Tim and Meredith, both beaming from ear to ear. Wang Yong, Uncle Jun, Yan and others he recognised who had helped him so much.

There in the corner sat Frederick and Louise Pembroke. She too was smiling, while Mr Pembroke looked like he'd eaten a sour lemon.

"Wha," he coughed. "What is this about?" He felt Mary's hand clasp his and grip him tightly.

"Come Leo, have a seat." She led him to a table near the room's centre.

Once he and Mary were seated, someone struck a glass with a knife and all chatter stopped. Yan assisted Wang Yong to his feet and the elderly, distinguished gentleman looked around the room. He nodded to them all as his eyes shifted from person to person. Leonard couldn't stop smiling and was unable to fathom what was going on. He looked at Mary for answers, but none were forthcoming. Instead he felt her support, warmth, and most of all, her love.

"Mr Hardy — Leonard," began Mr Yong. "Along with Chen Jun, we took the initiative to invite those close to you, to attend this occasion to acknowledge all you have done. The effects of your dogged determination and resilience will ripple through Wellington for some time. Yet, you have overcome considerable adversity, and not entirely without, er, some blemishes. Regrettably, people died, citizens of this fair town were hurt, robbed, swindled and even murdered. The deception and corruption were systemic. Without your perseverance, a criminal enterprise would have flourished and gained a substantial foothold. And like a festering plague, if left unvanquished, would have been difficult if not impossible to eradicate. We all owe you a debt of gratitude." Wang Yong raised a tea cup. "I propose a toast — to Leonard!"

Everyone raised glasses or cups and echoed, "To Leonard!"

Leonard looked down at his hand, which Mary still held, and slowly shook his head. After a brief moment he looked up. "I, uh, I, have no words, I don't know what to say."

"That's a first," interjected Tim, which brought a hearty laugh.

Leonard turned to his friend and smiled, then self-consciously faced the room again. "Thank you, but your acknowledgements are undeserved."

Over the course of dinner, Leonard spoke to everyone and thanked them for their help and for coming. With Mary at his side, he approached Mr and Mrs Pembroke's table. After a brief chat, he was about to leave to speak with Mr Yong when Mr Pembroke tugged the sleeve of his jacket.

"I implore you Mr Hardy, please curtail your consumption, it is not acceptable to arrive at work under the effects of alcohol."

Leonard knew that Mrs Pembroke advocated temperance, but … he looked puzzled. "Sir?"

"Don't get drunk, lad!"

Mrs Pembroke smiled.

"Leo, Mr Pembroke doesn't wish for you to drink excessively because you have work tomorrow," Mary clarified.

Leonard's head whipped around to face the *Evening Standard*'s interim publisher, senior reporter and editor.

"Eight a.m. Mr Hardy, don't be tardy!" Mr Pembroke's face cracked into a warm smile. "Welcome back, Leonard. We'll discuss details when you're in a better state of mind, eh?"

Leonard smiled so hard it hurt. "I'll be there, sir."

The evening came to an end and Leonard approached Wang Yong to again offer his appreciation and to say goodnight. Most people had departed and returned home. Mary, Bridgette, Tim and

Meredith still remained along with Wang Yong, Uncle Jun and Yan.

"Before you leave, Leonard," said Wang Yong. "We have a gift for you." He turned and gave Yan a nod. "Please accept this gratuity as atonement for your unfortunate losses."

Again, Leonard was puzzled.

Yan, who sat beside him, reached under the table and handed Mr Yong a simple hemp bag. "Please, take this with our gratitude."

Leonard accepted the bag and offered his thanks.

"Open it, Leo," encouraged Mary, who was eager to see the gift.

Leonard opened the bag and stared at its contents in disbelief. Inside were two bundles, each wrapped in brown paper and secured by twine. He'd seen these before. Elijah Riley handed three of these packages to Wang Yong's representative in the warehouse. If he estimated correctly, the two bundles equalled two hundred pounds. It was a huge sum of money.

Yan and Wang Yong were grinning. "Rebuild your home, Leonard," he said.

"I can't accept this, it is, uh …"

"Yes, you can," said Tim moving to stand behind him. "According to written statements gathered by the police, no one has claimed the money impounded at the warehouse. If the Rileys claimed the money, then that is an admission of guilt. After a thorough search, only one-hundred pounds was recovered. Certainly, no one has filed any claim stating that this money," Tim pointed to the bag Leonard held, "was either lost or stolen. I believe it's yours, Leo." Tim straightened and turned to Mr Yong. "If I may ask, sir, how … how did you manage to obtain all this money?"

Wang Yong paused as he considered his response. "Let me say this. And I will not repeat it to anyone. Do you understand?"

Everyone nodded.

Satisfied, Wang Yong continued. "Our ransom demand was not for one hundred pounds as we initially agreed. After consultation, we decided to increase our ransom demand to three hundred pounds. However, to have our plan succeed, we needed to complete the exchange before the police arrived at the warehouse." Mr Yong inclined his head at Tim. "This is why we needed you to arrive early, Leonard. You were the only policeman to witness the ransom exchange and we thought your presence would aid in the prosecution of the Rileys."

Leonard looked puzzled. "How, how did you know?"

Wang Yong quickly glanced at Chen Jun. "He informed me of your arrangement with the police and how you were sworn in as a constable."

Leonard turned to Uncle Jun who shrugged, "You silly boy, Leo."

Everyone laughed.

"Once we received the money," continued Wang Yong, "we immediately took two of the one-hundred pound bundles and placed them securely into our wagon, outside. It was always our intention to see you receive this money because the Riley brothers unfairly denied your house indemnity claim. This, after all," he indicated to the bag Leonard held, "is the Rileys' money, and rightfully yours."

"And if the inspector had witnessed the exchange, then he would have impounded the entire amount," added Leonard. "But do I need to report this, after all, was I not a sworn constable?"

Tim looked thoughtful. "If you report it, Inspector Gibbard will tell you that he has no record of this money and he will tell you that no one within the Riley enterprise has asserted that any money has gone missing or was stolen. I'm quite confident he will say you can accept this gift from Mr Yong."

Mr Yong smiled. "It matters not from where this money came, it is our gift to you," he smiled.

Leonard looked down at the two innocent bundles of wrapped notes. He wasn't so sure.

"Leonard, you have a house to build," Mary said. "Take it."

He looked up at her and swallowed. "*We* have a home to build."

Epilogue

The bullpen was mostly quiet. Someone sniffed and the sound of scratching pens dominated the heart of the *Evening Standard* newspaper offices. Leonard's head was down and he was busy writing. Occasionally Mr Pembroke scoffed or said an unsavoury word in response to a document or article he read that failed to meet his expectations. Periodically he'd raise his head and, with a practised eye, survey the room and his charges to ensure his staff were suitably occupied.

When the bullpen door latching mechanism engaged and issued its dependable warning, all heads turned as one and stared at the door to see who was about to enter. With eager anticipation, the reporters within the bullpen had almost an entire second to wait, and they weren't disappointed as they immediately recognised their unexpected visitor. Inspector Gibbard entered, paused momentarily and as a senior policeman was want to do, confidently assessed the room, and its occupants, before turning to Mr Pembroke.

"Why, Inspector Gibbard, it is indeed a pleasure to see you. Can I, uh, be of some assistance?" asked Mr Pembroke as he removed his reading spectacles and stood abruptly to greet the visitor. His pillow tumbled to the floor.

"Good morning, Mr Pembroke. Please excuse the interruption. I wonder if I may have a word, uh, in uh … confidence with you …"

"Of course, sir. Ah, perhaps the conference room will be best, eh?"

"… and Mr Hardy."

Leonard's eyes opened wide.

"Oh, uh, of course." Mr Pembroke turned quickly to Leonard. "Mr Hardy!" and looked back to the inspector with a growing sense of foreboding. "Uh, does he require his notebook, inspector?"

"No, that won't be necessary."

Leonard dropped his notebook back onto his desk at the same time his heartbeat increased in tempo.

"Mr Hardy, the conference room, please," instructed Mr Pembroke as he waited near the open bullpen door.

Leonard hurriedly made his way from his desk, his stomach in knots.

"It will be alright, lad," whispered Mr Pembroke as Leonard squeezed past him to lead the way.

Leonard and Mr Pembroke sat in the musty conference room with growing anxiousness. As yet, the inspector had not smiled and obvious to them both, looked tense and pensive. With hands clasped behind his back, he stood gazing at the dusty painting of a horse hanging on the wall.

"How may we assist you, Inspector?" asked Mr Pembroke.

Inspector Gibbard turned around to face Leonard, his expression cold and unfeeling. "Mr Hardy, I regret to inform you that your life is in imminent danger."

"What!" Leonard shot to his feet.

"Inspector!" shouted Mr Pembroke in an uncharacteristic outcry.

The inspector took a big breath and stepped closer. "Leonard," he said in a softer voice, "an unimpeachable source has come forward and informed me that Mr Joshua and Elijah Riley have secured the services of an individual, as yet unknown, to ensure you cannot, and *will not*, testify against them at their upcoming trial."

Leonard sunk back into his chair.

Mr Pembroke placed his hands over his face. "Dear God!"

"I'm sorry, Leonard. You and Miss Worthington must both go into immediate seclusion."

End

Author's Notes

Writing historical fiction is a pure delight, and only possible with the help and assistance of so many people with far greater knowledge than I, who are willing to share their expertise with me. Any errors, omissions and inaccuracies are entirely my own. This book is a work of fiction and any resemblance to characters, either living or dead, is purely coincidental and unintentional.

Obtaining accurate information about life in New Zealand's capital city, Wellington, during the 1880s isn't always easy. As always, in all my writing, I attempt to honour historical accuracy and weave fiction through fact. When records no longer exist, or when subject specialists simply don't know or can't agree, then through extensive research, I revert to logic and common sense and exercise my writer's creative prerogative.

For the penniless and destitute drunkards, drinking methylated spirits was a cheaper alternative than consuming conventional alcohol. Methanol, a major component of methylated spirits, is a nondrinking type of wood-alcohol and is poisonous to humans. Consuming methylated spirits will result in permanent blindness through the destruction of the optic nerve and the central nervous system, proving fatal — hence the origin of the saying, *blind drunk*. In 2007, methanol was removed from over-the-counter-purchased methylated spirits in New Zealand.

Within the framework of this story, Agatha Gringle's father,

Balthazar, was drinking methylated spirits and already suffering the effects of blindness. If he hadn't been murdered, he would certainly have passed away within a very short time. In reality, many people resorted to the toxic alternative because of availability and cost, and died as a result.

For many years, at the eastern end of Courtenay Place, near the tram shelter and Pohutukawa trees, vagrants and homeless drunks would often congregate and spend their nights inebriated and begging for money as I described. For the keen historians of Wellington, those same Pohutukawa trees where Leonard witnessed the drunks sheltering were, at great expense, uprooted and replanted on Liardet Street, along the perimeter of Macalister Park in Vogeltown, where they still grow today.

Our newspapers were important, and obviously were the only real source of news and information. Competition was fierce, yet their existence was often fuelled by advancing the political interests of the paper's publisher. The *Evening Standard* newspaper is purely fictional and has no relationship to any publication, either then or now, and was created by me without bias or a political agenda. However, I do hope that the *Evening Standard* newspaper feels as real to you as it does to me.

The word *Oriental* was commonly used by the west to depict people of east and southeast Asian descent. In the past, the word has also been used to also describe their cultures and countries. To many, the use of the adjective *Oriental* is objectionable and considered racist. In the context of this novel, the use of the word *Oriental* is not intended as an insult but rather to accurately describe people of the Orient in the same way the word was used during the time period of this novel. I apologise if I have caused offence.

The Chinese played an important role in New Zealand's early colonial history, and they suffered unfairly by being targeted and ostracised as unwelcome immigrants and social outcasts. This belief extended to all corners of the community, including parliament. New Zealand Liberal politician, William Pember Reeves, shockingly described his anti-Chinese sentiments by stating they are, "*dirty, miserly, ignorant, a shirker of social duty, and a danger to public health*." His opinions and those of other influential community leaders fuelled the existence of anti-Chinese organisations such as the *White Race League*, the *Anti-Asiatic League*, and the *Anti-Chinese Committee* that proliferated throughout the country and well into the twentieth century.

Within the period that this story takes place, opium was not a banned or illegal substance. It was, however, required to be labelled as a poison and vendors of the drug were legally obliged to register. Contrary to popular belief, not all Chinese were habitual opium users, and it was largely due to Chinese community pressure that opium for recreational use was finally outlawed in New Zealand. The Opium Prohibition Act of 1901 made it illegal to smoke and import the drug and the police were awarded extraordinary powers to search premises for the narcotic without a warrant.

The freedoms that Bridgette, Mary and Meredith enjoyed as nurses at Wellington Hospital are purely a result of my fertile imagination. Under the watchful eye of the Matron, nurses did not enjoy such liberties as I have afforded them during the time period of this story and worked extremely hard, with severe restrictions in a most honourable profession.

During the Victorian era that this novel was set in, doping racehorses with performance-enhancing drugs was not illegal. Introduced by Americans, it wasn't until the turn of the century that doping race horses became a true menace and the practice commonplace. During its most prolific use, experts surmised that 50 percent of race horses were under the influence of artificial stimulants to improve performance. In 1903, the U.K prohibited horse doping and in 1912 saliva tests were introduced to determine if any horse tested positive for stimulants.

The practice of administering performance enhancing drugs to animals is unbelievably cruel. Many stories are told of race horses, under the influence of drugs, that ran at unbelievable fast speeds. One story in particular horrified me when I learned that a particular thoroughbred was so *high* that it completed a race, and unable or unwilling to stop, ran directly into a brick wall and killed itself. The poem in the beginning of this novel is appropriate and certainly heartfelt.

Thank you for reading.
Paul W. Feenstra

Other historical fiction books

by

Paul W. Feenstra

Published by Mellester Press

Boundary

The Breath of God (Book 1 in Moana Rangitira series)

For Want of a Shilling (Book 2 in Moana Rangitira series)

Gunpowder Green

Into the Shade

Falls Ende short story eBooks
1. The Oath
2. Courser
3. The King

Falls Ende full length novels
Falls Ende – Primus (eBooks 1,2 & 3)
Falls Ende – Secundus
Falls Ende – Tertium
Falls Ende – Quartus
Falls Ende – Quintus

Leonard Hardy's
A Sinister Consequence
A Questionable Virtue

Ingram Content Group UK Ltd.
Milton Keynes UK
UKHW050804100523
421509UK00009B/63

9 781991 182449